Management of Secondary Education in India

Management of Secondary Education in India

Quality, Performance and Administration

K. Sujatha
P. Geetha Rani

NUEPA

SHIPRA

ISBN: 978-81-7541-502-7

First Published in India in 2011

Management of Secondary Education in India: Quality, Performance and Administration

Published by:
SHIPRA PUBLICATIONS
H.O.: LG 18-19, Pankaj Central Market, Patparganj, Delhi-110092, Tel: 91-11-2223 5152, 2223 6152
Br.Off.: 4617/18, Ansari Road, Darya Ganj, New Delhi-110002, Tel: 6594 6453, 9810522367
E-mail: info@shiprapublications.com
www.shiprapublications.com

Foreword

India has been the cradle of an ancient civilization as well as the host to one of the fastest growing economies of the world, currently. India is recognized as a leader in Information and Communication Technology (ICT). It is also creditable that the country has taken a big jump in universalizing elementary education by launching the Right to Education Act. While provision of primary education for all could ensure a reasonable improvement in the overall status of human development, it is unlikely that the country will significantly succeed in reducing poverty and creating a more equitable society without adequately focusing on improving secondary education. While primary education is a basic enabling factor for participation and freedom, for leading a life with dignity and overcoming basic deprivation, secondary education is the gateway for prosperity, for transforming the economy and establishing social justice in any country. It opens the world of work to the youth of the country and contributes to socio-economic development of the community. But, mere expansion of secondary schools, more of the same, is not likely to help. It has to radically transform its basic character in tune with the demands of the emerging knowledge intensive economy, and the far-reaching impact of the globalised market, and the fast changing structure of the knowledge generation establishment under the framework of the evolving intellectual property regime.

It is in this context that NUEPA has undertaken a research study on 'Secondary Education in India' in Collaboration with International Institute for Educational Planning, Paris. The research study report is being published in two volumes covering different aspects of secondary education. The present book "Management of Secondary Education in India" specifically focuses on provision of facilities, internal efficiency, extent of private tuition, teacher management, planning and management of curriculum and textbooks, administration of secondary education including conduct of public examinations. The book highlights the widely varying conditions characterizing development of secondary education in different parts of the country. It is clear that *Rashtriya Madhyamik Shiksha Abhiyan* (RMSA) to be successful should be adaptive to local contexts; a pan-national model of financing and implementation is not likely to work. Also, any development programme in a large federal country such as India demands that the Central Government and State Governments work in close partnership in its design and implementation. Furthermore, it should be noted that a major proportion of secondary schools are in the private sector adding more complexity to the effort to expand secondary schools.

That the volume is being brought out when the RMSA is taking shape is a very significant. The findings of the study reported in the book would hopefully provide direction to further progress in the implementation of RMSA. At the moment, NUEPA is actively involved in building a robust Secondary Education Management Information System (SEMIS) to support the implementation of RMSA. The present volume brought out by Professor K. Sujatha and Dr P. Geetha Rani based on extensive empirical work should add further value to NUEPA's efforts in contributing to the development of secondary education in India. Let me congratulate them and record my deep appreciation for putting together such a comprehensive volume on secondary education in India.

March, 2011

R. Govinda
Vice-Chancellor
NUEPA

Preface

The network of the educational system in the second highest populous country like India is vast in size. Though provision of access is a precondition to educational progress, particularly in improving the agenda of human development but is not a sufficient condition for development of education. In addition to access it is the effective functioning of the schools that determines the quality and in turn translates the efforts into progress. The quality and performance of Indian education system is a major concern and has not received adequate attention. In this context, it is appropriate to examine the quality, performance and management of secondary education in India from a critical perspective.

The present book on "Management of Secondary Education in India: Quality, Performance and Administration" examines various aspects such as the quality and availability of infrastructure and academic facilities in secondary and higher secondary schools; extent of transition, drop-out and repetition, performance of students in public examinations; the nature and extent of private tuition; planning and management of curriculum including textbooks. This book also examines management of secondary education by covering features like administrative structures at various levels, process of establishment, recognition and upgrading of schools, inspection and supervision, teacher deployment, conduct of public examinations etc.

The uniqueness of this book lies in the comparative perspective of management of secondary education from macro to micro-level. The comparative analysis integrates all India, sixteen major states, four sample states i.e. Andhra Pradesh, Kerala, Maharashtra and Uttar Pradesh which are diverse in educational and economic development and case studies of schools.

The present book is part of the major research study on Secondary Education in India funded by NUEPA which was undertaken as part of a Comparative Study on Secondary Education in Developing

Countries initiated by International Institute for Educational Planning (IIEP), Paris.

We would like to thank Mrs. Francoise Caillods, Deputy Director (Retd.), IIEP, Paris for providing the broad research design and her valuable guidance. I am grateful to Professor R. Govinda, Vice-Chancellor, NUEPA for his immense support to publish the present book. I acknowledge with thanks Professor B.P. Khandelwal, former Director, NIEPA for his cooperation and support in undertaking the research study.

I appreciate and thank the research project staff, Dr. Gobind Pal, Dr. Mithilesh Kumar Singh, Dr. N.K. Mohanty and Mr. Pankaj Kumar Singh for their able assistance. I thank Mr. Satish Kumar, NUEPA who without worrying about time or pain, assisted in word-processing the document. I appreciate Mr. Pramod Rawat and Mr. Amit Singhal of Publication Unit, NUEPA for their cooperation and patience in bringing out this publication. I also appreciate Shipra Publications for their interest and cooperation for bringing out the book in its present form.

K. Sujatha

Contents

1

Introduction

Secondary education provides an indispensable link to the whole education that forms the inter connectivity to the higher education system, by providing the required input. As an important point of transition secondary education offers a significant perspective for understanding and analysis of prevailing educational scenario in the country. Research evidences shows that secondary education is the fastest growing sector in most of the countries further emphasising the need of universalisation of secondary education. No country in the world could achieve sustainable development without providing opportunities for secondary education. Though secondary education forms an integral part in the development of the entire education system, very few studies have examined the related issues and problems of secondary education in India. Recently, World Bank (2009) has come out with a document, looking at the aspects of access and equity, management, quality and financing of secondary education in India. However, the present study intends to provide a comprehensive picture of secondary education in India with special emphasis on infrastructure provision, internal efficiency, the prevalence of supplementary tutoring–an entirely unexplored area of secondary education in the Indian context, curriculum development, management of secondary education, and teacher management. The following are the research questions that the study intends to explore and analyse.

Some of the research questions that arise on the basis of available evidence on secondary education and analysis of recent trends are as follows:

1. What is the extent and nature of infrastructure provision in secondary schools?

2. What is the level of quality and internal efficiency of secondary schools?
3. What is the nature of supplementary tutoring in secondary education?
4. What is the administrative and management mechanism of secondary education?
5. How the curriculum is developed at secondary level and how public examination is conducted?

Given the research questions of the study, the framework for analysis will include national, inter-state, regional, district and school level data. The study covers four selected states, their regional, inter-district and schools representing different levels of development (education, economic and industrial). Thus the present book attempts to examine the research questions from macro and the micro level.

Sampling constitutes an important aspect of research design as entire process of data analysis and interpretation depends on the method of sampling. In this study macro level analysis is based on primary and secondary data collected from various sources, while at the micro level we have used sampling techniques to select specific schools representing majority of the traits prevalent in the research universe. However, the sampling procedure was quite different as instead of taking random samples, we have selected the criteria and used them to select schools for case studies. Therefore, it is important to clarify few of the processes and procedures of sampling adopted in this study.

As the study is an integration of both macro and micro level analysis, it was necessary to select specific areas while following broad national pattern in other case. There are three level of analysis made in this study. Firstly, in order to provide a holistic dimension on secondary education its process and pattern i.e. infrastructure provision, internal efficiency, curriculum development, management of secondary education, and teacher management and functioning of secondary schools the study relied heavily on national data collected from divergent sources including Selected Educational Statistics and documents of Ministry of Human Resources Development, data from other government organisations and national and international reports etc. The first part of the description is based on the national level patterns, where educational trends of 17 major states have been discussed. For better representation, the rural-urban difference is also accounted for at the level of inter-state analysis.

The second level of analysis depicts the inter-state variation highlighting the patterns and processes of secondary education in selected sample states. In fact, in order to closely look at this phenomenon and focus on particular issues, it was essential to select a few states, consequently Kerala, Maharashtra, Andhra Pradesh and Uttar Pradesh were considered for the purpose of detailed analysis.

Characteristics of Sample States

The basis of selection of state was indicators of development. For example, Kerala is an educationally developed state, Maharashtra is educationally and economically developed state, Andhra Pradesh is moderately developed both in terms of income and education, while Uttar Pradesh is an underdeveloped state in terms of these development indicators (see Table 1.1). Importantly, these four states constitute, nearly 40 per cent of the total population of the country and around 30 per cent of the territory as well. The table below depicts the variation among the sample states in terms of population, area, sex ratio, literacy and female literacy, per capita income and also their level of educational development in terms of schools and enrolment in secondary education

With regard to secondary education institutions, the four sample stats cover around 30 per cent of the schools in India while their enrolment coverage is 40 per cent of the total secondary enrolment in the country.

States in India are comparatively large and varied in size, structure, political context, and socio-economic set up. The variations are not only limited to inter-state level but also at the intra-state level. In order to make an in-depth study of these sample states, we further stratified them into regions. There are different regions in the state again divided on the basis of their level of development[1] . For instance, Maharastra is evolved as a socio-cultural unit of 3 broad regions, Western Maharashtra, Marthawada and Vidharbha. However, for administrative purposes, the state is divided further into six regions. Andhra Pradesh comprises of three natural regions, based on historical, cultural and economic backgrounds, namely, Coastal region, Rayalseema, and Telangana. Kerala can be divided into three regions on the basis of its physical features, namely the forest highland region, the low land region bordering the sea and the mid land region consisting of Southern, Middle and Northern Region.

Table 1.1: Selected Indicators on Sample States and India

	Population (in millions)	*Area (sq. km)*	*Sex Ratio*	*Literacy*	*Female Literacy*	*Per capita Income (in Rs.)*	*No. of Districts*	*Secondary Schools*	*Enrolment (in millions)*
	2001		2001	2001	2001	2004-05	2001	2003-04	2003-04
Andhra Pradesh	76.21	275068	978	70.32	51.17	23153	23	16427	2.88
Kerala	31.84	38864	1058	90.92	87.86	27048	14	4157	1.15
Maharashtra	96.88	307713	922	77.27	67.51	29204	34	8706	4.55
Uttar Pradesh	166.20	238,566	898	57.36	42.97	11477	70	12387	5.8
India	1028.61	3287590	933	65.38	54.16	23241	516	145962	35.01

Source: Census, 2001, Selected Educational Statistics, 2003-04, National Accounts Statistics, Central Statistical Organisation.

Uttar Pradesh is divided into four geographical regions Central, Bundelkhand, Eastern and Western Regions.

Taking cognisance of these regions and their development parameters, efforts were made to segregate them into smaller units. In the context of Indian state, these units are districts.
Therefore, four districts were chosen, from these four states for further study and analysis. These districts are moderately developed districts of respective states. The reason behind this sort of classification lies in the fact that these districts will help in providing the total picture that includes both developed and backward areas. These districts are Thiruvantapuram (Kerala), Pune (Maharashtra), Nalgonda (Andhra Pradesh) and Varanasi (Uttar Pradesh).

The aggregate data collected at national, state and even at the district level rarely reflect the dynamics taking place at the institutional level in terms of the role of delivery mechanisms and functioning of schools. Therefore, school level data were collected and analysed. For this purpose, 49 schools from four districts of four sample states were chosen. The basis of school selection was their level of performance in public examination at secondary level (X-XII) level in the past five years. In taking the public examination results as indicator it was emphasised that the consistency in the performance must be the criteria. Hence, 'results of schools' with different levels of performance namely the good, moderate and poor were selected as case studies. These schools for better representation of the universe cut across types of management, rural-urban and type of school in terms of their in-take (boys and girls).[2]

There are 49 schools in our case study. Each state has 12 schools, Uttar Pradesh has 13 schools. At the school level, information regarding infrastructure, performance in public examination, staffing, teaching-learning method, nature and extent of private tuition, investment in private tuition and socio-economic status was collected from a pool of informants consisting of the head teacher, teachers and students. The study covered a total number of 4, 945 students, covering 20 per cent of the total number of students from lower and higher secondary classes of the 49 schools. Similarly, all the head teachers and 50 per cent of teachers were interviewed to obtain their perspective.[3] A total of 346 teachers were interviewed from these schools and their opinions were recorded. Students were interviewed to provide data on the extent of private tutoring, money paid for private tuition, socio-economic status of parents etc.[4] The school records and headmasters' opinion formed the basis of information regarding the caste categories of students, Parent Teacher Association, infrastructure, staffing and teaching-learning method. The perspectives of teachers form an important dimension of the study as they are transacting the curriculum and engaged in the teaching-learning process. More importantly, the investigators in the process of field survey collected first hand information and recorded their observations thus, ensuring reliability and validity of data. These data were not only used to describe case studies but have also been referred in appropriate sections. However, the following section provides a brief overview of secondary education in terms of its size in India.

Educational Scenario: An Overview

The post-independent India inherited a poor educational infrastructure from scratch to the massive agenda of educational development. In fact, the Constitution of India guarantees education to all of its citizens. According to the Article 45 of the Constitution, the state shall provide free and compulsory education to the children below fourteen years of age. In order to fulfil these Constitutional mandates and obligations the Indian state has taken several steps to set-up educational provisions in general and school education in particular. A brief glance at Table 1.2 shows the magnitude of educational system in India. The network of the educational system in the second highest populous country like India with its vast size, comprises of 1286 thousand educational institutions having 239.2 million students with 6223 thousand teachers covering different levels of school education (see Table 1.2).

The educational facilities include 787.8 thousand primary schools 325.2 thousand upper primary schools and 113.8 thousand lower secondary schools, 59.2 thousand higher secondary schools, 14.17 thousand higher educational institutions and 294 universities including deemed universities and institutions of national importance in the country. During 2007-08, these educational intuitions enrolled 135.5 million students in primary, 57.2 million in upper primary, 28.2 million in lower secondary, 6.25 million in higher secondary and 10.01 million students in higher education. Such a network of institutions has been developed over a long period of time. India has one of the largest networks of educational institutions in the world.

Table 1.2: Education in India at a Glance: Total Number of Institutions, Size of Enrolment and Number of Teachers (2007-08)

Educational Institutions, Category	*Number of Institutes (in '000)*	*Size of Enrolment (in Millions)*	*Number of Teachers (in '000)*
Primary	787.8	135.5	2315.1
Upper Primary	325.2	57.2	1780.1
Secondary	113.8	28.21	1175.0
Higher Secondary	59. 2	16.25	28.21
Tech. /Indus./Arts & Crafts$ Institutes	4.8	0.71	n.a.
Polytechnic Institutes$	1.1	0.37	n.a.
Teacher Training Institutes$	1.3	0.05	n.a.
Higher Education Institutions$	14.17	10.01	456.74
Universities#	0.29	*	*

\# Includes deemed Universities and Intuitions of National Importance;

* Include in Higher Education Institutions;

** Figure does not include teachers in Technical/Industrial/Arts & Crafts Institutes, Polytechnic Institutes and Teacher Training Institutes.

Source: Selected Educational Statistics, 2007-2008. MHRD, GOI, 2006. $ = Data refers to 2003-04.

Institutional Expansion

The phenomenal growth of education in India can be gauged from the fact that in 1950-51 there were only 209 thousand primary schools, 13.6 thousand upper primary schools and 7.4 secondary and higher secondary schools. Compared to the existing situation mentioned earlier it pales into insignificance. However, it needs to be emphasized that the current educational development profile reflects the improvement of access conditions in a broader perspective. There had been phenomenal expansion of educational facilities at all levels of school education and more so in case of secondary education (see Table 1.3).

The expansion of secondary schools cannot be seen in isolation as it has both forward and backward linkages with other sectors of education, especially the lower levels of school education. More importantly, achievement in elementary education is a pre- requisite for the growth of secondary education besides various other factors, such as accessibility, availability, affordability and social demand etc. At primary level, expansion of educational institutions made in the last few decades is quite commendable. From the decade of 1950s to 2007-08 there has

Table 1.3: Number of Institutions by Levels of School Education in India

(*Figures are in '000*)

Year	Primary	Upper Primary	Secondary	Hr. Secondary	Sec. and Hr. Secondary
1950-51	209.7	13.6	7.4*	–	7.4
1960-61	330.4	49.7	17.3*	–	17.3
1970-71	408.4	90.6	37.1*	–	37.1
1980-81	494.5	118.6	39.3	12.3	51.6
1990-91	560.9	151.5	59.5	19.2	79.8
2000-01	638.7	206.3	87.7	38.4	126.1
2001-02	664.0	219.6	91.4	42.1	133.5
2002-03	651.3	245.3	90.7	46.4	137.2
2003-04	712.2	262.3	99.1	46.8	145.9
2007-08	787.8	325.2	113.8	59.2	173.0

* Includes Secondary and Higher Secondary/ Intermediate/ pre-university/ Jr. college/pre-degree Institutions.

Source: Selected Educational Statistics, Various issues, MHRD, GOI, New Delhi

been a 3-fold increase in the number of primary schools. Similarly, at upper primary and secondary levels the schools have grown by around 19 and 13 times between the periods of 1951 to 2007-08. Though increased number of schools reflects importance attributed to education, it does not reveal the extent of facilities available in terms of distance and coverage of population. Towards this we need to examine access conditions (for details see Sujatha and Geetha Rani, 2010).

Demand for Secondary Education: Growth of Enrolment

India has witnessed an exponential increase in the number of students enrolled at all levels of school education in the last five decade, as discussed earlier. The magnitude of students enrolled at secondary level of education has been as a result of growth of enrolment and expansion of institutions over the years. The growth rate of enrolment varied at different levels and also at different periods of time (see Table 1.4).

The total enrolment during 1950-51 to 2000-01 had increased at the primary; upper primary and secondary stages by 6, 14 and 20 times respectively. A look at the enrolment and decadal growth rate suggests that during 1950-70, there has been more than five-time increase in the growth of enrolment at secondary level. This figure,

Table 1.4: Growth of Enrolment at Secondary Levels in India

Year	*Secondary*	*Hr. Secondary*	*Secondary and Hr. Secondary Together*
1950-51	1.5*	–	1.5
1960-61	3.4 (8.5)*	–	3.4 (8.5)
1970-71	7.6 (8.4)*	–	7.6 (8.4)
1980-81	7.1	4.1	11.2 (4.1)
1990-91	14.5 (7.4)	6.4 (4.6)	20.9 (6.4)
2000-01	19.0 (2.7)	9.9 (4.5)	28.9 (3.3)
1950-2000	40.6 (5.0)**	2.04 (4.5)**	73.6 (6.1)

Note: Figures in parentheses indicate the Compound Annual Growth Rate (CAGR) over decades

* - Includes Secondary and Higher Secondary, Intermediate/pre-university/Jr. college/pre-degree Institutions.

** From 1980-81 to 2000-01

Source: Selected Educational Statistic, Various Issues, MHRD, GOI, New Delhi.

of course, includes intermediate/ pre-university/junior colleges/pre-degree institutions – the names by which higher secondary sections have been known. The trend of enrolment also points that 1970s can be truly called as the 'golden period' of enrolment as more students joined the schools during this period. However, it may be noted that though the enrolment for primary education has shown an increase in terms of absolute numbers, its growth rate has actually declined, when compared to that of 1950-60s. At the all India level, one can discern the cumulative growth of CAGR with increase in the level of school education till secondary stage during the period 1980-81 to 1990-91, while in the decade of 1991-2001 there has been continuous increase of growth rate for enrolment at all levels, including the higher secondary stage.

There was a sudden decline in the growth rate of enrolment at secondary level during the 1970s as after 70s the enrolment started stabilizing. The shift to 10+2+3[5] pattern after educational restructuring led to the enrolment in Grade VIII being clubbed with upper primary stage for the national level accounting of educational statistics. However, during 1980s, the enrolment for lower secondary education had more than doubled from 7.1 millions to 14.5 millions. This substantial rise was not an overnight phenomenon, rather it was because of the factors like increase at the lower level. This growth was not independent rather influenced by efforts to increase the enrolment at the base. In the 70s, enrolment at upper primary level rose significantly, the result of which could be found in the subsequent increase in enrolment at lower secondary level during the 1980s. Many other factors, viz. growth of institutions, fee concessions, free lower secondary education in some states, etc. were responsible for this increase. The compound annual growth rate remained at about the same level in the last decade for higher secondary level.

Role of Different Agencies at Secondary Level

Private participation in providing secondary education has a long tradition in India, dating back to pre-independence period. Secondary education was largely managed by the private agencies but was being funded by the government under grant-in-aid system. The basic philosophy behind the grant-in-aid system was to motivate the local effort and cooperation in managing secondary education. Over the years, state governments had increased the size of grants and financed almost all the expenditures of the private aided schools. Consequently, private managements have come to establish large number of institutions with corresponding number of teachers and students.

The beginning of the new millennium has very critical significance in the context of Indian education in general and secondary education in particular. Though the liberalization process was a decade old, the real effects of liberalization began to take shape during this period and the second phase of liberalization only hastened the pace of change. Consequently, a perceptible difference could be found in the nature and functioning of secondary education in India in terms of access, participation and the types of supply mechanisms. A glance at the number of secondary schools, their coverage and the managements that operate these institutions will facilitate to take note of these transformations at the macro level.

At the all India level, during 1973-74, the private aided secondary schools were the majority, the government was running a little more than one-third of secondary schools and the proportion of private unaided schools was trivial (see Table 1.5). During the last three decades, the percentage share of private aided schools declined sharply from 57 to 34 per cent, while the share of private unaided sector increased significantly, more than four times, the proportion of government schools registered a very marginal improvement. There

Table 1.5: Growth of Secondary Education Institutions by Type of Management in India

(*in per cent*)

Year	*Govt**	*Pvt Aided*	*PUA*	*Total (in Nos.)*
1973-74	37.4	57.0	5.6	–
1980-81*	48.59	51.42	–	47972
1985-86	45.94	43.98	10.08	61638
1990-91	44.05	43.63	12.33	78678
1991-92	43.51	43.37	13.13	81470
1992-93	43.82	41.77	14.42	83490
1993-94	47.03	37.80	15.17	89226
1994-95	45.32	37.84	16.85	92774
1995-96	45.02	36.62	18.36	96952
1996-97	45.70	36.19	18.10	100205
2001-02**	42.45	33.99	23.56	133492
Growth Rates^ (1984-85 to 1996-97)	3.85	2.49	10.62	4.79

^ Growth Rate is calculated by fitting a semi-log linear regression equation of the form Y = a + bt.

Note: Government includes local body schools as Local Body schools are fully managed and funded by the state governments.

* No separate information is available on private aided and unaided schools from 1980-81 to 84-85.

** Selected Educational Statistics.

Source: Education in India Vol.1 (S).

has been a consistency in the substantial rise in the proportion of unaided schools, especially since mid-80s. These schools effectively filled the gap created by the decline in number of private aided schools. Thus by 2001-02, the private unaided sector had grown to cover nearly one-fourth of secondary schools. However, government with 42 per cent schools has replaced the private aided sector as the major player in delivering secondary education, followed by private aided sector with about one-third of total schools. This clearly reflects the dwindling state of private aided sector and to some extent government schools, as they had a growth rate of 2.5 and 3.85 per cent respectively. In contrast, private unaided schools grew at a rate of 10 per cent. It evidences the higher pace of growth of private unaided schools, particularly since late 80s. In other words, this changing trend suggests the inadequate investment of the government on secondary education, on the one hand, and the increasing participation of private sector on the other.

Along with changes in the proportions of schools under different managements, coverage of students in different managements had also changed significantly over the decades. Following the introduction of macro economic policies that included stabilization and structural adjustment policies, a fiscal squeeze was experienced in all social sector investments in many developing countries, including India in the beginning of 1990s. As a follow-up of the economic reform packages, expenditure compression trickled down to public expenditure on education. As a result, many state governments not only refrained from opening new schools but also discouraged the practice of grant-in-aid. New economic policy consisting of Structural Adjustment Programme (SAP), liberalization, globalization of economy and opening of markets not only affected the economy but also the society in general and education in particular. These new policies brought with them improved access and choices for consumers, a higher level of income that resulted in burgeoning of middle class with enhanced purchasing power. The consumer choice and enhanced income level coupled with state polices on 'no-grant-in-aid' and declined investment on secondary education led to the growth of private unaided sector of education.

Given this backdrop, the present book examines the quality of infrastructure provision, internal efficiency, the prevalence of supplementary tutoring–an entirely unexplored area of secondary education in the Indian context, curriculum development, management of secondary education, and teacher management.

NOTES

1. It is not within the purview of the study to examine the dimensions and reasons of their particular status but based on common indicators these regions are divided on the basis of development indicators.
2. Secondary schools can be classified as co-education schools, exclusively for boys and exclusively for girls. In Uttar Pradesh the number of girls' schools at higher secondary level is more and is a state pattern. However, we have all types of schools in our sample.
3. In case of Andhra Pradesh all students and all teachers were interviewed as class size and numbers of teachers are less. For example, higher secondary sections are largely independent in Andhra Pradesh thus reducing the total number of students and teachers. On the contrary in other three states the number of sections and teachers are more.

4. The data regarding the economic status of their parents and amount paid for private tuition were collected from students thus, the reliability and validity of such an observation have limitation.
5. This pattern (ten years of schooling) comprises of 5 years of primary, three years of upper primary and two years of lower secondary, followed by two years of higher secondary and three years of first university degree. This means ten years of schooling before higher secondary education.

2

Infrastructural Provisions: Size and Nature

The transformation of the globe from a 'growth-based' economy to a 'knowledge based' economy and increasing emphasis on 'human development' have brought education into the forefront of development debate. Education defined in terms of capacity building, enhancement of skills, experience and insight is an integral part of any human resource development package and hence, the need to have a critical look at the educational scenario in general and the quality of education in particular. In the analytical framework of educational assessment it is believed that access and enrolment, though, play dominant role in making education reach out to larger sections, do not themselves ensure educational progress, especially school effectiveness. They are, of course, parameters of development of education rather than being measures of standards of quality education. In this chapter, an attempt has been made to look at quality of education from a critical perspective as the last chapter had thrown light on the degree of demand, access to and participation in education. The quality of education depends, among other things, on the availability of physical and academic facilities.

Provision of physical and academic facilities is the precondition for effective functioning of schools and for achieving academic excellence. The serious efforts of different agencies to supply secondary education reflect the extent of provision of physical facilities and creating appropriate teaching learning conditions. Availability of facilities in a school can be divided into physical and ancillary facilities. Further, physical facilities are sub-divided as infrastructure and academic facilities. As far as physical facilities or physical infrastructure is concerned one can include availability of permanent buildings, adequate classrooms. The academic facilities comprise laboratory, library and teaching-learning aids. In addition the quality provisions include educational qualification and training of teachers, favourable teacher-pupil ratio, teaching load and availability of subject teachers, co-curricular activities with a mindset towards academic learning etc. Ancillary infrastructure refers to the presence of well-marked school compound, playground, drinking water, urinals and separate toilets for girls, etc. In this chapter, the attempt is to look at the extent of availability of these facilities. Secondary data from AISE, DISE and also field level information collected from sample schools are used for analysis. It may be noted here that information in respect of both AIES and DISE is limited to few aspects and hence, at most, throw light on macro level scenario. But, for a holistic understanding of secondary education, it is necessary to go beyond the given data. Hence, secondary data are supplemented with micro level data collected from sample schools.

The analysis of physical facilities, particularly the availability of school building and other ancillary facilities is carried out in the following section. This is followed by an examination of the quality of teaching-learning provisions, particularly related to teacher characteristics. In the last section, concluding observations are made.

PHYSICAL INFRASTRUCTURE

A school building not only provides an identity to school, separating it from others, but it is also essential for effective teaching-learning activity in the classroom and for facilitating teachers, students, records, and safeguarding materials from the vagaries of weather.

Contrary to the common belief, there has been improvement in infrastructural facilities in the last one decade as is clear from the seventh all India educational survey (2002) compared to sixth all India educational survey (1993), as shown in Table 2.1.

Along with huge expansion of schools at all levels, there has been a considerable increase in the extent of availability of permanent building facilities, more so for secondary schools. At all India level, 85 per cent of all schools have pucca buildings as against only 67 per cent during the year 1993. The extent of pucca buildings gradually rises with the increase of level of schooling. 92 per cent of higher secondary schools in 2002 had pucca buildings as compared to only 84 per cent

Table 2.1: Physical Facilities in Secondary and Higher Secondary Schools Location in India (in %)

	Secondary				*Higher Secondary*			
	7th AIES (2002)		*6th AIES (1993)*		*7th AIES (2002)*		*6th AIES (1993)*	
Type of Buildings	*Rural*	*Urban*	*Rural*	*Urban*	*Rural*	*Urban*	*Rural*	*Urban*
Pucca Building	85.65	92.01	63.66	81.99	89.92	94.57	78.54	89.19
Partially Pucca	10.41	6.52	25.69	14.00	8.81	5.00	17.88	9.02
Kuchcha Thatched	3.26	1.28	10.05	3.74	1.14	0.36	3.25	1.54
Tent	0.16	0.08	0.15	0.12	0.05	0.04	0.04	0.09
Open Space	0.52	0.10	0.50	0.14	0.08	0.04	0.28	0.16

Source: Sixth and Seventh All India Educational Surveys, NCERT, New Delhi

Note: *Pucca Building*: A school building is to be treated as pucca if it has its walls and roof made of the following materials.

Wall Material: Burnt bricks, stones (duly packed with lime or cement), cement concrete or timber, plywood, artificial wood of synthetic material and PVC.

Roof Materials: Tiles, G.I./Metal/asbestos sheets, concrete, bricks, stone, timber, plywood, artificial wood of synthetic material and PVC.

Partly Pucca Building: A school building is to be treated as partly pucca if it has its walls made of the above mentioned materials but roof is made of the materials other than those mentioned above such as bamboos, grass, thatch, etc.

Kuchcha Building: A school building, the walls and/or roof of which are made of material other than those mentioned above such as unburnt bricks, bamboo, mud, grass, reeds, thatch, loosely backed stones is to be treated as a kuchcha building.

during 1993. At secondary level, there has been significant increase of pucca buildings in last decade, which has gone up from 69 per cent to 88 per cent in 2002. Similar trend is witnessed at primary and upper primary levels, having 84 per cent and 86 per cent of pucca buildings respectively as against 65 per cent and 68 per cent in 1993.

The progress is evident in terms of increased percentage of schools having pucca buildings and simultaneously declining percentage of schools run in partially pucca and Kachcha houses. Despite improvement, yet 12 per cent of secondary and 8 per cent of higher secondary schools did not have pucca buildings. Further, it may be noted that 9 per cent of secondary schools and 7 per cent of higher secondary schools are functioning in partially Pucca buildings, while 2.61 per cent of secondary schools and 1 per cent of higher secondary schools have kachcha buildings, Similarly, 0.13 and 0.04 per cent of secondary and higher secondary schools respectively are run in tents and significantly, 0.38 and 0.06 per cent of secondary and higher secondary schools function in the open spaces. Though statistically, and in terms of percentage, these number look insignificant, viewed in the context of absolute numbers and the phenomenal increase in secondary schools, it drives home the point that lot needs to be done to improve the conditions of secondary schools in India. It also shows that more than one tenth of secondary schools and 7 per cent of higher secondary schools do not have all-weather buildings. However, more number of schools conducted in open space are found in rural areas.

Inter-State Variation

The improvement in building facilities is not only at national level but also impressive increase has been witnessed among different states in previous decade. While all the states have improved extent of permanent buildings some of them made remarkable progress.

All the 17 major states showed considerable growth of pucca buildings at secondary level in preceding decade. While some of the states had steep increase of pucca buildings, in a few states there was only marginal improvement. There is a wide range of variation among different states in the extent of provision of school buildings (see Table 2.2). There has been 20-30 per cent increase in the extent of pucca buildings among different states during the period of 1993 to 2002. The inter-state disparities had narrowed during 1993 to 2002, yet few states are lagging far behind others. Among 17 major states, while six states have above ninety per cent of schools with pucca buildings five states had lower than national level average.

In the economically better off states like Punjab and Haryana, 97 per cent to 99 per cent of secondary and higher schools have pucca buildings, topping the country in this respect. Fascinatingly, Rajasthan, that is educationally and economically backward and is popularly referred to as one of the "BiMARU" states, has almost 99 per cent secondary schools with pucca buildings. Educationally and economically backward hilly state Assam has the lowest position as only a little more than one third of secondary schools have pucca buildings (35%). However, Uttar Pradesh which is also one of the most backward (BiMARU) states had higher percentage of pucca

Table 2.2: State-wise Share of Pucca (Permanent) Building at the Secondary and Higher Secondary level in 1993 and 2002 (in percentage)

States	*Secondary*				*Higher Secondary*			
	7th AIES (2002)		*6th AIES (1993)*		*7th AIES (2002)*		*6th AIES (1993)*	
	*No. of Schools**	*Pucca Building*	*No. of Schools**	*Pucca Building*	*No. of Schools**	*Pucca Building*	*No. of Schools**	*Pucca Building*
Andhra Pradesh	12371	89.06	12371	89.06	2730	86.45	1292	77.01
Kerala	1419	91.68	1419	91.68	1596	92.23	295	78.98
Maharashtra	13181	86.28	13181	86.28	3481	94.25	2372	83.68
Uttar Pradesh	4441	92.21	4441	92.21	7036	95.49	4311	89.56
Assam	*675*	*35.11*	*675*	*35.11*	*675*	*35.11*	597	41.21
Bihar	*597*	*58.96*	*597*	*58.96*	*597*	*58.96*	500	83.60
Gujarat	4629	86.78	4629	86.78	2452	95.84	1835	94.77
Haryana	3442	98.98	3442	98.98	1632	98.59	536	97.76
Himachal Pradesh	1320	70.76	1320	70.76	807	77.57	241	65.56
Karnataka	7739	92.31	7739	92.31	1771	96.50	1276	89.89
Madhya Pradesh	4087	82.02	4087	82.02	4000	88.03	2913	82.66
Orissa	*507*	*48.32*	*507*	*48.32*	*507*	*48.32*	383	77.28
Punjab	2230	96.82	2230	96.82	1748	97.94	744	96.10
Rajasthan	5616	97.95	5616	97.95	2915	98.70	1204	97.67
Tamil Nadu	4356	84.23	4356	84.23	4065	87.43	2250	66.76
West Bengal	4785	81.76	4785	81.76	2891	92.11	1265	90.12
All India**	75844	87.74	75844	87.74	41997	92.18	23662	83.97

Source: Sixth and Seventh All India Educational Surveys, NCERT, New Delhi

Note: The data for Assam, Bihar and Orissa are not available in 7th AIES. Hence, DISE data (NIEPA), 2003, which include upper primary with secondary and higher secondary are used.

*The data on number of schools in numbers.

** All India includes all the States and Union Territories of India

buildings. Startlingly, educationally and economically developed state of Maharashtra lags behind many sates with only 86 per cent secondary schools having pucca buildings. Similarly, some of the states like Tamil Nadu and Gujarat, that are considered educationally and economically medium level developed have apparently poor infrastructure for schools as nearly 15 per cent of the schools lack pucca buildings. Interestingly Himalayan ridge state Himachal Pradesh, that showed impressive achievements in terms of literacy and universal elementary education has been able to provide permanent buildings to only two thirds of secondary schools. Educationally developed state like Kerala is no different from educationally backward state like Andhra Pradesh in provision of the extent of pucca buildings for secondary schools (91%). The educationally and economically backward states like Bihar and Orissa understandably have low per cent of pucca school buildings.

As far as higher secondary schools are concerned, the situation the situation is better both at national level and among different states with Gujarat and Karnataka, Maharashtra, West Bengal joining Punjab, Haryana and Rajasthan in having more than 90 per cent of schools with permanent buildings. Further, in most of the states, almost 90 per cent of higher secondary schools have pucca buildings. In other words, very small proportion of higher secondary schools is run in Kachcha houses, tents or open space.

RURAL-URBAN DIFFERENCES

The extent of different types of school buildings not only differs among different states but also rural urban disparities are obvious in most of the states. Apparently urban schools have better infrastructure in the form of pucca buildings compared to rural schools. 92 per cent of urban secondary schools have pucca buildings as against 86 per cent in rural areas. One-tenth of rural secondary schools had partially pucca buildings compared to 7 per cent in urban areas. Further, higher percentage of schools having non-permanent buildings (kachcha buildings/open space) is in rural compared to urban areas. Similar situation prevails at higher secondary level also with rural areas comparatively having lesser extent of pucca buildings (see Table 2.3).

The rural-urban disparities vary among different states. However, in case of three states that have the highest per cent of schools with pucca buildings i.e., Punjab, Haryana and Rajasthan rural-urban disparities are visibly absent. Similarly, in case of Kerala and Andhra Pradesh there is no difference on this count between rural and urban localities. Contrarily, in states with lower percentage of pucca school buildings, there is a sharp differences between rural-urban schools, with the later category having concentration of pucca buildings. However, in the preceding decade, the gap between rural-urban areas in percentage of pucca buildings has narrowed drastically. The extent of improvement in school buildings is striking in rural areas than in urban areas leading thereby to narrowing the disparity. In rural areas there had been 22 per cent increase in the extent of pucca buildings at secondary level as against 10 per cent in urban areas. There is

Table 2.3: State-wise Type of Building at the Secondary Level in Rural and Urban Areas (%), 1993 and 2002

	7th AIES (2002)				*6th AIES (1993)*			
	Rural		*Urban*		*Rural*		*Urban*	
	*No. of School**	*Pucca Buildings*	*No. of School**	*Pucca Buildings*	*No. of School**	*Pucca Buildings*	*No. of School**	*Pucca Buildings*
Andhra Pradesh	8285	89	4086	88	4762	75	2197	80
Kerala	1053	91	366	93	1621	78	565	84
Maharashtra	8825	83	4356	93	6498	57	3339	82
Uttar Pradesh	2802	92	1639	97	1849	78	684	91
Gujarat	3265	83	1364	96	2937	80	831	94
Haryana	2551	99	891	99	1667	98	507	98
Himachal Pradesh	1167	68	153	94	916	39	109	82
Karnataka	4635	92	3104	93	3219	73	1761	83
Madhya Pradesh	2510	76	1577	92	1673	64	998	90
Punjab	1758	96	472	98	1717	93	437	96
Rajasthan	3857	98	1759	98	2643	96	687	97
Tamil Nadu	2419	89	1937	89	2344	44	1041	70
West Bengal	3542	78	1243	93	3182	62	1405	86
All India**	50929	86	24915	92	47870	64	17694	82

Source: Sixth and Seventh All India Educational Surveys, NCERT, New Delhi.

Note: * Number of schools in numbers.

** All India includes all the States and Union Territories.

glaring variation among different states in the extent of increase of pucca buildings in rural areas. The percentage increase ranges from 1 per cent to 45 per cent among 17 states. In five states, the increase had been 12 per cent to 16 per cent while in two states it varied 25-30 per cent. In 3 states the percentage increase of pucca buildings was very insignificant, that is, 1-3 per cent. However, these sates already had a very high per cent of pucca buildings for secondary schools. In Tamil Nadu not only the percentage of pucca buildings has more than doubled in the last decade, from mere 44 per cent to 89 per cent but also the rural-urban disparity has also disappeared. However, in hilly backward state Himachal Pradesh, though there has been significant improvement in the extent of pucca buildings, yet the rural-urban difference is considerably large. This evidently proves that the secondary schools in rural areas are fast moving up at least in respect of acquiring permanent buildings, though they lag behind in other aspects.

At all India higher secondary level, there had been 11 per cent of increase of pucca buildings in rural areas compared to 5 per cent in urban areas (see Table 2.4). The rural-urban variation remained more or less same compared to previous decade. While in those states with high percentage of pucca buildings, there was very marginal increase. Among other states, the extent of increase of pucca buildings varied from 9 per cent to 17 per cent among 6 states. Likewise at secondary level, Tamil Nadu state had the highest percentage increase (17%) but with marginal decline in rural-urban disparity. The state Kerala has also witnessed notable increase in pucca buildings. West Bengal, which, though lags behind in terms of having permanent buildings for secondary schools, comes high in case of higher secondary schools (90.12%).

Improvement in rural context can be attributed to different factors. The National Finance Commission awards finances to states for rural

Table 2.4: State-wise Type of Building at the Higher Secondary Level in Rural and Urban Areas (%), 1993 and 2002

States	*7th AIES (2002)*				*6th AIES (1993)*			
	Rural		*Urban*		*Rural*		*Urban*	
	*No. of School**	*Pucca Buildings*	*No. of School**	*Pucca Buildings*	*No. of School**	*Pucca Buildings*	*No. of School**	*Pucca Buildings*
Andhra Pradesh	1365	83	1365	89	523	73	769	80
Kerala	1041	91	555	95	205	74	90	90
Maharashtra	2070	93	1411	95	1308	79	1064	90
Uttar Pradesh	3905	94	3131	97	2450	85	1861	96
Gujarat	1109	94	1343	97	769	93	1066	96
Haryana	892	99	740	98	252	99	284	97
Himachal Pradesh	643	75	164	87	167	59	74	81
Karnataka	879	97	892	96	696	88	580	92
Madhya Pradesh	1714	79	2286	95	1338	71	1575	92
Punjab	1177	98	571	98	366	96	378	96
Rajasthan	1643	99	1272	98	461	97	743	98
Tamil Nadu	1345	81	2720	91	1008	58	1242	74
West Bengal	1531	89	1360	96	609	86	656	94
All India**	21578	90	20419	95	11600	79	23662	89

Source: Sixth and Seventh All India Educational Survey, NCERT, New Delhi.

Note: * Number of schools in actual numbers.

** All India includes all the States and Union Territories.

development. This allocation has a strong component for construction of school buildings. And the backward and poorer states get higher allocation from Finance Commission. This facilitates to construct school buildings in rural areas. In the last fifteen years, the national government sponsored schemes like 'Operation Black Board' and District Primary Education Programme have very strong ingredient of construction of permanent buildings for primary and upper primary schools, mainly in rural areas. Normally, secondary schools are established by upgrading upper primary schools. Therefore, the secondary schools, established in the last decade, have the benefit of inheriting permanent buildings. The 73rd Constitutional amendment and consequent empowerment of local bodies through direct funding from centre to the district level bodies, to a large extent, has helped to improve rural infrastructure, especially school buildings, as these funds are mostly utilized for construction. Another important factor for increase of pucca buildings is 'Constituency Development Fund' provided to all the elected representatives. Most of the elected representatives of Parliament, State Legislative Assemblies, district and block level local bodies allocate part of the Constituency Development Fund for construction of school buildings. Also in few states, like Tamil Nadu the increase of pucca school buildings reflects the focus of state policy on rural secondary schools as part of a political compulsion. And it may also be explained that in many states, the private unaided sector is fast expanding secondary schooling facilities in urban areas, whereas in rural areas still government is the main provider of secondary education. Therefore, the governments consciously pay attention on rural schools. The case of Rajasthan shows that economic condition and educational backwardness of the state has little value in terms of providing infrastructure to schools. As historical reasons related with being former princely state, extreme weather conditions, elite characteristic of secondary education following norms by state government etc. are the main reasons for exceptionally exclusive permanent buildings for secondary schools in Rajasthan. In addition, one of the important reasons for increased percentage of permanent buildings can be associated with increased proportion of private unaided schools, especially in the last decade. Normally, unaided schools fulfil the conditions laid down by the central or state government affiliated bodies. In providing the building facilities. The private managements provide permanent buildings in order to face market competition and to attract students. Recently established private unaided schools are mostly located in surroundings of urban areas, as the availability of land and cost of it are considerations. Generally these schools are classified as rural and they mostly possess permanent buildings. This also has been one of the factors for increased proportion of permanent building facilities in rural areas. Thus, once mere urban-based private unaided schools become accessible, they are able to meet the demand of rural people. In many states, the private unaided residential schools are invariably located in rural localities, nearer to the urban centres. This has really helped rural people to avail quality facilities if they can afford the cost.

The poor state of building facilities in north-eastern hilly state of Assam and that of Himachal Pradesh in the north can be explained from different perspectives. In Assam, traditionally, family venture was the practice in establishing and running schools; hardly any strict norms prevailed regarding provision of buildings as education was more of social responsibility at low cost. Even after state has taken over the responsibility to provide secondary schools, the historical hangover of running schools in partially pucca or kachcha houses continued. In addition, being difficult and hilly and high altitude terrains, frequent floods, deeply infested by extremists activities, dwindling economic status of the state could be probable reasons for lack of permanent buildings at all levels of school education, more specifically at secondary level. Similarly, Himachal Pradesh, that is hilly state with less of infrastructure development, could not provide pucca school buildings, especially in tribal and interior rural areas. The practical problem in construction of pucca buildings in difficult hill terrains is obvious.

The availability of pucca school buildings alone does not ensure effective functioning of schools. The associated ancillary facilities are equally important. Hence, the size and nature of these facilities are examined.

Ancillary Facilities

Availability of drinking water facility, playground, urinals, separate toilet for girls, counselling and guidance service constitute largely the ancillary facilities (see Figure 2.1).

Student welfare facilities include drinking water, urinal, lavatories, lavatories for girls and playgrounds facilities for which the provision is better in higher secondary schools than secondary schools. While

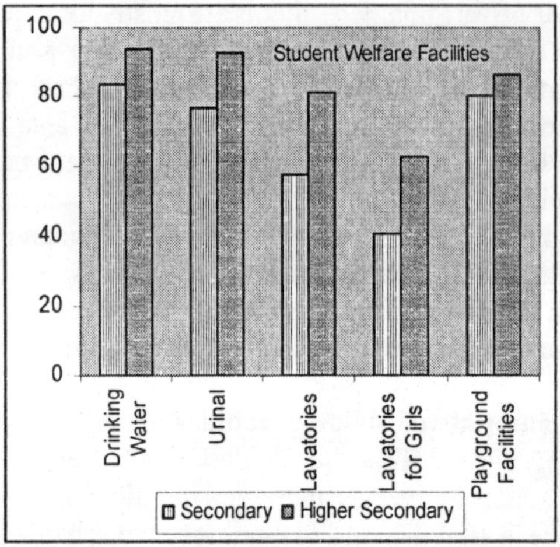

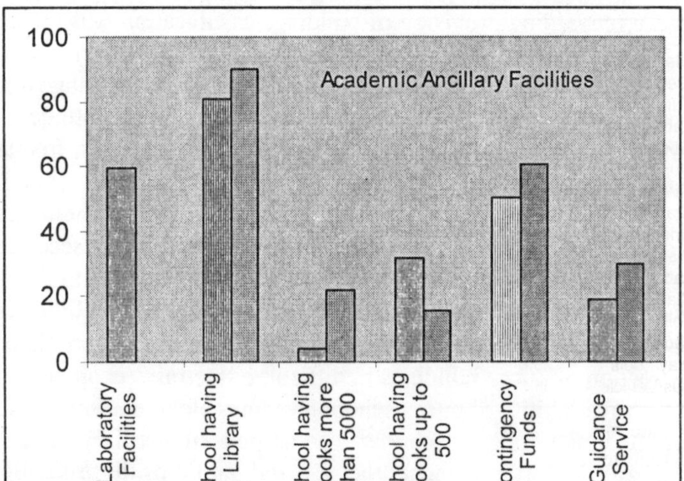

Figure 2.1: Percentage of Secondary and Higher Secondary Schools Having Different Facilities in India

Source: Sixth All India Educational Survey, NCERT, New Delhi

the academic ancillary facilities consisting of laboratories, schools with library, schools with a range of more than 5000 books and up to 500 books, contingency funds for teachers and guidance service for students are not better compared to the student welfare facilities. These academic ancillary facilities are equally important for improving the quality of secondary education, which is far from satisfactory. This information is little outdated but can be updated as and when the same kind of information is available either from 7th AIES or from other sources.

The national, state and regional level data present only a general picture of the situation. They rarely indicate about ground reality at school level. An important question is whether the buildings and classrooms are adequate and have congenial environment for teaching learning. A close look at school scenario drawn form the case studies provide more in-depth and micro level understanding and veracity of the situation (see Table 2.5).

Table 2.5: Percentage of Schools Having Different Facilities in Sample States

Basic Facilities	*A.P.*		*Kerala*		*Maharastra*		*U.P.*		*TOTAL*	
	Ade.	*In ade.*	*Ade.*	*In ade.*	*Ade.*	*In ade.*	*Ade.*	*In ade.*	*Ade.*	*In ade.*
School Blds.	41.7	58.3	75.0	25.0	83.3	16.7	58.3	41.7	64.6	35.4
Classrooms	33.3	66.7	75.0	25.0	91.7	8.3	58.3	41.7	64.6	35.4
Electricity	50.0	25.0	100.0	0.0	91.7	8.3	66.7	16.7	77.1	12.5
Furniture	33.3	50.0	75.0	25.0	83.3	16.7	50.0	50.0	60.4	35.4
Laboratory	16.7	16.7	75.0	25.0	91.7	8.3	66.7	33.3	62.5	20.8
Library	8.3	33.3	75.0	25.0	91.7	8.3	41.7	58.3	54.2	31.3
Computers	41.7	0.0	58.3	25.0	58.3	33.3	33.3	16.7	47.9	18.8
TV/Telephone	41.7	0.0	75.0	25.0	75.0	25.0	41.7	33.3	58.3	20.8
Staff Room	41.7	58.3	75.0	25.0	91.7	8.3	75.0	16.7	70.8	27.1
Drinking Water	91.7	8.3	83.3	16.7	100.0	0.0	66.7	33.3	85.4	14.6
Play Grounds	75.0	25.0	50.0	33.3	58.3	33.3	66.7	25.0	62.5	29.2
Lab. Equipts.	25.0	25.0	58.3	41.7	83.3	16.7	58.3	41.7	56.3	31.3
Classroom fan	16.7	16.7	33.3	66.7	75.0	8.3	58.3	41.7	45.8	33.3
Toilet	58.3	8.3	91.7	8.3	91.7	8.3	66.7	33.3	77.1	14.6
Ladies Toilet	58.3	16.7	83.3	8.3	100.0	0.0	58.3	33.3	75.0	14.6
Play Tools	25.0	41.7	41.7	41.7	50.0	41.7	41.7	25.0	39.6	37.5
Bus/Vehicle	8.3	0.0	33.3	8.3	8.3	8.3	16.7	8.3	16.7	6.3

* Ade. = Adequate; In ade. = Inadequate; The rest is not available which is not reported in the Table as it is self derived; A.P. = Andhra Pradesh; U.P. = Uttar Pradesh.

Source: Based on the data from Sample Schools (N = 48).

Despite improved building facilities at macro level, one-third of case study schools covered in four sample sates had inadequate classrooms to run all the classes. There is variation among the sample schools located in different states. In Andhra Pradesh 67 per cent of sample schools face shortage of classrooms as against only 8 per cent in Maharashtra. In Uttar Pradesh, 41 per cent of schools suffer from inadequate number of classrooms while one-third of schools in Kerala lack sufficient number of classrooms. Further, availability of facilities also varies from school to school based on locality, management types, residential and day schools. Though micro-level data from sample schools show that there is very little to choose between private aided schools and government schools regarding the adequacy of infrastructure, yet there has been a considerable variation in terms of claims made by various management groups regarding actual status of infrastructure. The case studies evidently prove that even schools considered as good schools too represent lack of adequate classrooms and building facilities. Some of the sample schools in rural areas have pathetically inadequate facilities and uncongenial environment These schools belong both to the good and the poor performing categories. Similarly, some of the schools, despite having pucca buildings, lack congenial learning environment due to shape and size of classrooms, lack of ventilation etc. (see Box 2.1 for the situation in ZP High School, Begumpet, Andhra Pradesh and Box 2.2 relating to ZP High School, Huzurnagar, Andhra Pradesh).

Box 2.1

The school has a pucca building of its own, with a compound wall and a bore well. Each class is provided with a room with sufficient number of long benches for the students and chairs and tables for the teachers. Classes VI and VII are accommodated in three rooms, with windows open to each other class. They are neither symmetrical nor orderly constructed, giving an appearance of a goods shed, where material is stored; not congenial for learning. As there are windows open for one class to another class, instruction in one class affects the other class. Ventilation is very bad, no electrification, no provision for fans, lot of suffocation is there. There are four big halls constructed recently. One hall is allotted for the Head Master and the staff. With the help of almirahs, partition is made. On the one end, the Head Master sits and the staff sit on the other end. There is no privacy. Classes X and IX are accommodated in the other two halls. RCC roof is laid on the walls only, without having pillars. Since it is a loose black soil, the foundation being not deep, roof laid on nine inches walls, resulted in cracks and one hall, which is not being used, is almost in a collapsing condition.

ZP High School, A.P. (2005)

Box 2.2

The infrastructure of the school is very poor and awfully inadequate. There are only four classrooms and the built-in area is inadequate. Due to this the school did not get the computers. There are no toilets in the school neither for teachers nor for students. Teaching aids (charts, maps), laboratory, library are not available to the students. Only two classrooms have furniture for students; rest of them are sit on the floor. The school does not have night watchman. Window pans are broken by local people who are using them for various activities during non-school hours and holidays. The school has electricity and the office-cum-staff room has fans and lights but no classroom has electric bulbs. Laboratory and library are only on paper. The school has spacious playground but it has no sports equipments for the students to play.

ZP High School, A.P. (2005)

Increased enrolment leading to deterioration of facilities is not so uncommon among some of the sample schools. This is more so, in case of old schools, especially in urban localities that were built long back with limited space. Currently, these schools with dilapidated buildings face tough situation with growing demand on the one hand, and on the other they could not expand the facilities due scarcity of space. In addition, some times functioning of the schools is affected by external disturbances like sound and traffic having direct effect on academic environment (see Box 2.3 as in Ashok Vidyalaya, Pune, Private Aided School in Maharashtra and Box 2.4: as in S.M. Choksey High School, Pune, Partially Aided school in Maharashtra).

Box 2.3

Ashok Vidyalaya has its building in the heart of the city. It is convenient for the students. But it doesn't have spacious verandah or playground. It creates hurdles in the free movements. The school works in one shift only. Also the traffic noise on the main road creates much more difficulties for the teachers while teaching. Truly speaking, the school doesn't get the advantage of calm and quiet surrounding. The school doesn't have its own transport facility. The students come to school by Rickshaw, PMT Bus or on foot. Some students have hostel facility. The classrooms are big, spacious and airy but do not have fan and proper electricity supply. Despite these difficulties, the teachers' hard work and good teaching adds to the development of the school. Toilets are available for ladies but there are no adequate toilet facility for gents. So it creates inconvenience. Teachers don't have separate staff room. They don't have special room for completing their daily work or they can't sit together to exchange their thoughts and ideas, or cannot have rest for few minutes.

Pune (Private Aided School) (2005)

Box 2.4

It is seen that the school does not have adequate school building. The classrooms are also small in size. The building was erected during 1945-48. The building was large enough to accommodate all the classes in one shift at that time. But due to increase in number of students, the area per student had shrinked to such a level that the management was forced to run the school in two shifts. The area of the classroom creates another problem. The old norm of 40 students per class could be well placed hygienically in 22' × 20'= 440 sq. feet area of the classroom (i.e. 10 sq. feet area per student). Now a days, minimum number of students in each classroom in urban schools is 60. Thus reducing area per student gives rise to many problems – personal, administrative, academic, social. The classroom can accommodate 20 benches of standard size. Hence the norm of 2 students per bench cannot be adhered and new norms of 3 students per bench creates all types of difficulties. *Financially it is not difficult to provide the necessary furniture to the school by the management. but lack of space is the problem which is too difficult to overcome.* Insufficient space is the cause to curtail many school activities. There are no classrooms available for crafts, drawing, music and many other extra curricular activities. There is no suitable hall to accommodate the computers and allied machinery. The school has no ground at all. Organizing the physical exercises and games for the entire school is not possible. Playing games is a must to create a healthy body and a healthy mind (and in future healthy citizens). Physical drills imbibe sense of togetherness in students. Being a city-school there is no open space around the school premises. Games like cricket, foot ball, rolling ball, kho-kho, wrestling, individual athletic items like running, long jump, high jump, for the students are not possible. Even for indoor games like table-tennis, badminton, there is no hall available. Any type of sports material is not available in the school. This is a major handicap and the school is devoid of any prizes in the games.

High School, Pune (Partially Private Aided) (2005)

There are several reasons behind this abysmal record. First of all, up-gradation of upper primary schools to secondary and higher secondary schools without looking at the feasibility of such an exercise. Mere up-gradation of schools without improving and adding necessary infrastructure did prove the undoing of many schools. Secondly, the norms regarding up-gradation of schools to secondary were never seriously follo1wed. Further, in case of private schools management making false claims, manage to get approval from education department by adopting dubious methods even without appropriate facilities. In case of government schools with the increase of enrolment, hardly new additional classrooms are ever constructed. The private unaided schools that are established on commercial basis yet adopt an attitude of squeezing the limited facilities in view investment considerations. However, they utilize the resources optimally.

Thus even if there is significant increase in the extent of pucca buildings, still the adequacy of classrooms and congenial environment for teaching learning remains far from satisfactory.

At micro level situation, the school case studies depict no better picture from that of the last decade. Only 62 per cent of sample schools have laboratories out of which in 20 per cent schools the facility is inadequate. The remaining schools do not have laboratories. In case of Andhra Pradesh, a majority of secondary schools didn't have laboratory, even those of them that have, are only for namesake. In Kerala, Uttar Pradesh and Maharashtra, more number of laboratories have an educational structure where secondary and higher secondary classes are integrated. Even among the integrated schools, the laboratory facilities are rare if they do not have science stream.

In this backdrop, one can certainly presume that unsatisfactory situation of ancillary facilities does affect the quality of teaching-learning process.

QUALITY OF TEACHING-LEARNING PROVISIONS

Teacher Qualifications

Teachers are integral part of the educational system and it is on them that the responsibility of quality of education mainly rests. Entrusted with the onerous responsibility of transacting the curriculum and indoctrinating the nuances of subjects in students, they have a major role to play. But then, in order to fulfil these obligations, a teacher must have necessary qualification, competency and experience. It is in this sense that teacher qualification and experience become important to any educational system, more so in secondary education that remains in the centre of educational hierarchy. Most important aspects in quality provisions include feasible teaching learning conditions like teacher-pupil ratio, availability of subject teachers, workload of teachers, pedagogical strategies, student assessment methods, remedial teaching, external and internal academic supervision, professional development of teachers etc. The prescribed norm for teachers in secondary schools in India is Bachelor's degree or first University degree along with training which is also known as Bachelor of Education that imparts necessary pedagogical skills to impart education. For the higher secondary classes, the aspirant teachers should have a master's degree or a post-graduation in a subject with or without training. We have discussed issues pertaining to the qualification of teachers in management chapter in detail. The composition of teachers with differential qualification varies, based on structure of schools. The structure of secondary and higher secondary education demonstrates a differential and divergent scenario. There are integrated schools having classes from V-X/XII, VI-X/XII or VII/VIII-XII. This varied structure of secondary education becomes important in the context of recruitment, deployment and allotment of classes to teachers. In these cases it is not unusual to find teachers of class-VI taking classes VIII, IX and X and the reverse is even commoner than that. Similarly, in some of the states like Uttar Pradesh, teachers of higher secondary level have to teach secondary classes and secondary teachers to teach in lower secondary classes for prescribed number of periods. These integrated classes are common in all the four sample states. While lower classes have advantage of being taught by higher qualification teachers the higher classes some time have disadvantage of being taught by unqualified teachers. According to all India Educational Survey (1993), only 33 per cent of teachers in secondary level had Bachelors' degree or above, while 61 per cent of them had passed higher secondary (see Figure 2.3 and Table 2.6). It means that 61 per cent of teachers with higher secondary qualification teach lower grades in secondary schools and teachers with Bachelor's degree qualification were given secondary classes and even had to teach lower classes depending on the demands of the school. Data on teachers' qualifications reveal that among the states of India, Assam had a very low percentage of teachers (8%) with Bachelor's degree and Uttar Pradesh had a high 68 percentage of teachers at secondary level with Bachelor's degree.

An interesting trend emerges from the Table 2.6. The states where there is higher percentage of qualified teachers i.e., graduates and above, had lesser percentage of less qualified teachers. For instance, Uttar Pradesh had the highest per cent of teachers with graduate and above qualification, while the least per cent of teachers with higher secondary qualifications. The same is true in a few other states like Madhya Pradesh, Rajasthan and Bihar. These states fall into the category of educationally backward states, while the reverse of the situations can be found in states like Assam, Kerala, Karnataka, Maharashtra, Gujarat and few other states. It may be noted, most of these states are educationally developed ones. This inverse kind of relationship between teacher qualification and educational development needs to be further explored in terms of the political patronage the teachers occupy in these states (for details see the section on teacher management in the chapter on Management of Secondary Education).

Table 2.6: Educational Qualification of Teachers in Secondary Schools in Sample States

States	*Levels by Qualification*		
	Higher Secondary	*Graduate and Above*	*Any other*
Andhra Pradesh	73.27	25.99	0.75
Kerala	88.35	10.14	1.51
Maharashtra	75.53	22.98	1.46
Uttar Pradesh	31.81	68.01	0.18
All India	65.97	32.92	1.12

Source: Sixth All India Educational Survey, NCERT, New Delhi, 1993.

The educational qualification of teachers varied among different states. Few states like Rajasthan and Madhya Pradesh have a higher per cent of teachers (50%-68%) with first-degree. Contrary to this, in many states secondary schools were integrated with upper primary classes, therefore, a large proportion of teachers were having higher secondary qualification. In these schools, while the lower classes have an advantage of being taught by higher qualified teachers, the secondary classes some time had disadvantage of being taught by less qualified teachers, particularly when the number of teachers are inadequate. In many integrated schools, there is no clear-cut demarcation between teachers of lower class and senior classes. In fact, teachers of class-VI and VII take classes for IX and X grade and vice versa. In case of higher secondary level, despite subject specialization, it is not uncommon to find that teachers of X-XII do duties of teachers of Classes IX-X.

In the last decade, there has been considerable improvement in educational qualification of teachers in general and secondary teachers in particular. In 2002 at all India level, more than 55 per cent of secondary teachers were with graduation and above qualification. And also one-fifth of teachers were having post-graduation degree. In fact, the educational level of primary school teachers has also increased impressively as 42 per cent of them were having graduation and above even though minimum required qualification being only higher secondary level (DIES, NIEPA, 2004). Further, educational profile of teachers in sample schools substantiates improving educational levels of teachers. Educational qualification of teachers teaching at secondary classes in sample schools of four states depicted that majority of teachers (60%) were with Bachelor's degree and another 38 per cent had post-graduate qualification.

The increased qualification of secondary teachers can be attributed to culmination of different reasons. While some of the states adopted a policy decision to separate the lower classes from secondary schools resulting in lowering the number of teachers with higher secondary qualification. Further in some states, higher secondary was de-linked from degree colleges and integrated with secondary level. One of the most important factors for increased educational level of teachers can also be due to dwindling employment opportunities in government sector, as in most of the states, there has been a ban on fresh recruitment, naturally the graduates and post-graduates turn towards teaching as the source of employment.

In case of higher secondary level, the educational qualification being post-graduation in specific subjects and largely all the states follow the norm. At all India level 98.73 per cent higher secondary teachers were having post graduation qualification. And in all the states the percentage varies from 95.18 per cent in Maharashtra to 99.67 per cent in Madhya Pradesh.

Trained Teachers

Since teaching is a skilled job and requires pedagogical of training, therefore, along with the general qualification, teachers are prescribed to have Bachelor's degree in Education as an additional prescribed qualification.

Table 2.7: Percentage of Trained Teachers at Secondary and Higher Secondary Level across Major States in India

State	*Secondary*			*Higher Secondary*		
	1980-81	*1990-91*	*2001-02*	*1980-81*	*1990-91*	*2001-02*
Andhra Pradesh	98	99	91	96	95	95
Kerala	98+	99	99	100	90	59
Maharashtra	95	95	98	92	97	99
Uttar Pradesh	93@	97	97	Na	97	97
Assam	28	31	30	35	25	30
Bihar	91	88#	99	93	90	95
Gujarat	99	100	99	93	100	99
Haryana	99	100	95	99	99	97
Himachal Pradesh	97	97	98	96	94	99
J & K	82	82	75	80	88	75
Karnataka	90	96	100	78	100	100
Madhya Pradesh	Na	Na	68	Na	na	75
Orissa	69	95	100	68	100	100
Punjab	99	99#	99	99	99#	99
Rajasthan	98	98	89	98	99	95
Tamil Nadu	100	100	100	98	98	100
West Bengal	60	73	86	56	70	86
All India	88	90	89	87	92	90

Source: Selected Educational Statistics, MHRD, GOI, New Delhi.

\+ Figure related to 1979-80

@ Classes IX-XIII

\# Figure related to 1989-90

However, emphasis on trained teachers has had a positive influence on recruitment policy of teachers. As a result national average of trained teachers at different levels of school education stands as 86 per cent and 87 per cent at primary and upper primary levels respectively in 2002-03. At secondary level, 89 per cent of teachers are trained. But interestingly, it has a marginal change at all India level. It declined from 1 per cent to 2 per cent in the last decade (see Table 2.7). Though there has not been much change in the extent of trained teachers at the national level but variations are remarkable at the state level. Some of the states *viz.* Karnataka, Kerala, Gujarat and even Orissa have cent per cent trained teachers and a higher average than the national one. In contrast with this figure, Assam has only 30 per cent of trained teachers at secondary level, without any improvement even in last two decades, followed by Madhya Pradesh with one-third of secondary and one-fourth of higher secondary teachers of being untrained and surprisingly, it has remained so since the last few decades in case of Assam and half a decade in Madhya Pradesh. While Uttar Pradesh, Maharashtra and Kerala maintained the status quo in the extent of trained teachers, some states have shown a decline of trained teachers in the last decades. States like Andhra Pradesh, Jammu & Kashmir and Rajasthan fell in this category. The decline of trained teachers was about 7-9 per cent in these states, which is matter for great concern considering large number of teachers in these states.

At higher secondary level, 90 per cent of teachers are trained at all India level. There has been marginal decline in the extent of trained teachers with variation among states. While in some states there was significant improvement in the extent of trained teachers, in few states, however, size of trained teachers has considerably declined. Some of the sates have 100 per cent trained teachers and Kerala has low trained teachers at higher secondary level as their percentage declined steeply during 1991-2001. The decline can be attributed to the de-linking of higher secondary from degree colleges. In light of this data it is cautionary to note that the data on untrained teachers do not tell us about subject level untrained teachers at secondary and higher secondary levels which is a cause of greater worry.

One of the important reasons for high degree of untrained teachers in some states is lack of adequate teacher training facilities and accumulation of backlog of untrained teachers. In addition, in a few states like Assam pre-service teacher training is not a compulsory condition for appointing teachers. In case of Andhra Pradesh, the reason for decline in the extent of trained teachers is mainly due to appointment of para teachers and contract teachers in recent years, coupled with exemption from training for scheduled tribes to be appointed as teachers. It is also true that most of the untrained teachers are normally concentrated in rural schools.

From the above analysis it can be drawn that secondary education in India is characterized by lack of subject teachers, overworked teachers, lack of proper assessment and performance evaluation mechanism, ritual teaching, *ad hocism*, and redistribution of teaching resources. Mere development in the front of pupil-teacher ratio is not the main problem; it is the lack of technical inputs and attitude to *ad hocism* that plagues the system and kills it from within.

Teacher-Pupil Ratio

Teacher-pupil ratio is one of the indicators of quality. It assumes significance in the context of secondary schools because of increased enrolment in secondary schools, higher transition and need for quality education at this level as it acts as an entry point for further and higher education.

Table 2.8: Teacher-Pupil Ratio at Higher Secondary, Secondary and Upper Primary Levels across Major States in India

State	1985-86			1995-96			2001-02		
	Upper Pri.	Sec.	Hr. Sec.	Upper Pri.	Sec.	Hr. Sec.	Upper Pri.	Sec.	Hr. Sec.
Andhra Pradesh	42	32	16	42	32	47	39	34	38
Kerala	32	28	24	30	29	52	28	29	19
Maharashtra	38	24	36	39	31	35	30	54	41
Uttar Pradesh	23	35	34	40	56	56	34	43	43
Assam	30	28	24	28	23	29	25	21	32
Bihar	40	34	32	42	37	30	54	45	23
Gujarat	40	26	26	42	31	30	38	28	43
Haryana	35	34	25	39	35	27	22	25	29
Himanchal	19	30	18	19	32	28	16	28	28
J & K	22	22	20	18	08	10	19	18	20
Karnataka	43	43	23	51	23	36	39	25	58
Madhya Pradesh	28	28	NA	37	40	33	29	29	27
Orissa	32	17	40	32	17	45	36	23	51
Punjab	17	23	23	21	27	30	17	26	29
Rajasthan	31	20	NA	32	26	30	40	29	29
Tamil Nadu	43	28	29	50	44	39	37	36	34
West Bengal	47	32	30	61	45	39	51	49	47
India	35	27	29	38	29	35	34	33	36

Source: Selected Educational Statistics, MHRD, Govt. of India.

The teacher-pupil ratio at all India level in primary, upper primary, secondary and higher secondary ranges as 43, 34, 33 and 36 respectively during the year 2002. In fact, there is a wide variation in the ratio among the states. At secondary level it varies from a high

54:1 to a low of 18:1 in Maharashtra and Jammu and Kashmir respectively. While teacher-pupil ratio in primary and upper primary levels remained more or less same in the last decade, at secondary and higher secondary level it has declined but marginally. However, over the years in some states the pupil-teacher ratio at secondary level has increased significantly while in a few states the ratio has gone down. In ten out of 16 major states, the teacher-pupil ratio is below the national average. Among four sample states in Maharashtra there has been steep increase of teacher-pupil ratio from 31 to 54:1 and contrarily, in Uttar Pradesh it declined considerably from 56 to 43:1 in the last five years. While in Andhra Pradesh, the ratio increased marginally from 32 to 34:1, in Kerala the ratio remained the same.

At the higher secondary level, the PTR ranges from 54:1 in Karnataka to 19:1 in Kerala as the highest and lowest respectively. Though at all India level the increase of PTR in HS is very negligible, there has also been considerable increase in some states. Among seventeen major states, the PTR had increased in seven states and in the remaining, the ratio has decreased in last five years. However, in Karnataka, Gujarat and Orissa the there has been significant increase in PTR. In four sample states, the PTR has come down in all except in Maharashtra. In Kerala, the PTR steeply declined from 52:1 to 19:1 during last five years. The increase of PTR is mainly due to large increase of enrolment without corresponding increase of number of teachers. Normally state administration considers the average daily attendance of students as the main criteria in providing teachers rather than the enrolment. Among all the states of India, Kerala has a favourable ratio due to the state's specific emphasis on education. In fact, Kerala is a state with surplus teachers and dwindling number of students due to change in its demographic patterns. And also the sudden fall of PTR at HS level is due to delinking of HS from higher education and establishment of separate HS schools and provision of adequate subject teachers. However, higher educational awareness and better public investment have made Kerala attain a very low PTR ratio than the nation.

In most states, the PTR is marginally higher in rural areas than urban areas both in Secondary and HS levels. However, the rural-urban disparity is glaring in only few states like Tamil Nadu, West Bengal but the difference is marginal in other states. Among the four sample states, Uttar Pradesh has higher rural urban disparity in PTR. Kerala is characterized of equality in rural-urban localities for obvious reasons. One of the important reasons for higher PTR in rural areas is increased enrolment in rural areas. And also normally, the vacant posts are filled up faster in urban areas than in rural areas. Usually some teachers posted in schools located in rural areas are reluctant to work and hence manage to be posted elsewhere or take long leave. This is more prominent among government school teachers, particularly women teachers.

In all the four sampled states and among the sample schools, 92-97 per cent of posts are filled up. 86 per cent teachers are permanent, 11 per cent are temporary and the rest are employed on contract basis. In Andhra Pradesh, only 67 per cent of teachers in sample schools are permanent, the rest are temporary or are on contract, in U.P. 79 per cent are permanent, in Maharashtra 85 per cent are permanent and in Kerala highest 93 per cent of teachers are permanent. In some of the states, the number of temporary, para-teachers and contract teachers have increased in the last decade or so, in view of government's inclination towards cost-saving methods (see Table 2.9).

The question of para-teachers needs a special mention because their appointment is more a question of political expedience than of educational efficiency. These teachers work in a state pervaded by lower salary, low expectation and under a permanent threat of insecurity. This in turn does affect their level of confidence and competency and thereby takes secondary education towards a state of permanent difficulty.

Class Size

Quality of education achieved through better teacher-pupil ratio in

Table 2.9: Nature and Status of Teachers' Posts in Sample Schools

State	*Nature of Teachers' Posts*			*Status of Teachers' Posts*	
	Permanent	*Temporary*	*Contract*	*% filled*	*% vacant*
Andhra Pradesh	67.47	28.31	4.22	90.66	9.34
Kerala	85.21	11.04	3.97	99.53	0.43
Maharashtra	92.73	5.26	2.01	97.70	2.30
Uttar Pradesh	79.34	20.06	0.60	93.30	6.70
Total	86.19	11.42	2.44	96.60	3.40

Source: 48 Sample Schools in Four States.

the framework of secondary education is quite different from primary education. In fact, at secondary and higher secondary level it is not only PTR but also number of subject teachers according to number of sections per class.

One of the key areas of qualitative improvement in school education is the size of section in general and that in secondary and higher secondary education in particular. Size of the section assumes importance because it determines the dynamics of classroom curriculum transaction, individual attention to students, student assessment and feedback, remedial measures, etc. Since it is imperative to transact curriculum among a variable section of students, it is essential on the part of the teacher to be aware of new methods of teaching and contextualizing innovative pedagogical innovations in different and difficult classroom situations. In this sense, it may be said that in order to have a more effective teaching-learning system, the size of the section becomes an important ingredient. In addition to teaching learning aspect, size of the section also matters in terms of establishing meaningful rapport and interaction with teenage students. However, these can be possible within a definite size of section and unviable section size will affect the intensity and motivation of both the teacher and the taught.

The data from the sample schools show that the average size of the section for classes IX to XII vary among the four states. In IX class, the average size of section varies with 45 in Kerala as the lowest and 63 as the highest in Maharashtra and Uttar Pradesh. In X grade the average section size ranges between 41 and 69 in Andhra Pradesh and Uttar Pradesh respectively. At higher secondary level, in XI class the number of students per section varied between 54 in Kerala and 88 in Uttar Pradesh. In the final class of higher secondary (XII), the average size of class was 51 in Kerala and 82 in Maharashtra (see Table 2.10).

To a large extent, Kerala and Andhra Pradesh have more acceptable class size. However, there is high inter-school variation in all the four states. The interschool variation is very large in Uttar Pradesh and Maharashtra. The two states, Kerala and Andhra Pradesh not only have feasible section size but also have less inter-school variation. While Kerala has schools having large number of sections both in secondary and higher secondary classes, Andhra Pradesh has very small number of sections for different classes. It

Table 2.10: Average Size of Sections and Percentage of Sample Schools with Different Range of Section Size

	Secondary							Higher Secondary						
	Size of section	*<40*	*41-50*	*51-60*	*61-70*	*71-99*	*Above 100*	*Size of Section*	*<40*	*41-50*	*51-60*	*61-70*	*71-99*	*Above 100*
Andhra Pradesh	43	5	5	1	1	0	0	–	–	–	–	–	–	–
Kerala	43	5	5	1	0	1	0	50	2	2	8	0	0	0
Maharashtra	62	1	2	2	5	1	1	96	1	0	1	1	3	5
Uttar Pradesh	58	2	3	1	1	3	2	46	3	2	1	1	2	1
Total	51	13	15	5	7	5	3	58	6	4	10	2	5	6
Percentage		27	31	10	15	10	6		18	12	30	6	15	18

Note: In the state of A.P., sample schools do not have higher secondary level. One School in Maharashtra and two schools in U.P. do not have higher secondary level.

evidently illustrates that the average size of schools in Kerala is relatively larger.

There are different factors for large size of sections. It can be attributed to increased enrolment and due to lack of physical facilities and additional teachers to form the sections according to norms. The other reason behind the large size of sections is due to policies of state governments. In Uttar Pradesh and Maharashtra, most of the schools are government aided private management schools. Due to financial constraints, the state governments have not given consent to aided schools for sanction of additional teacher posts corresponding to increased enrolment to facilitate formation of separate sections. As a result the schools have large sections. And also in recent years, large number of private unaided schools were established. These schools are usually motivated by profits and refrain themselves from investing in the appointment of additional teachers and creating more facilities; they rather choose to continue with large class size. The reasons for feasible section size in Kerala and Andhra Pradesh have different explanations.

In Kerala, state government follows the policy of providing additional teachers to maintain section size according to the state educational norms both for private aided and government schools. Secondly, in recent years the student enrolment has declined due to demographic changes and also good number of surplus teachers were transferred to government schools. Some of the field observations in Kerala evidently prove that in private aided schools, the enrolment figures are inflated in order to obtain additional teachers as sizable amount of money changes hands in teacher appointment.

In Andhra Pradesh, there has been considerable expansion of schools at secondary level particularly in rural areas to meet the increased enrolment. As a result, the average size of school is small with viable class size. The situation of higher secondary schools in Andhra Pradesh is also not much different from that in Uttar Pradesh and Maharashtra as all the students of particular academic stream are often clubbed into one section irrespective of number of students. The class size at times goes up to 100-120 even in case of science stream. This scenario is found both among government and private unaided schools.

Teaching Workload

Another long-standing problem with the Indian secondary education is teaching more than one subject by the teachers. Though there are prescribed state level educational norms and guidelines clearly indicating subject specifications, prescribed number of teaching hours etc., they are rarely followed. As a result, secondary school teacher invariably have to teach more than one subject. Inadequacy of teachers, large number of sections, lack of subject teachers seems to be the reasons behind this problem.

It is quite common to find a mathematics teacher taking science classes and vice-versa as well as a social science teacher teaching English. More than that, teachers recruited to teach arts, music, dance, drawing and physical education are invariably given additional responsibility of teaching, though in junior classes. This duly raises questions regarding the quality and seriousness of instructional transaction as each discipline at the secondary level requires appropriate pedagogy and technical competency. Further, introduction of new courses like computer, general knowledge, environmental education, value education, human rights etc. is rarely associated with new appointments. Rather, this additional responsibility goes to a teacher who is already teaching a different subject. However, this problem is not unique to India, or to few states or even to few schools. In fact, in all states, most schools, despite difference in management, performance and location, are afflicted with this problem. There are arguments for and against this practice, e.g. many African countries defend this practice on the ground that secondary school teachers should have the capacity to teach two subjects and must be trained for that but in case of India, it is a practice, despite having norms in contrariety to it (see Table 2.11).

The data from sample schools show that 40 per cent teachers are entrusted with teaching additional subjects and 60 per cent of teachers teach one subject. There is variation among four states in the percentage of teachers teaching more than one subject ranging from

Table 2.11: Number and Percentage of Teachers in Sample Schools Teaching One Subject and More than One Subject

States	*One Subject*	*More than one Subject*	*No. of Schools with 100% Teachers Teaching more than one subject*
Andhra Pradesh	28 (47%)	32 (53%)	2 (16%)
Kerala	94 (82%)	20 (18%)	0 (0%)
Maharasthra	68 (51%)	67 (49%)	1 (8%)
Uttar Pradesh	28 (51%)	27 (49%)	1 (8%)
Total	218 (60%)	146 (40%)	4 (8%)

Source: Field Survey.

53 per cent to 18 per cent in Andhra Pradesh and Kerala respectively, whereas in Maharashtra and Uttar Pradesh, about 50 per cent of teachers teach more than one subject.

The common combination of subjects taught by teachers is social science and English or regional language and science and Mathematics. It is also not uncommon that science and mathematics teachers teach English language. Lack of adequate subject teachers were reported as main reasons behind such a scenario in sample schools. Many teachers found it as a compulsion. Some of the problems related with teaching different subjects include lack of subject knowledge and pedagogical training. For example the social studies teacher or science teachers are trained in respective subject methodologies, and lack fundamental understanding of teaching methodologies of language, in addition to subject content. However, things are changing for the better as Kerala and Andhra Pradesh have employed strict norms to appoint qualified teachers to teach English and Physical sciences, the subjects which were earlier taught less professionally.

In India, at secondary level, 65 per cent of teachers with a first-degree from University in science and 8 per cent with post-graduate qualification teach science, though there are huge inter-state differences and disparities (AIES, 1993). The number of teachers having a graduate or post-graduate degree and teaching science in secondary schools is 88 per cent in Kerala and only 58 per cent in Madhya Pradesh. So is the case with mathematics as around 64 per cent of teachers with graduate and post-graduate degree taught this subject. The figure varies from 96 per cent in Kerala and Andhra Pradesh. But it is surprising to note that an educationally developed state like Maharashtra has only 38 per cent qualified teachers teaching mathematics, though most of the teachers were appointed long back when opportunities for mathematics graduates were better in other sectors than in teaching. However, changes have taken place in the recruitment policy of teachers over the years wherein more number of trained teachers in mathematics are recruited. This can be seen from the sample schools where majority of teachers handling mathematics are trained graduates in mathematics.

Teaching Hours

All the sample state governments prescribe a number of periods for teaching of week for different subjects ranging from 24 to 30 per week. In the sample schools, in Kerala, on an average, a teacher teaches 21 periods in a week as against 31 periods in Uttar Pradesh. In Maharashtra and Andhra Pradesh the number of teaching periods per week seemed to be just the same (29). However, in Maharashtra and Uttar Pradesh there were large inter-school variations in terms of teaching load. In Kerala and Andhra Pradesh not only number of teaching periods but also inter-school variation is less. The inter-school variation in teaching load may be due to lack of adequate number of teachers and delay in recruitment of teachers. However, in recent times, some states like Andhra Pradesh adopted a policy of rationalization of teachers in order to ensure equitable distribution of teachers based on requirement (see Table 2.12).

Table 2.12: Average Teaching Load Per Week among Sample Teachers in Sample Schools

Sample Schools	A.P.	Kerala	Maharashtra	U.P.
1	31	23	27	34
2	32	21	33	31
3	28	22	30	26
4	26	24	28	19
5	27	20	28	40
6	31	24	16	29
7	27	24	33	34
8	27	27	32	38
9	36	19	32	29
10	n.a.	20	35	23
11	32	17	30	30
12	32	22	27	38
Average	29	21	29	31
Minimum	26	17	16	19
Maximum	32	27	35	40

Source: Sample Schools.

Teaching Methodology

The success of teaching largely depends on the type of method that one uses for transacting the curriculum. Indian education system in general and secondary education in particular has been lagging in this since long. Pedagogy in case of secondary education has invariably been restricted to completion of syllabus and textbook based approach. As a result students have been reduced to passive listeners in a process of completion of syllabus leaving little for innovation, discussion, critical analysis etc. Further, owing to shortening of working days due to various engagements of teachers as well as socio-political and natural vagaries even this exercise is not often completed and that being so, the result is often haphazard and piecemeal. Learning becomes a casualty in the process when emphasis is laid on mundane and routine classroom exercises rather than on developing competence, critical thinking and mastering of learning.

Though similar arguments were levelled against all levels of education and more so in case of primary education in last decade, primary education system has tried to remove this tag. Through inputs from various projects and interventions at various levels, primary education system has adopted a more comprehensive, sensitive and child-centered approach, making efforts to make learning activity a joyful exercise. But the tides of change have not affected secondary education nor have there been policy measures to change the pedagogy at secondary level. Some efforts have been made in changing the pedagogy in teaching a few subjects but even these initiatives have remained operative more in theory than in practice.

Analysis of responses from teachers from sample schools about teaching methodology shows that about 60 per cent of respondents teach through lecture method in order to explain the facts and figure of the course while another 20 per cent make students slightly more involved by providing them opportunities to ask questions as a design to clear doubts. As far as science and mathematics are concerned, there are discerning trends of difference from a pronounced lecture mode. Science teachers use lectures, experiments, demonstration and fieldwork for better effect but again very few teachers go beyond the lecture mode to impress a particular point. Similarly, in mathematics the favourite mode adopted by teachers is to solve a few problems and ask the students to solve the rest; the second method is to ask the students to solve the problems themselves and ask the teacher in case of difficulty. As far as language teaching is concerned, teachers usually follow the textbook method with little or no variation. In fact, it has been found in case study in Andhra Pradesh that teachers do not follow hints mentioned in the textbooks to teach a particular subject. Surprisingly, even 40 per cent of teachers are not aware of such hint questions.

Completion of Syllabus

As discussed earlier, teachers lay more emphasis on completion of syllabus than on qualitative improvement in delivering the lessons as completion of syllabus stands as an objective criterion of teaching capability. As a result, normally teachers follow the annual calendar and monthly plan to complete the syllabus. But a look at the school calendar and workload of teachers provides a glimpse about the difficulty of the task. This has made most teachers to take extra classes and tutorials to finish the course on time. The study of sample schools reveals that one-fourth of teachers take extra classes to complete the course due to shortage of time and their involvement in non-academic work. In Kerala, due to a severe shortage of working days for various reasons,* 34 per cent of teachers take extra classes to complete the syllabus. This is not only limited to Kerala. It is found in all the four selected states though with a degree of variation. This only shows how a serious profession like teaching has been reduced to the mundane task of completion of syllabus in a rapid, hurried and haphazard manner.

However, there are also a few schools under private sector and also residential schools that follow very structured teaching schedule and complete coverage of syllabus well in advance and revision of important aspects of curriculum is also repeatedly done, combined with continuous evaluation of students to assess and organize remedial teaching.

Home Assignments

One of the common practices prevalent at all educational levels in India in all schools is the technique of 'home assignment' used by teachers. Home assignment is a mechanism to monitor the progress of students and provide them feedback on their performance. More than sixty per cent (61%) of teachers responded by saying that they give home assignments to students on a daily basis, around 28 per cent teachers give home assignments on a weekly basis while 10 per cent teachers give home assignments as and when required. Though it is very difficult to gauge the efficacy of this system in the absence cross-examination from students, it can be assumed albeit arguably that a feedback on performance of students is rarely passed on. Around 20 per cent of teachers mentioned that they take the help of class monitors in evaluating home assignments. There were cases where home assignments were never regularly checked and this trend is more prevalent in government schools. However, it may be added

* This aspect is analysed and discussed in detail in the chapter on management.

that due to some accountability, things are better off in private management schools and with the exception of schools with dynamic and diligent head teachers determined to supervise things, home assignments have been a casualty in government schools across the states. In-depth discussion with teachers showed that correction of home work was done in routine manner rather than being used as an improvised tool to break new barriers in the teaching-learning process.

As far as problems in learning process are concerned, teachers did admit the existence of the problem. However, they blamed it on lengthy curriculum, poor academic record of students, low socio-economic background of students, lack of practice etc. More than fifty per cent of teachers (51%) held the syllabus responsible for learning difficulty, 37 per cent to overcrowded classrooms, 19 per cent to lack of practice, 16 per cent to poor academic records and 18 per cent blamed the poor socio-economic status of the students and thereby lack academic support at home. Though the teachers did not bring their own performance to scrutiny, it must be said that they did not put the blame squarely on students. In fact, the proportion of blame on various factors varied on the basis of locality, student strength and infrastructure.

Additional Responsibilities

Another aspect of teachers' problem in India is the overburdening of teachers. Teachers are burdened even within the school premises and are entangled in different tasks. They have to work and take different responsibilities as class teachers, members of school committees, advisors on student bodies, part of administration etc. In a sense there are a number of responsibilities for a teacher, both in curricular and co-curricula activities. Studies from sample schools revealed that 45 per cent of teachers are class teachers, 1/4th are involved in co-curricular activities of school, 11 per cent represent school level committees, 4 per cent of them are in charge of student bodies and another 4 per cent are entrusted with responsibilities pertaining to school level administration. Some other teachers are members and functionaries of teachers' bodies, clubs, admission bureau, examination branch, evaluation section, time-table committee and various other miscellaneous activities.

Academic Supervision

Supervision has been a key component of educational administration and school management but, of late, this aspect has faced severe strain. The external supervision that dominated government school system for far too long has been diluted, often missing altogether. Rapid expansion of secondary schools without creating adequate supervisory infrastructure has spelled doom for school supervision. Information pertaining to supervision of sample schools states that only 32 per cent of schools have never been supervised in last two years, 25 per cent of schools were visited only once in the last year and 45 per cent of schools were visited twice in a year. Even when external supervisors have visited the schools, the teachers rarely receive the feedback making the entire exercise redundant (see Table 2.13).

Table 2.13: Percentage of Schools Visited by Inspector and Receiving Feedback

State	*Frequency of Visit*					*Receiving Feedback*
	Once	*Twice*	*Thrice*	*More than 3 times*	*Never*	
Andhra Pradesh	27.27	18.18	18.18	9.09	27.27	72.72
Kerala	33.33	16.66	0.00	16.66	33.33	50.0
Maharashtra	16.66	41.66	25.0	0.00	16.66	58.33
Uttar Pradesh	16.66	25.0	8.33	0.00	50.0	33.33
Total	23.40	25.53	12.76	6.38	31.91	53.19

Source: Field Survey.

As a result, most of the schools depend on internal academic supervision machinery. In response to a question on academic supervision to head of institutions, it was found that 51 per cent head teachers supervise the teachers, in case of 21 per cent of sample schools, the supervision is done by senior teachers, 15 per cent sample schools' head informed of teachers being supervised by inspection officers, and only 5 per cent schools identified community members (people) as supervisors. In case of primary and upper primary level, there has been a structure and hierarchy for academic supervision and at secondary level the mechanism is in shambles.

To make matters worse, in the absence of rigorous supervisory mechanism no appropriate alternative system is in place. However, in some states, efforts have been made to assess secondary school teachers through the achievement of students in public examination at the end of secondary school. The result of this assessment is further linked to the service conditions of teachers precisely to their increment.

At the institutional level, the head teacher is entrusted with the task of supervising the teachers and grading them on the basis of class performance, discipline, rapport with students etc. They have also devised a formula to fix the accountability of teachers and introduced Teacher Performance Appraisal (TPA) scheme. In states like Maharashtra TPA rankings have been linked to mobility in hierarchy and promotion.

In this section, we have dealt with various dimensions of problems and their degrees affecting secondary education in India. We have highlighted physical, technical and academic difficulties that have jeopardized the performance and end product of secondary education. At length, we have dealt with the problem persisting at the macro level as well as at micro level. Absence of physical facilities is a common problem for secondary education at all levels. Similarly, the problem of privatization, political interference and regional deprivation are generic problems, stunting the growth of secondary education at the macro level. Mere expansion of facilities or introduction of norms do not necessarily bring all round development in a system, rather it requires serious efforts to identify the anomalies and prescribe remedial measures besides monitoring its administration. It is also important to note that of late the qualification of teachers teaching at secondary level has gone up and so is the case with their training, but the question is how best we can tap this resource to usher in a qualitative transformation in secondary education making it sound, suitable and systematic.

Teachers' In-Service Training

The quality of teaching depends squarely on the quality of teachers. But quality, being in itself a changing variable, needs constant updating and addition. At the recruitment level, quality of teachers can be controlled by rigorous criteria of qualification and expertise but in a fast changing new world, one has to update his information in order to make him relevant to the present context. As it happens in case of a skilled worker in an industry who has to constantly update his competency level to face the challenges of time and technology, so is the case with the teacher who has to reinvent himself to understand and explain new concepts and theories. In the context of India, majority of teachers being permanent employees and having joined the profession quite early definitely require updating of their knowledge base. In an era of fast changing information and rapidly moving frontiers of knowledge, it is imperative and essential that teachers, being vanguards of knowledge, must arm themselves with the latest information. Else, they will teach Divided German and United Russia and thereby will make a poor caricature of general knowledge and geography. However, this constant updating of knowledge base cannot be possible without institutionalizing a system of training for teachers already in service. This is not an easy task when we consider the magnitude of the problem. There are 1.7 million secondary and higher secondary teachers and out of which there are one million at secondary level spread over the length and breadth of the country. Providing them any sort of in-service training is a huge challenge, but considering the need for such a programme, some arrangements at the national, state and regional level have been made.

At the state level, State Councils of Educational Research and Training (SCERT) conduct in-service training programmes for teachers. States like Uttar Pradesh and Maharashtra have taken teacher training seriously and have established state level supporting institutions to professionalize the training system. In Uttar Pradesh, apart from SCERT, there are institutions like SIEMAT (State Institute of Educational Management and Training), State Institute of Science Education, English Language Teaching Institute and Bureau of Psychology. All these institutions deal with specific disciplines and components of training and some of them train master trainers and help in further decentralizing the programme. Maharashtra too has developed institutional framework, apart from SCERT. Of late, education departments of specific universities, known as Institute of Advanced Studies in Education (IASE), with an interest on training component, have come forward to impart training to secondary school teachers. This pattern is found in Maharashtra, Kerala and Andhra Pradesh. In some states, Boards of Secondary Education are involved in imparting teacher training but more often than not, Boards are concerned with examination only. Andhra Pradesh does have another supporting institution in the form of State Institute of Technology but it is more in the field of preparing tele-films and programmes. In the absence of such supporting institutions, the teachers at the secondary level have to depend on SCERT for in-service training.

Despite massive problems, these training institutions have tried their best to cater to the needs of teachers. The essential parts of these trainings have been to help the teachers in transacting the curricula and familiarizing them with various aspects of course contents. The introduction of new subjects like population education, environmental education, human rights education requires a degree of understanding and appreciation which these teachers lack and hence, the need for in-service training. States like Maharashtra have made in-service training at definite intervals compulsory for teachers and linked it with their promotions. In recent years, many states have shown interest to provide in-service training to teachers of schools who have fared poorly in public examinations. A sample survey conducted in a selected district of state like Andhra Pradesh showed that 32 per cent of teachers did not have any in-service training while rest of them had at least one opportunity. In the sample schools, no teacher had in-service teacher training in last two years whereas in Maharashtra, 21 per cent of the teachers in sample schools had opportunity of teacher training.

Training for Head Teachers

Since training forms an integral and important part of professional career, there has been some need for training of head teacher as he heads the smallest and the most important administrative structure at the grass-root level. In U.P., SIEMAT has made efforts in training the head teachers because school management requires some managerial skills. Since head teachers are selected on the basis of seniority and experience, they have little or no change of being introduced to the art of management. In states like Andhra Pradesh, West Bengal and Kerala, the teachers' unions have taken initiative in organizing special professional training for teachers and head teachers.

Despite the importance of training and the huge need for training as well as establishment of specialized institutions for training, the situation has remained bleak. Major problems in the training sector are technological, motivational, logistical, financial, and temporal. Training is not a routine activity, nor it can be served as a medicine. Training requires dedication and motivation from trainees and at the beginning, there is no such motivation for teachers to go for a training programme. Except Maharashtra, no other state has made in-service training a mandatory criteria or essential for career growth and a part of service condition. An in-service training, in any way too, does not bring any substantial benefits to a teacher, as a result the motivational level for such training drops considerably. Logistical problem is evident in any training programme and more so, at the state level. Application, confirmation, permission are indeed very cumbersome processes and they are doubly disadvantageous for teachers beyond the boundary of state capital. At the level of training imparting institution as well, there are problems pertaining to disbursement of T.A., D.A. to participants, arrangement for boarding and lodging takes more time and energy than organizing the training programmes. Finance has been a major problem in many activities and more so in case of training programmes as many still think it as an unnecessary expense. There has been low budgetary allocation for training programmes, making it very difficult for training institutions to conduct large-scale training programmes. Apart from these, time is also a constraint in complete realization of the potential of training programmes. Conducted for short durations, training programmes usually fail in accomplishing their tasks as the programme comes to an end before the trainees acclimatize with the problem and start grasping the nuances. Similarly, over-emphasis on curriculum and less emphasis on content and pedagogy have made in-service training toothless. Further, though training institutions are involved in research, they rarely use research component in training programmes, making them over-ripe with theory and far from reality.

The quality of education, among other things, depends upon on the availability of physical and academic facilities. Availability of physical facilities in terms of permanent buildings have improved over all and enormously in the rural areas across states, barring a few hilly states. With regard to ancillary facilities, in terms of student welfare the size of provision though better, yet its nature in terms of adequacy as revealed from case studies is far from satisfactory. As regards academic ancillary facilities in terms of laboratories and libraries, equally important for quality education, these are not even covering half of the existing schools in majority of the states, including also the sample states.

Further, in terms of important aspect of the quality of teaching-learning process, the macro level analysis on quality provisions such as educational qualification and training of teachers, teacher-pupil ratio etc. suggest a definite improvement across states including sample states. Micro level analysis from case studies such as teaching load, availability of subject teachers, co-curricular activities, etc. also bring out that the situation needs to be improved, given the pressure on demand and skills required at the secondary level.

The analysis categorically shows that mere expansion of facilities does not necessarily bring the development; rather it requires serious efforts to identify the anomalies and prescribe remedial measures besides monitoring and administration. It is important to note that physical as well as human resources in terms of buildings and other facilities in addition to qualification of teachers and training at secondary level have improved. The moot question is how best can we tap this resource to help qualitative transformation in secondary education.

REFERENCES

NCERT (1982), *Fourth All India Educational Survey,* National Council of Educational Research and Training, New Delhi.

NCERT (1992), *Fifth All India Educational Survey,* National Council of Educational Research and Training, New Delhi.

NCERT (1998), *Sixth All India Educational Survey,* National Council of Educational Research and Training, New Delhi.

NCERT (2002), *Seventh All India Educational Survey,* National Council of Educational Research and Training, New Delhi.

3

Internal Efficiency of Secondary Education

Provision of access is a precondition to educational progress, particularly in improving the agenda of human development but is not a sufficient condition for development of education. In addition to access it is the effective functioning of the schools that determines the quality and in turn translates the efforts into progress. The effectiveness of schools is largely captured through internal efficiency of the schools. Though school effectiveness is important for all levels of schooling, it has particular relevance for secondary education for a variety of reasons. For example, secondary schools have to operate in the context of large and diverse catchment areas, with students from different levels of learning and more importantly within the framework of uniform curriculum. Hence, effective functioning of schools and internal efficiency of the system are very important in judging the overall performance of secondary education.

In the present chapter, an attempt has been made to examine the internal efficiency of the system in terms of transition, repetition, dropout rates and performance of students in public examinations at the end of secondary level. In an efficient system of education, all those enrolled should complete the cycle and seek for admission in the next higher level of education. The completion of the cycle depends on the indicators of efficiency, *viz.* transition, repetition and dropout and the performance in public examinations. The first section of the chapter attempts to examine these indicators at the secondary level. The performance of students in the public examinations is examined in detail in the second section of the chapter. The last section deals with the inter linkages at the micro level between these indicators as well as in identifying areas which influence the performance of the students, drawing evidences from school level. However, as mentioned earlier, the framework of analysis is based on examination of these phenomena at the national level, mapping of interstate, select sample states, inter-region and inter-district variations and study of micro level reality through case studies of select schools.

TRANSITION RATE

Transition rate refers to the number of students joining from one level to the next level out of the total passing out students and expressed in percentage terms. Ideally, the transition rate should be 100 per cent at every stage, if universalisation of secondary education is to be achieved. A smooth transition process demonstrates the quality and competency of the system in addition to reflecting the importance accorded to education by the households. The extent of transition rate to secondary level primarily reflects the demand for secondary education; however, transition rate also depends on several academic and socio-economic factors.

The transition rate from primary to upper primary and on to secondary level shows that at the national level, 89 per cent of students who complete primary education, join the upper primary level (Grade VI) and 87 per cent of those who complete upper primary level (Grade VIII) transit to secondary education. In the last few years, there has been impressive increase in student enrolment at the secondary level (particularly in Grade IX), part of which can be attributed to improvement in the transition rate. Further, the transition rates for the year 2000-01 depict that these have improved when compared to those of earlier years, both in case of primary to upper primary and from upper primary to secondary levels. The increase in transition rate during 1999-2001 has been higher at secondary level compared to upper primary level. The transition rate from primary to upper primary level has been 5 per cent more than that in 1995-96 and it increased by about 9 percentage points at the secondary level during the same period. The significant increase in enrolment in upper primary and secondary stages in the last five years affirms increased transition rate at all levels of school education (see Figure 3.1). It is on this indicator that India, though improved, fares poorly at international level, and still requires increasing the transition rate by 11 per cent at upper primary to achieve universalisation of elementary and, even more to achieve universalisation of secondary education. The transition rate in India is not only low in absolute terms but also

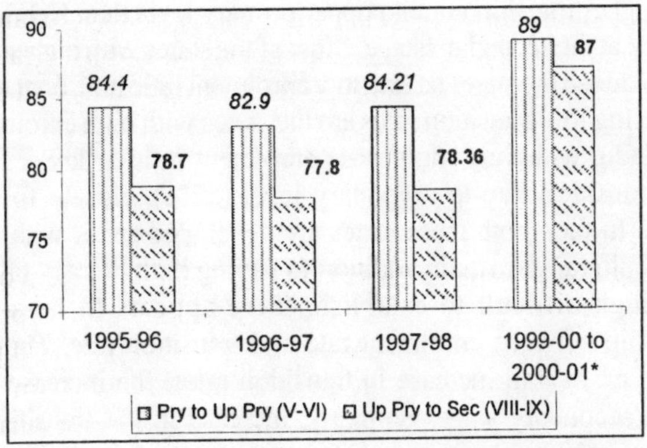

Figure 3.1: All India Transition Rates at Selected Years

Source: Education in India, 1995-96, 1996-97 and 1997-98. Department of Education, Ministry of Human Resource Development (MHRD) Government of India, New Delhi, 2002 and 2003.

low in comparison to many developed and developing countries of the world (UNESCO, 2004). The difference in transition rates becomes more glaring in the case of secondary education that does not receive much of the state patronage in India. Contrary to many developed and developing countries, compulsory education stage in India is limited to only eight years of schooling (6-14 years of age). National commitment and obligation for the elementary stage, which has boosted the enrolment, is largely missing when it comes to secondary education.

Not only the transition rates in India are low, but there are wide variations among the states also. An examination of transition rates in 17 major Indian states shows that six of them had more than 90 per cent transition rate to upper primary level while only three states had more than 90 per cent transition rate to secondary stage (see Annexure Table A1).

In as many as 11 states, the transition rates to upper primary level are higher compared to secondary level. On the contrary, in other states like Andhra Pradesh, Assam, Bihar, Gujarat, Jammu & Kashmir and Madhya Pradesh, the transition rates are greater at secondary stage compared to transition rates at upper primary level, despite three of the states being backward, both educationally and economically. In an attestation to our earlier observation, it may be said that educationally and even economically backward states like Rajasthan and Orissa have shown higher transition rate to upper primary level than Kerala; and, on par with it at the secondary stage. Most of the states with higher transition rates are indeed the states having low enrolment ratio and, on the contrary, those having low transition rates are the states with high enrolment ratio. Tamil Nadu, with very high gross enrolment ratio at lower levels has lowest transition rate to secondary level (57%), closely followed by Haryana. In fact, both these states are developed states with industrial and agricultural growth, in addition to having high literacy rate.

Though difficult to establish, there appears to be a negative relationship between enrolment rate and transition rate. Though there has been an overall increase in transition rates, the increase has been lower at secondary stage. Similarly, increase in the transition rate at secondary level has been very marginal in most of the states, except in one or two states where it has significantly improved. In a few states, the transition rate to secondary level, however, decreased during 1995-1997, though the decrease was only marginal (see Annexure, Table A2).

This may be due to the fact that in the backward states, only a few, that too with better socio-economic background, enrol in the education system and have both the means and the determination to complete the cycle. In the developed states, on the other hand, many, including those from low socio-economic groups, join the system but fail to complete the cycle owing to economic, academic and other reasons. However, the trends of transition among different states though vary from each other do not necessarily corroborate with their respective levels of development. Rather, the state policies with regard to detention or non-detention influence the transition rates to a great extent.

Table 3.1: Transition Rates in Sample States

State	*Primary to Upper Primary*			*Upper Primary to Secondary*		
	1995-96	*1996-97*	*1997-1998*	*1995-96*	*1996-97*	*1997-1998*
Andhra Pradesh	78.5	78.7	80.7	91.7	90.9	90.0
Kerala	93.0	93.1	93.8	83.0	83.4	83.3
Maharashtra	86.2	87.8	89.6	86.2	86.7	89.4
Uttar Pradesh	86.6	87.2	87.2	73.5	74.7	81.0
All India	84.4	82.9	84.2	78.7	77.8	78.4

Source: Education in India, 1995-96, 1996-97 and 1997-98. Department of Education, MHRD, GOI, New Delhi, 2002 and 2003.

Among the sample states, Kerala, with its universal literacy and primary education, had higher transition rate at upper primary level but not so at the secondary level. In fact, educationally developing states like Andhra Pradesh and economically and educationally advanced states like Maharashtra have done much better than Kerala, having about 90 per cent transition rate. Uttar Pradesh obviously occupies the lowest position among the four sample states, with only 80 per cent transition rate from upper primary to secondary level. However, improvement in the transition rate at secondary level has been higher in Uttar Pradesh.

Various reasons influencing the transition to secondary education level can be explained in terms of supply and demand factors. Supply related aspects include provision of access to schooling, affirmative action, quality of inputs etc. On the other hand, demand aspects include socio-economic and demographic and technological change, besides the value attached to education. Access related factors are improved proximity to secondary schooling facility, improved roads and transport facility, and integrating upper primary section with secondary section. Physical proximity of the school to the residence not only leads to increased enrolment but also contributes to higher transition rates. As already pointed out elsewhere, the physical access to secondary schooling increased significantly in the recent years, more particularly in rural areas and has led to increased transition rate. Presence of a secondary school in close vicinity certainly facilitates higher transition, especially in case of girls.

Improved road and transportation facility also has an effect on transition rate. Not only many states have improved the transportation facility but also have reduced the cost of transportation substantially by providing concessions to students. Some of the states are Tamil Nadu, Maharashtra, Andhra Pradesh, Kerala, etc. As a result, quite a few students commute daily to secondary schools located even at a far away place. Some prefer to commute, though school exists in the vicinity, on the grounds of quality.

In addition, a closely related factor influencing the transition rate is the integration of upper primary section with secondary schools. The chances of students completing upper primary in a secondary school and entering secondary stage in the same school are much more than of students completing it in an another exclusive upper primary school or a school attached with a primary school. Mostly, in rural areas, upper primary schools are upgraded to secondary, resulting in an integrated structure. Though access may not necessarily result in higher transition but it certainly facilitates the process of transition.

Besides, offering monetary and non-monetary incentives in the form of free tuition or waiving of examination fees, awarding scholarships, free textbooks, free uniforms etc. encourage more number of children to enter secondary education and to continue. In this respect, majority of the states (including the sample states) are providing free secondary education or charge a very nominal amount in government or private aided schools. Tuition-free education, though necessary, is not sufficient enough to encourage the transition, particularly to secondary education where direct and indirect costs are not insignificant. Scholarship schemes partly take care of these costs, but not as much as to induce continuing secondary education in case of certain categories. Boarding and lodging facilities, particularly for girls, SC/ST students have a positive impact on transition rates as indicated by the micro level information on residential schools. The concessions, welfare schemes, boarding and lodging facility, and above all, free secondary education to these sections prompt them to pursue additional years of schooling, which in turn leads to increase in enrolment and transition rate at secondary level. The paternalistic attitudes of the government and its policy for affirmative action too have been responsible in increasing the demand for secondary education. The students from marginalized sections, belonging to scheduled castes and scheduled tribes, are more and more entering into the secondary education system. This can be profoundly found in three of the sample states, except Uttar Pradesh.

The overall improvement in the quality of education at the lower levels improves the transition to secondary levels. The initiatives for improving teaching-learning conditions at the lower levels had an effect on transition rate to the next higher levels, which in turn influenced the transition at secondary level. Government efforts to improve the quality of primary education, particularly under District Primary Education Programme, might bring dividends as has been underlined by the baseline survey conducted at different points of time, which found improvement in the achievement levels of students at primary level. Such qualitative change at primary level might have led to more students going to the higher Grades.

State policy on non-detention and promotion directly influences the transition rate. Automatic promotion and non-detention policy followed by many states at primary and by a few other states at upper primary increased the transition rates. As part of this policy, all those students, who satisfy stipulated attendance, are promoted. Though all those promoted need not enter the next Grade but all those detained cannot. This way, the non-detention policy has a positive impact on transition rates. However, such transition as reported from the micro level studies has a negative impact on the school effectiveness in general and internal efficiency in particular. Secondary schools have larger catchment areas with students coming from a number of upper primary schools and many of these students would have been promoted due to non-detention policy.

The socio-economic changes have also played their part in improving the transition rates. Reduction in poverty and increase in economic capability of people in the country and in many states, have helped increase not only enrolment but also transition to secondary education. The parents, otherwise willing and aware of the value of education, could not send their children to school earlier because of their poverty and low income. Such like economic and social factors as also reduction in poverty, lack of job opportunities with lower levels of education and general rise in awareness among people, etc. influence the transition rates.

Planned development, infrastructural improvements and better communication facilities have played a dominant role not only in bringing the children to the school by providing access and opportunities but also in making parents aware about the importance of education. Provision of education at doorsteps, as it is euphemistically called, has certainly paved the way for educating those children for whose reluctant parents distance and difficulty of travelling had been a problem earlier. Similarly, the spread of media, both print and electronic, as well as entertainment industry, has been successful in creating awareness among people about the value of education. Today more and more people are viewing education as a necessity rather than a luxury and as such more parents are sending their children to school than ever before.

Increasing educational opportunities and standards of education have also raised the minimum qualification for all types of jobs. As a result employment opportunities for people with lower educational levels have dwindled over the years. This has really spurred enrolment and retention more so in case of upper primary education. Even for the post of peons, semi-skilled or semi-technical jobs, secondary education has become the minimum qualification, forcing many aspirants for lower jobs to seek enrolment at secondary level. The students intending to pursue vocational training courses have to have secondary certificate, thus making it mandatory for many such aspirants to complete secondary education first. It can be said that though aspiration for higher education has brought many students into the fold of secondary education, aspiration for employment too has its contribution.

Similarly, the growing economy has also put up its own demands, and education is one of them. Decreasing dependence on agriculture sector and a shift to industrial and service sectors, requires a change in skills and competency. This can be achieved through education, and hence, increase in enrolment. This trend has also been bolstered by lack of employment opportunities in rural areas. Stagnation of rural employment, and low productivity of agriculture, have also pushed people from rural to urban areas, necessitating a change in their skill levels and specialization. In both the cases, those who have remained in rural areas and those who have moved to urban areas have no alternative but to depend on education for survival and success. It is this imperative that has fostered the growth of secondary education. The recent demand did not come from upper strata of urban society but from the realization of the need of education among the Indian rural masses. The lack of employment opportunities in rural and tribal areas had greatly reduced the opportunity cost of education. It had given the accessibility and incentives to parents who were not too pessimistic in sending their children to schools for a few more years of schooling. It is in this context, that one can view the improved transition at different levels of education in India in general, and secondary education in particular.

When many of the first generation learners transit to secondary education, are they able to complete the secondary education cycle successfully? In this context, it is important to examine the pattern of repetition and dropout rates, as these are important indicators of internal efficiency.

REPETITION RATES

Repetition refers to the occurrence of failure at one level and the attempt to repeat the same Grade next time. Repetition rate is defined as the ratio of number of students repeating the Grade to the total number of students in the Grade, expressed in percentage terms. Repetition has an important role to play in the determination and analysis of quality of education at the school level. Repetition rate indicates both failure of the students as well as of schools and also the wastage of resources. The higher the repetition rate, the more the wastage of resources and the lower the quality of education. Ideally, the repetition rate should be close to zero.

Repetition occurs normally due to detaining of a student in the same class as a result of poor academic performance and, in some cases, because of less than stipulated attendance. Some of the states like Andhra Pradesh, West Bengal and Jammu & Kashmir, have adopted a policy of non-detention with automatic promotion to next the higher class based on minimum prescribed attendance. There is variation among different states with regard to classes up to which non-detention policy and automatic promotion is followed.

In India, the repetition rates, though small, still exist at all levels, including the primary stage, despite many states following non-detention policy. At all India level, the repetition rates are slightly more in upper primary (4.9%) and secondary (7.4%) compared to primary (3.7%) level. It ranges between 12 and 0 per cent at primary level, 11.63 and 0 per cent at Upper primary and 22.19 and 0 per cent at Secondary level among the major states (see Table 3.2).

Table 3.2: Percentage of Repeaters at All India Level in Four Sample States

State	*Primary (I-V)*	*Upper Primary (VI-VIII)*	*Secondary (IX-X)*
Andhra Pradesh	0.00	0.00	0.00
Kerala	4.95	8.97	5.98
Maharashtra	5.39	3.13	2.75
Uttar Pradesh	1.06	5.63	22.19
All India	3.7	4.9	7.4

Source: Education in India, 1997-98. Department of Education, MHRD, GOI, New Delhi, 2003.

Inter-state comparison of repetition rates suggests a large variation at all levels (see Annexure, Table A3). There is a category of states where repetition rate is either nil or marginal (Andhra Pradesh and Bihar) at all levels of school education which can be attributed to the practice of non-detention policy. The second category of states shows the trend of low repetition rate at lower levels of school education and higher repetition rate with increasing levels of schooling (Rajasthan, Madhya Pradesh, Uttar Pradesh and Assam). It may be noted that all these states are economically and educationally backward. This also indicates that the states adopt non-detention policy at varying degree at various stages of schooling. The third category of states shows a picture where the repetition rate decreases along with the increase of levels of schooling (Bihar, Maharashtra, Gujarat). The fourth category consists of states that have more or less similar repetition rate at all levels of schooling. These categories interestingly include states with different levels of socio-economic and educational achievements. However, it can be said that these repetition trends are largely determined by the state policies in relation to non-detention and degree of their implementation.

Further, the grade-wise repetition rate at secondary level (Grade IX-X) facilitates for a closer examination of the phenomenon. Repetition is not only limited to stages of education but is also prevalent at grades. In order to arrive at a definite picture of the preponderance and implication of repetition rate, the study has further probed the issue going into the secondary grade level. Since non-detention policy is rarely followed at this level, the understanding and implication of repetition becomes rather clear at this stage. As many states have terminal examination at upper primary level, the states tend to show an increase in the repetition rate at this level. Consequently, many states have double digit repetition rate at this stage of schooling. However, when we look at Grade X, the repetition rate is very high. It has increased significantly in Uttar Pradesh and Madhya Pradesh as well as educationally progressive state of Tamil Nadu, which is also reflected at the national level (see Annexure Table A3).

Among the sample states, while Andhra Pradesh officially has no repetition rate at any level,* Uttar Pradesh has the highest (22.2%) repetition rate at secondary level (see Table 3.3).

Table 3.3: Percentage of Repeaters by Grades in Sample States

State	*Grade VI*	*Grade VII*	*Grade VIII*	*Grade IX*	*Grade X*
Andhra Pradesh	0.00	0.00	0.00	0.00	0.00
Kerala	6.36	9.78	10.69	10.79	0.01
Maharashtra	3.61	2.07	3.76	4.88	0.00
Uttar Pradesh	5.88	5.98	4.91	9.16	34.56
All India	5.10	4.37	5.17	5.62	9.38

Source: Education in India, 1997-98. Department of Education, MHRD, GOI, New Delhi, 2003.

In case of Kerala, the extent of repetition rate at primary and secondary levels is lower and less than upper primary stage. This is a because of the policy of non-detention at primary level and detention of students at upper primary level based on academic performance. The filtering at upper primary level results in declining retention rate at secondary level which is unique to the state. Maharashtra has a

* Most states (including Andhra Pradesh) have an annual examination at the terminal stage of upper primary education i.e. either at Grade VII or at Grade VIII.

decline in repetition rate at each successive stage (5.4% at primary, 3.1% at upper primary, and 2.8% at secondary). On the contrary, in Uttar Pradesh, the repetition rates increased from one per cent at primary to a staggering figure of 22.2 per cent at secondary level. The repetition rate of students at Grade X in Uttar Pradesh is quite high (nearly one-fourths of total students) and is definitely an area of concern. In the light of this evidence, it may be said that in addition to higher demand, the increasing transition rate that was evident in states like Uttar Pradesh and Madhya Pradesh (discussed in the previous chapter) to some extent was the result of repetition and stagnation.

However, this information on repeaters is a little old and also points to macro level picture. In the backdrop of increased enrolment and participation rates at the secondary level among states especially after 90s, it becomes necessary to look at the issue of repeaters at institutional level. Moreover, the micro level picture may not necessarily reflect the actual position. Further, the state level data were for the year of 1997-98 and since then educational scenario has rapidly changed, thus requiring additional and current input for critical analysis. Therefore, in this section an attempt has been made to examine state level trends from the data obtained through case studies of selected schools (2003-04).

Comparisons of class-wise of repetition rates in the case study schools in four sample states indicate different pattern. Andhra Pradesh has no repeaters and Uttar Pradesh has the highest number of repeaters in Grade X (38.8%), much above the all India rate of 21.0 per cent. Kerala and also Maharashtra have high repetition rates in all the Grades, except in Grade X (see Table 3.4).

Table 3.4: Enrolment and Percentage of Repeaters by Grades in Samples Schools in 2002-03

State	*Grade VIII*		*Grade IX*		*Grade X*	
	Enrolment	*% of Repeaters*	*Enrolment*	*% of Repeaters*	*Enrolment*	*% of Repeaters*
Andhra Pradesh	1036	1.9	937	2.2	755	16.15
Kerala	4192	2.8	3970	4.5	3273	4.03
Maharashtra	2805	15.6	2518	15.9	1721	30.3
Uttar Pradesh	1356	4.7	2528	13.5	2432	38.8
Total	9389	6.8	9953	11.2	8181	21.0

Source: Field Survey (N=48).

DROPOUT RATES*

Another factor that leads to low transition rate along with repetition is dropout rate. Indian school education is characterized by astronomical dropout rate. The problem of dropout extends beyond quality of school education and is associated with several socio-economic factors. It is considered more serious a problem than repetition in the Indian context. The high dropout rate has been one of the most important factors for slow educational development in the country. Very high dropout rates have always put a question mark over the capacity of schools in retaining their students, the quality of teaching, ability of teachers and above all efficacy of the system itself. Similarly, socio-economic and cultural aspects equally play important role on students' capacity to continue in the system. However, continuing efforts in the direction of tackling dropout has resulted in its decline in the last few decades, as the following statistics suggest (see Figure 3.2).

At the all India level, during 2001-02, out of a batch of students who joined in first grade, 66 per cent dropped out before completing Grade X, while more than half of the students (55%) left the system

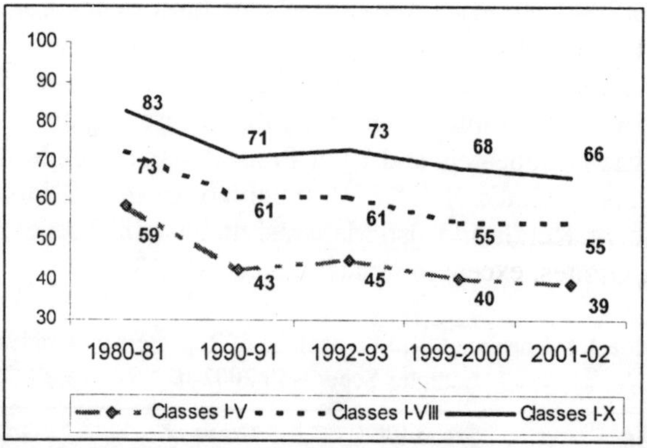

Figure 3.2: Drop-out Rates at Primary, Elementary and Secondary Stages in Selected Years in India

Source: Selected Educational Statistics, 2001-2002, Department of Education, MHRD, GOI, New Delhi, 2003.

---

* Dropout rate is defined as the percentage of pupils who drop out from a given Grade or cycle or level of education in a given cycle/school year. The formula for estimating the dropout is given as: Gross Dropout rate for Grades I to V = {1-(Enrolment in Grade V during 2001-2002/enrolment in Grade I during 1997-1998}*100.

without completing upper primary level i.e. Grade VIII and 39 per cent dropped out in at the primary stage itself. The extent of dropout rate is very high at primary level and it is comparatively less at secondary level (see Figure 3.2). The dropout rates among the disadvantaged groups, like Scheduled Castes (SC–72%) and Scheduled Tribes (ST–81%) are much higher than the national average at all levels (see Table 3.5). Only less than one-fifth of Scheduled Tribe students and one-fourth of Scheduled Caste students succeed to reach Class X while others dropout. The dropout rate at secondary level among Scheduled Castes and Scheduled Tribes is considerably higher than others.

In last two decades, the dropout rate has reduced significantly at primary level. Contrary to this, the dropout rate in upper primary and secondary level has increased though marginally in the last decade, both at all India level and also in some of the states. This trend needs to be viewed along with increased repetition rate, which may be pushing many of the repeaters out from school system, especially at the secondary level. Available data conforms to the possibility that dropout rates increase with successive levels of education as the opportunity cost of education rises and the need for earning wages beckons the young students. And also, with increased transition and enrolment at secondary level, the possibility of more dropouts too increases.

There are large inter-state variations (see Annexure, Table A4), ranging from zero in Kerala to 63 per cent in Rajasthan at primary level (Grade I-V). At elementary level Bihar has the highest dropout rate at 74 per cent and the lowest is again in educationally developed state of Kerala at 0 per cent. Similarly at secondary level, while Kerala has 16.64 per cent dropout rate, it is 83 per cent in Bihar. Unlike transition rates, the dropout rates are less in developed states and more in backward states. Except Madhya Pradesh, all the BiMARU states have alarmingly very high dropout rates at the elementary stage, and the trend continues at the secondary level. Interestingly, the state of Madhya Pradesh shows sharp decline in dropout rate which is not only below the national average but is just behind the educationally developed Kerala. Despite non-detention policy adopted in most of the states, high dropout rates continue to negate the pace of educational development especially at elementary level.

Dropout rates vary not only at interstate level but also on the basis of social groups. The dropout rate among the disadvantaged group of SC and ST is higher than the general population and varies between states. In Bihar, 90 per cent of students belonging to this category dropout between Grades I-X, while Kerala has the lowest dropout rate among the Scheduled Castes. Very high dropout rate in backward states is mainly because these states are predominantly inhabited by socio-economically poorer sections, including SCs, STs and other backward communities, among which dropout rate is very high as the following statistics would indicate. In India, the dropout rate at Grades I to X was 73 per cent for SCs, 81 per cent for STs as against 66 per cent for all categories at the secondary stage in 2001-02. It exceeded 90 per cent for SCs/STs in Bihar.

Among the sample states, Kerala has the lowest dropout rate and in fact, the state did not have any dropout till elementary level. Therefore, the 16 per cent dropout rate in Kerala at secondary level is quite high when compared to other states. In Andhra Pradesh 70 per cent of students dropout before reaching Grade X and a majority of them dropout (63%) even before reaching to the upper primary level (Grade VIII). In Uttar Pradesh, a majority of students do not complete secondary education and dropout in between (59%). Maharashtra is better than Andhra Pradesh in this regard, but is far behind Kerala, particularly in secondary education (see Table 3.5).

Among the sample states, Kerala with the lowest and Andhra Pradesh with the highest dropout rates represent two extreme situations. Andhra Pradesh, with many initiatives to improve education among the SCs/STs, could not make much progress in arresting the dropout rate among the disadvantaged groups. Uttar Pradesh characterises educational backwardness by reporting very high dropout rates in general and also the second highest among the Scheduled Caste in particular.

Gender wise dropout rates clearly suggest that girls dropout more

Table 3.5: Dropout Rates by Grades by Social Groups and by Levels of School Education in Sample States in 2001-02

State	*Grades I-V*	*Grades I-VIII*	*Grades I-X*	*Scheduled Caste Grades 1-X*	*Scheduled Tribe Grades 1-X*
Andhra Pradesh	43.03	63.09	70.12	77.59	87.78
Kerala	0.00	0.00	16.64	27.20	57.20
Maharashtra	7.37	37.03	52.28	57.98	73.93
Uttar Pradesh	49.40	60.11	58.98	68.96	43.22
All India	39.03	54.65	66.04	72.71	81.17

Source: Selected Educational Statistics 2001-02. Department of Education, MHRD, GOI, New Delhi, 2002-03.

often than boys in all sample states and also at the national level, except Kerala. Kerala is a unique case where there is no dropout till elementary level. Even at the secondary level dropout of boys is more than girls to the extent of 12 percentage points. On the contrary, extreme difference can be found in case of Uttar Pradesh starting from primary to secondary levels. Gender gap in dropout rates increases as levels of education move up. The same holds good for Maharashtra as well but at a moderate rate. Andhra Pradesh, despite making serious efforts to fill the gender gap at primary level, still around 3.4 percentage point difference can be observed at the secondary level (see Table 3.6).

Table 3.6: Dropout Rates by Gender and by Levels of Education in Sample States in 2001-02

State	*Primary (I-V)*			*Elementary (I-VIII)*			*Secondary (I-X)*		
	Boys	*Girls*	*Gender Gap*	*Boys*	*Girls*	*Gender Gap*	*Boys*	*Girls*	*Gender Gap*
Andhra Pradesh	42.6	43.5	-0.9	61.3	65.2	-3.9	68.5	71.9	-3.4
Kerala	0	0	0	0	0	0	20.7	12.5	8.2
Maharashtra	6.1	8.7	-2.6	35.4	38.9	-3.5	48.9	55.9	-7
Uttar Pradesh	45.8	54.9	-9.1	55.9	66.8	-10.9	53.4	69.4	-16
India	38.4	39.8	-1.4	52.9	56.9	-4	64.2	68.6	-4.4

Source: Selected Educational Statistics 2001-02. Department of Education, MHRD, GOI, New Delhi, 2002-03.

At the backdrop of improving transition rate, both repetition and dropout rates look quite discomforting, particularly while examining internal efficiency. Given this kind of discouraging trend, an attempt has been made to analyse the performance of students in public examinations at secondary and higher secondary levels.

PERFORMANCE IN PUBLIC EXAMINATIONS

In the context of secondary education, public examination system in India and its result have very prominent position. Examinations are necessarily held to test the learning ability and competency of a student, in a sense, through a mechanism of assessment and evaluation. Students in the school system have to appear at the public examination, both at the completion Grade X at the secondary level and at the end of Grade XII at higher secondary level. There are national and state level bodies entrusted with the task of conducting these examinations. At the national level, Central Board of Secondary

Education (CBSE) and the Indian School Certificate for Secondary Education conduct examinations for central government schools, like Central Schools and Navodaya Vidyalayas (pace-setting schools), private (unaided) management schools, and such other schools according to their affiliation. All the states also have State Boards of Education to conduct public examinations at secondary level. The national level boards cover very small proportion of secondary schools, as a majority of secondary schools are managed by the state governments besides a host of private aided secondary schools, which are also affiliated to state level Boards of Secondary Education. These boards conduct examinations for the schools that are affiliated to them and follow their prescribed curriculum. These examinations have assumed significance because these bodies are empowered to award certification and the certification becomes an instrumentality for higher education and selection to professional courses.

There have been doubts, debates and discussions regarding the reliability, validity and appropriateness of public examinations. It is true that these examinations rarely test the learning capacity, the application of mind and human sensibility. The critiques point out that these examinations are devoid of practical realities and biased towards chance and subjectivity. They nonetheless have remained the only available instrument for evaluation and assessment of the transacted curriculum and have also received recognition and approval over their results from government, teachers and parents. This has made the examinations generally an acceptable indicator of performance of students as well as schools. In order to maintain integrity and efficiency, these agencies follow well-laid procedures for conducting examinations, as discussed in detail in the chapter on Administration and Management of Secondary Education.

In the context of the analysis of internal efficiency of schools, the performance in public examinations as an indicator of quality has, however, some limitations. Performances in public examinations are often determined by several factors like quality, reliability and validity of test, level of preparation and other external factors in addition to teaching-learning process in the school. Further, performance levels in public examinations do not necessarily reflect the competencies of the students. The whole concept of public examinations system and their conduct in itself is a topic of serious debate in India which is yet to be resolved. We do share some of these concerns but in the context of the scope of the present study we have used it as one of many indicators. However, the public examination system, its management and problems are highlighted (see Appendix, Box).

Trends in Public Examinations at All India Level

The number of students who appeared in the public examination, and their results are simply mind-boggling. The number of students who took secondary examination (at 10th standard) in the year 2000 was 11.8 million as against 8.8 million in 1991. Similarly, the number of candidates appearing for higher secondary examination was as high as 3.99 million in 1991 and 4.66 million in 2000. The increase is not limited to a particular state or locality, rather it was similar across the country.

At the All-India level, the pass percentage of students in secondary (Grade-X) examination had varied between 44 to 60 per cent during 1991-2004. It ranged between 48 to 70 per cent in the higher secondary examination during the same period. The time series data on secondary schools public examination results did not show any particular trend but had fluctuated around 40-50 per cent. However, the pass percentage in Grade XII was better than Grade X. In fact, compared to the year 2000 the pass percentage during the last four years has substantially increased (see Figures 3.4 and Annexure, Table A5).

Unlike other indicators *viz.* repetition and dropout, girls have been consistently performing well in public examinations compared to boys. Over the years, it has been observed that girls have consistently out-performed boys in public examinations. The differences between the performance of boys and girls have varied from 3.8 to 12.0 percentage points at the secondary and between 5.5 and 16 percentage points at the higher secondary levels during 1991-2000.

Inter-state Variation in Examination Results

There are significant differences among states in terms of teaching-learning conditions, composition of students, extent of different management schools, nature and management of examination system, in addition to political and social contexts. More importantly, a common core curriculum has been adopted in the entire country despite vast diversity among the states. Therefore, national average pertaining to performance in public examinations does not exhibit or reflect the

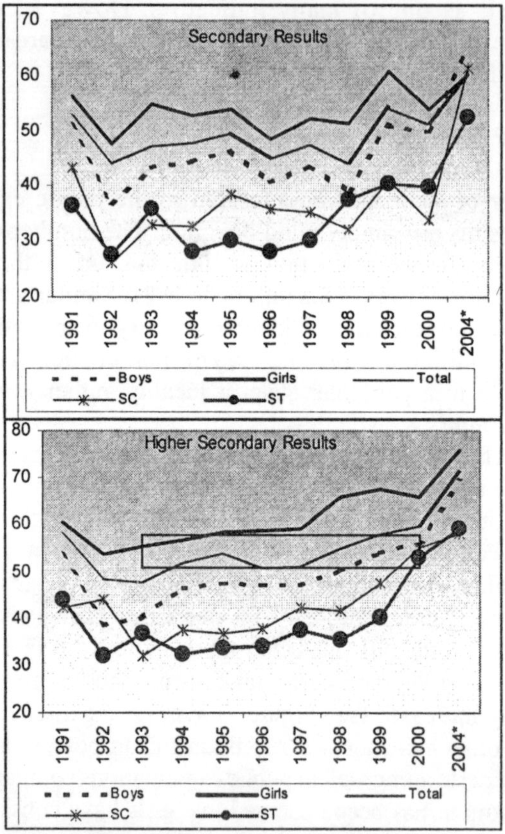

Figures 3.4-3.5: Trends in Pass Percentage According to Gender and Social Group in SSC and HSC Examinations (All India)

Source: Results of Secondary, Higher Secondary and Intermediate/PUC Examinations, 1991-2000, MHRD, GOI, New Delhi.

variations in efficiency of schools in different states. Considering these variations it would be interesting to examine the performance of students in public examinations across different states. Like other aspects of education, public examination results also show significant variations among the states. However, a common feature is that there is no consistency in the extent of pass percentage in public examination results among the states (see Annexure, Table A6).

In few states like Tamil Nadu and West Bengal the pass percentage in public examination has been more than the national average with little fluctuations (see Annexure, Table A6). There is no state with a consistent increase or decrease in the pass percentage rate. However, there are a few states that have very poor record in pass percentage. The fluctuations are so high that a state with highest pass rate in a year is also the state with the lowest pass rate in some other year. For example, Haryana which had the highest pass rate in Grade X public examination (82%) in 1991 also had a very low pass per cent (32%) in 1998. Similar trends can be found in some other states. Unlike other indicators of progress and efficiency, it is very difficult to place any state as the best or the worst performing state based on the trends in examination results.

Considering the average of pass percentage over the last ten years, Tamil Nadu, and West Bengal had the best average along with central board's *viz*. CBSE and ICSE. The poor performers have been Madhya Pradesh and Assam. Madhya Pradesh not only had poor pass percentage (29%), but also continued with it for quite some time. This is a state where a large proportion of lower secondary schools are private unaided schools.

The scenario of public examination results at Grade XII is quite different from that of Grade X. Except in a few states, the pass percentage rate at higher secondary level is higher than at the lower secondary level. Some of the educationally and economically backward states *viz*. Rajasthan, Orissa, Bihar and Uttar Pradesh, show very high pass percentage rate at higher secondary and a lower pass percentage rate at lower secondary level. Quite interestingly, Madhya Pradesh which had only 29 per cent pass rate (the lowest in the country) had remarkably a higher pass percentage at higher secondary level (79.5%) in the same year.

Differences in Performances: Gender and Social Groups

The national pattern continues to repeat itself at the state level with girls performing better in the examinations. However, the extent of this difference in performance between boys and girls varies from state to state. While Kerala reported zero per cent gender difference in the performance at public examinations, Uttar Pradesh had the highest gender variation. Interestingly, educationally fast developing state like Punjab and economically backward state like Assam have lower percentage of gender variation. It is not unusual to find states with strong patriarchal values like Uttar Pradesh and Haryana with wider gaps in performance between boys and girls where women are subject to tremendous hurdles to overcome the existing prejudices but it is difficult to explain prevalence of substantial gender gap in performance levels in Karnataka (see Annexure, Table A7).

There are many explanations behind this disparity, most of them being commonly held beliefs like that girls spend more time in studies than boys as they have less work at home. But held to scrutiny, it is found that girls in fact spend more time doing household chores and domestic work in rural India than boys. Though there is no empirical evidence to substantiate the presumption regarding girl's better performance and related respective socio-economic status and sociological underpinnings, but it may help us in understanding the phenomenon. It is quite possible that the economic status of girls continuing in secondary and higher secondary levels is better than that of boys at least in terms of averages. Due to better socio-economic background, these girls can concentrate on their studies and have done well while boys from poor backgrounds have numerous distractions including the necessity to earn the livelihood. The other reason is sociological which is rooted in the mindset of 'fear of failure', which is more intense girls. Failure in examination in case of girls always hangs like Damocles' sword over their head. Failure will not only lead to discontinuation of their study but will also bring them shame and ridicule. This has probably motivated them to do well at the first opportunity leading to better pass percentage. This also explains why girls' performance is far better than that of boys in states known for discrimination against girls.

Akin to its geographic features and population characteristics India exhibits similar traits of diversity and differences in its educational achievement and performance of different states. The differences in socio-economic levels of its population, their educational choices and preferences as well as levels of ability, have significant effect on the performance in public examinations and consequently on results. The Scheduled Castes and Scheduled Tribes, for whose development, the Constitution had made special provisions in guaranteeing education and employment, lag far behind other groups in terms of educational achievement, particularly in performance in public examinations. At secondary level, the pass percentage of these groups has not only been lower than that of other groups but also they did not show any sign of improvement in the last decade. Therefore, the absolute difference in their pass percentage did not decline. Though some improvement is observed in higher secondary results, yet without much decline in the differences; the results of other groups also improved. Within these groups, pass percentage has been more for Scheduled Castes compared to Scheduled Tribes though there were some instances of tribal students doing well (see Figures 3.4-3.5 and Annexure, Table A5).

Among the sample states, Uttar Pradesh has the highest number and Kerala the lowest number of candidates appearing both for the X and XII Grade public examinations. The pass percentage in Grade X public examinations, though fluctuating, showed some improvement in all the sample states during the last decade, more so in the last five years. Andhra Pradesh not only had the highest pass percentage but also maintained consistent improvement in the last few years in Grade-X examination. Uttar Pradesh, on the other hand, has shown very fluctuating trend while averaging around 56 per cent. Maharashtra has shown a consistent increase in the pass percentage rate with slight variation. However, Kerala though showed an increase in the pass rate during 1991-2000, but the pass rate has reduced during 2000-2004 (see Table 3.7).

At higher secondary level, Uttar Pradesh has the highest pass percentage rate though it has been fluctuating over the years; Andhra Pradesh is placed at the bottom among the sample states. However, both Andhra Pradesh and Maharashtra have shown consistently improving pass percentage rate. The poor pass percentage rate at higher secondary level in Andhra Pradesh is surprising considering that a large proportion of higher secondary schools are private unaided. The pass percentage rate in Grade XII has been better than in Grade X in all three states, except in Andhra Pradesh, as most of the weak students are weeded out at the Grade X public examination and relatively academically sound students join XII Grade. This may be one of the reasons for better results in Grade XII public examinations. In most of the states, pass percentage is not related to size of the system, as Kerala with its small size did not show any better performance. Among the non-sample states, some big states like Bihar and West Bengal had better results both in Grade X and Grade XII examinations.

Low pass percentage in 10th Grade may be one of the reasons for high pass percentage at higher secondary level. Since

Table 3.7: Pass Percentage in Public Examinations (Grade X and XII) in Sample States in India

State	Secondary						Higher Secondary					
	1991	1995	2000	2004	Avg.	Rank	1991	1995	2000	2004	Avg.	Rank
Andhra Pradesh	48	60	55	80	61	7	21	28	44	55	37	18
Kerala	51	N.A.	76	59	62	6	60	54	68	59	60	8
Maharashtra	48	51	52	60	53	14	50	49	62	63	54	10
Uttar Pradesh	61	61	32	72	56	11	81	73	68	91	78	3
All India	55	53	53	60	54	13	58	54	52	71	55	9

Source: Results of Secondary, Higher Secondary and Intermediate/PUC Examinations, 1991-2000, Department of Education, MHRD, GOI, New Delhi.

performance in higher secondary is a very crucial and a decisive factor to get admission into higher education, especially professional courses, it influences to achieve better results. At higher secondary level, having different subject streams too plays a role in better performance as the students opt for the subjects in which they have interest and potential for performance. In addition, compared to lower levels, the teaching-learning conditions at higher secondary level are generally better. On the basis of trends and analysis of public examination results and the management type, it can be said that there is a negative relationship between the proportion of private unaided schools and performance in public examinations, particularly when the proportion is extremely high. For example, Madhya Pradesh with higher proportion of private unaided schools at lower secondary level has poor examination results and so is the case with Andhra Pradesh at higher secondary level. Similarly, states like Bihar with almost zero per cent of private schools at higher secondary level has much better performance at public examinations. However, looking at the reliability and integrity of examination system, it is difficult to provide a reasonable answer to this issue.

District Level Variations

The differences in results among states are well understood, given the differences in the policies and programmes related to quality, curriculum, management and examinations. But differences within a state and among districts exist in view of wide regional disparities. However, it is not a regular phenomenon for any one district to have either good or poor results. Similarly, examination results are not necessarily related with levels of development of districts. The inter-district variation in public examination results is conspicuous among the four sample states (see Annexure, Figures A1-A4).

Irrespective of population size, levels of education and economic development, all the sample states showed large inter-district variation in examination results. Among 23 districts in Andhra Pradesh, the highest and the lowest pass percentage ranged between 89.5 per cent and 61.59 per cent in Warangal and Hyderabad districts respectively. While Hyderabad, the state capital, is more urbanized with high literacy, yet in examination results it occupied the lowest position, whereas Warangal, being educationally lagging behind, comprising more rural areas with considerable percentage of socio-economically disadvantaged population, topped in public examination results. In this state, 11 districts had less than average pass percentage of the state. The inter-district variation in Kerala is significantly high as the highest and the lowest pass percentages vary between 80 per cent and 45 per cent respectively. Unlike in Andhra Pradesh, the districts with high pass percentage are also the districts with high literacy and economic development. Similarly, the districts with low pass percentage in public examinations are those which, otherwise, are also backward, educationally and economically, in the state. However, some of the districts in the state, even though economically backward, did perform well. These are the districts which have high proportion of unaided private schools. Quiet interestingly, in an educationally and industrially developed state like Maharashtra, not only the inter-district disparities are less but the variation between the highest and the lowest pass rate is also small, although the relatively backward districts evidently have low performance in public examinations. Both educationally and economically backward large state of Uttar Pradesh, with as many as 70 districts, and having the largest number of students appearing for public examinations at secondary level in India had pass percentage in most of the districts, below the state average; more interestingly, several districts had the same level of performance, with a very few districts reaching state level performance if not higher pass percentage. Thus, the performance in public examinations is not only low across the states; the uneven performance of students across different districts within the same state reflects differential in facilities and variation in the quality of education.

The extent of inter-district variation differs among the four sample states. While in Andhra Pradesh, more than 90 per cent of districts had more than 60 per cent pass rate in X Grade public examination in 2002, the percentage of districts achieving the same result was 64 per cent in Kerala and 74 per cent in Maharashtra. No district in Uttar Pradesh had this distinction. The pass percentage was less than 30 per cent in more than 70 per cent of the districts in Uttar Pradesh. Except in Andhra Pradesh, there are no districts with more than 80 per cent pass rate at secondary level (see Table 3.8).

Table 3.8: Distribution of Percentage of Districts According to Pass Percentage at Secondary Level

Range of Pass Percent	*Andhra Pradesh**	*Kerala*		*Maharashtra*		*Uttar Pradesh*		*Total*	
	X	*X*	*XII*	*X*	*XII*	*X*	*X II*	*X*	*XII*
>40	0	0	0	0	5.71	90		45.9	1.7
41-60	8.7	35.4	0	25.7	57.2	10.0	12.9	40.2	24.4
61-80	82.6	64.3	100	74.3	34.8	0	77.1	12.7	67.2
80>	8.7	0	0	0	2.85	0	10.0	1	6.72

* HSC not available for Andhra Pradesh.

Source: Based on Boards of Secondary and Higher Secondary Education in Sample States, 2002.

However, the picture was different with respect to higher secondary public examination. Kerala and even Uttar Pradesh were better with 100 per cent and 87 per cent of districts respectively, with more than 60 per cent pass rate. Maharashtra showed large inter-district variations in higher secondary examination results among all the sample states. Uttar Pradesh did not show significant inter-district variations.

Further disaggregated and micro level data depict inter-school variations in terms of pass percentage (see Table 3.9).

Table 3.9: Distribution of Schools According to Pass Percentage in Grade X Examinations in Three Sample Districts (During 2002-2003)

Range of Pass percent in Exams	*Trivandrum (Kerala) percent of Schools*	*Pune (Maharashtra) percent of Schools*	*Varanasi (UP) percent of Schools*
	Grade-X	*Grade-X*	*Grade-X*
Up to 40	14	4.7	53
41-60	29	12	29
61-80	12	36	10
80 and above	45	48	8

Source: Based on Boards of Secondary and Higher Secondary Education in Sample States, 2002.

This has been tested in the backdrop of data available from the sample districts. Pune (Maharashtra) district has more inter-school variation with only less than 5 per cent of schools with less than 40 per cent pass rate, while in Varanasi (Uttar Pradesh) more than 50 per cent of schools have less than 40 per cent of pass rate. While Trivandrum (Kerala) and Pune has a majority of schools with more than 80 per cent of pass rate, only 8 per cent of schools in Varanasi have 80 per cent of pass percentage. This means that while there is a large concentration of good performing schools in Trivandrum and Pune the contrast is true in case of Varanasi with large concentration of poor schools. Uttar Pradesh has less interschool variation with higher percentage of schools showing poor performance.

Public Examination Results among Different Management Categories

Since secondary schools belong to different management categories, it is imperative to examine the extent of performance in public examinations by management. Generally private schools follow either central syllabus or state syllabus, however, the government and private aided schools in the state are affiliated with state boards and curriculum (see Table 3.10). The analysis of public examination results by management is confined to four sample states.

Table 3.10: Pass Percentage in Grade X and XII Public Examinations by Type of Management in Sample States, 2002

State	Management Type	Grade X	Grade XII
Andhra Pradesh	Govt.	59.72	20.54
	Govt. Residential	88.30	29.74
	Private Un-aided (State Affiliated)	75.76	53.18
	Private Unaided (CBSE)	91.20	90.93
Kerala	Govt.	48.76	62.30#
	Private Aided	64.85	74.06#
	Private Unaided (State Affiliated)	97.49	91.17***
	Private Unaided (CBSE Affiliated)	94.17	91.17
Maharashtra	Govt.	71.81*	68.98*
	Private Aided and Unaided (State Affiliated)	76.76**	80.45**
	Private Unaided (CBSE Affiliated)	93.49***	94.00***
Uttar Pradesh	Govt.	43.94	73.98
	Private Aided (State Affiliated)	41.97	72.22
	Private Unaided (CBSE Affiliated))	43.24	72.88

* Includes both Government and local body schools of Pune District.

** Includes both private aided and private unaided schools of Pune District.

*** CBSE Results of Maharashtra.

\# Pass Percentage in 2003.

Examination results in different management type schools vary among the four states. In all the states, private unaided schools had higher pass percentage both in Grade X and Grade XII. Among these private unaided schools those affiliated to CBSE had a better pass rate than those affiliated to State Boards, except in Kerala at lower secondary level and in Uttar Pradesh at higher secondary level. However, the difference between the pass rate of private unaided and other management schools varies among the sample states. Interestingly, in Uttar Pradesh, at lower secondary level schools affiliated to State Board, irrespective of management, had more or less similar level of pass percentage rate which was quite low.

Though in Andhra Pradesh government schools lag behind others, the residential schools that are operated by government for the rural and disadvantaged children have far better results (87%), comparable with unaided CBSE affiliated schools and higher than the private unaided schools following the state syllabus. Such high performance of students in residential schools could be attributed to structured school schedule, intensive teaching-learning process and high accountability of teachers and heads of the school, in addition to provision of adequate facilities and administrative support. In Kerala, at lower secondary level, a little more than half of the students fail in the public examination in government schools, whereas in private aided schools two-thirds of students have succeeded in the same examination. The state also shows similar trend at the higher secondary level. Interestingly, in Maharashtra, the difference in pass percentages among government and private aided schools is very little; however, it has increased at the higher secondary level. Uttar Pradesh presents a different scenario where the performance among government, private aided and private unaided schools affiliated to the State Board varies a little with a pass per cent varying from 39-44 per cent. However, the schools affiliated with CBSE had better results (77%) although it is much less compared to other three sample states.

Unlike in other states, surprisingly in Uttar Pradesh, the lower secondary public examination results of unaided schools affiliated with state syllabus are as poor as in government and aided schools. Contrary to common belief that the performance of private unaided schools is better than of the government schools, is rather in failing, particularly in the context of Uttar Pradesh and Madhya Pradesh. One of the reasons for such a low performance of unaided schools can be attributed to mushrooming of these schools in smaller towns and rural areas of these states without quality conditions. This also substantiates the inherent logic of operational inefficiency of private unaided schools when expanded beyond a particular level. In fact, many schools may not invest on quality provisions as they have to provide education at a lower cost unlike private schools affiliated to CBSE and located in urban areas.

Performance and Quality

In India, the minimum percentage of marks required to pass a public examination is 33 per cent or more in aggregate at the secondary level. Divisions and ranks are accorded based on the aggregate marks secured by the students. The number of students passing with first division and distinctions can be taken as a better indicator for determining internal efficiency. For example, in order to move a more competitive and demanding levels of educational cycle, mere passing an examination is the enough, rather it is the quality of performance that matters in the end. Rather than mere pass rate, the achievement levels of students in terms of accruing different divisions could illustrate the efficiency of the system. However, in the absence of consistent data for all the states and boards, we have examined this aspect only for the four sample states.

Among the four states, the percentage of students passing with different divisions varies (see Table 3.11). In Andhra Pradesh, a majority of students in 2003 passed with first division, in Kerala maximum students were placed in third division, while in Maharashtra and Utter Pradesh a large percentage of students had second division at lower secondary level. Andhra Pradesh not only has increased consistently pass per cent at Grade X but also has shown improvement in terms of percentage of students getting first divisions. The state of Maharashtra witnessed a significant improvement in the performance levels of students during 2001-2003, resulting in doubling the proportion of students placed in first division. However, in both Kerala despite improvement in pass percentage in Grade X public examinations did not show progress in levels of performance in accruing higher Grades. On the other hand, Uttar Pradesh not only had poor pass percentage but also continued to have lower achievement levels during the period of 2000-2003.

Uttar Pradesh showed no improvement, both in quantitative and qualitative terms, despite prevalence of malpractices. The other two sample states, though having more first divisions than U.P., are nowhere near to A.P. achievement; though in Maharashtra the first divisioners almost doubled during 2000-2003. In Kerala, the percentage of students passing in third division is very high compared to both first and second division, and no state, including U.P., has been better in this regard. A.P. has very low number of those in the third division.

Table 3.11: Division-wise Pass Percentage in Grade X Public Examinations in Sample States

Year	*Andhra Pradesh*				*Kerala*				*Maharashtra*				*Uttar Pradesh*			
	Pass %	*I*	*II*	*III*	*Pass %*	*I*	*II*	*III*	*Pass %*	*I*	*II*	*III*	*Pass %*	*I*	*II*	*III*
2000	55	51	33	16	55	31	19	50	50	18	41	41	30	7	66	27
2001	67	58	29	13	55	33	20	47	55	NA	NA	NA	35	7	63	30
2002	68	58	29	13	59	37	19	44	61	30	46	24	42	7	64	29
2003	75	64	26	11	62	34	20	46	67	37	45	19	42	9	65	26

Source: State Boards of Secondary and Higher Education in the four sample states.

At higher secondary level too, Andhra Pradesh retained its top position with a high number of students obtaining first division among the four states (see Table 3.12). Also in this state, one-fourth of students got second division and a negligible percentage was placed in third division. Contrary to this, a majority of students in Uttar Pradesh secured only second division and a very few (less than one-fifth) students obtained first division. A little less than half of the students in Kerala and a little more than one-third of students in Maharashtra were able to secure first division. In these two states, like Uttar Pradesh, a considerable percentage of students were placed in second division. All the four states have shown an increasing trend of students obtaining first division though the percentage varies in each state. However, the improvement was marginal.

Table 3.12: Division-wise Pass Percentage of Grade XII Public Examinations in Sample States

Year	*Andhra Pradesh*				*Kerala*				*Maharashtra*				*Uttar Pradesh*			
	Pass %	*I*	*II*	*III*	*Pass %*	*I*	*II*	*III*	*Pass %*	*I*	*II*	*III*	*Pass %*	*I*	*II*	*III*
2000	39	60	29	12	56	29	41	31	61	31	50	20	68	12	63	25
2001	40	67	25	9	58	37	39	24	66	NA	NA	NA	71	10	64	26
2002	40	68	24	8	59	36	33	30	65	37	48	16	73	13	67	21
2003	55	69	25	6	62	48	34	18	63	38	48	13	73	19	68	13

Source: State Boards of Secondary and Higher Education in the four sample states.

Subject-wise Performance

Grouping the student's performance into divisions indicates the aggregate achievement of learners. This aggregate performance does not denote the performance of students in individual subjects which may vary among the students. This aspect of student's achievement is very important considering the uniform curriculum, pedagogy and teaching-leaning process at the state as well as school level. An attempt is made to analyse the performance of students in different subjects at Grade X level public examination in the following section.

At secondary level, the pass percentage varies from subject to subject and from state to state in a given subject (see Table 3.13). In first language, i.e., generally the medium of instruction and also the mother tongue, pass percentage is relatively high. The other subject in which the students perform better is the social studies, however, a majority of students who fail in Grade X usually have difficulty in qualifying in mathematics, English and science.

Table 3.13: Subject-wise SSC Results in Sample States at Grade X in 2003 (in%)

Subject	*Andhra Pradesh*	*Kerala*	*Maharashtra*
1st Language	91.97	84.37	84.97
2nd Language	92.36	36.19	84.62
3rd Language	88.66	52.63	90.02
Mathematics	86.39	45.91	76.13
General Science	87.24	51.09	92.94
Social Studies	93.66	67.84	89.32

Source: State Boards of Secondary and Higher Secondary Education in Sample States, 2003.

Note: Subject-wise Grade X results were not available for Uttar Pradesh.

In all the subjects, Andhra Pradesh had more than 85 per cent pass rate, followed by Maharashtra. Kerala had very low pass rate in all the subjects, more so in subjects like mathematics and the second language. It may be noted that having high pass percentage in every subject does not guarantee overall high pass rate unless the same students pass in all the subjects. This is unlikely to happen and hence pass rate in individual subject is higher than overall pass percentage.

Stream-wise Analysis of Performances at Higher Secondary Level

As the level of education moves up, the secondary students have option of choosing their streams and subjects based on their performance in the previous public examination besides the individual aptitude and interest. However, so far as combination of subjects and categorization of streams are concerned, there is no uniformity among the states. For further analysis and critical examination of the issue, we have focused on performance of students in arts, sciences and commerce streams (see Annexure, Table A8).

The number of students appearing in Grade XII examination is larger in the science stream than any other streams. Generally, the pass percentage is more in science stream compared to arts stream in many states.

Within science stream, the pass percentage is more in stream of mathematics-physics-chemistry combination, compared to the Biology group in Andhra Pradesh. Even in Arts group, mathematics-economics-commerce group students performed better than even biology stream students. This shows that students have performed well in the Science as well as in Arts streams with mathematics combination. In addition to these, the students who opt for Science stream, usually seek private tuition to improve their levels of performance. However, there is little doubt that students in Arts, comprising history, economics and civics (HEC), have fared poorly in comparison to other streams in Andhra Pradesh. In Kerala also, the pass percentage is more in Science stream (70%), than in Commerce (53%) and Arts (51%).

In contrast, in Uttar Pradesh and Maharashtra, the pass percentage was more in Commerce stream, followed by Science and Arts streams. Division-wise and stream-wise results again suggest that students are doing better in Science stream. In all the sample states, more than half of the students secured first division in science stream whereas not more than 40 per cent of students could secure first division in Arts group.

The students appearing in public examination at higher secondary level with arts and humanities streams without the combination of mathematics have performed poorly compared to other streams. Interestingly at Grade X students have performed better in social studies and find mathematics difficult while the results at higher secondary level shows mathematics as a scoring subject. The reasons for such a trend includes: (i) The students with high performance levels in Grade X generally choose science stream including mathematics, followed by commerce; (ii) those who did not fare well have to opt for arts subjects; (iii) generally arts and humanities streams are available in government schools where related facilities are probably poor.

Performance in Public Examinations: School Level Dynamics

The foregoing discussion on performance in public examinations has shown a mixed trend and variations at different levels. Though these indicators provide an overview and a macro level picture, they do not reveal the real dynamics at the school level. In order to capture the micro level situation, primary data from 49 school case studies from four sample districts of four states have been examined. These case study schools belong to different managements and locations.

Based on the performance in the public examination at Grade X over a period of five years (see Annexure, Table A9) these schools can be categorized into following different categories. The first category consists of those schools which have high pass percentage and high percentage of students with first division and have been consistent in their performance.

The second category of schools belongs to those schools which have improved their performance in public examination compared to previous years and have consistently been improving. The third group of schools are those which have shown a declining trend in their performance graph in public examinations over a period of time. The last category, the fourth, refers to schools with consistently poor performance in public examinations. These different categories of schools belong to different management types, and are found in rural-urban localities and have diverse socio-economic composition of students (see Table 3.14).

Table 3.14: Performance in Public Examinations – Case Study Schools

Category	*Location*	*Type of Management*		
		Govt	*Private Aided*	*Private Unaided*
Consistently good performing schools	Urban	3	2	5
	Rural	2	2	1
Improving schools	Urban	2	2	1
	Rural	3	3	0
Schools with declining performance	Urban	2	1	0
	Rural	2	3	2
Consistently poor performing schools	Urban	4	0	2
	Rural	2	3	2

Source: Case Studies of Sample Schools.

The schools defined as good schools do not constitute a homogeneous group either on the basis of available infrastructure, school size or location. In fact, most of these schools complain lack of adequate physical and infrastructure facilities. However, the common features in these schools are planned teaching-learning process *viz.* completion of syllabus, revision of courses, continuous and comprehensive evaluation of student's performance, giving feedbacks to students, organization of remedial teaching etc. Most of these schools enjoy a degree of functional autonomy in carrying out the teaching-learning activities and have regular headmasters. A lot of efforts are made in these schools acquainting the students with possible patterns of examination-special preparation and discussion, in fact, the approach is examination oriented. Some of the good schools are government schools located in rural areas and cater especially to disadvantaged groups. However, these schools are residential government schools.

The critical factors influencing the performance of the schools can be broadly categorised as internal and external. Internal factors consist of system level and institutional level factors. Within the institutional level, the academic factors on the one hand and leadership and congenial environment on the other hand, greatly influence the performance of the schools. External factors would comprise of the community and PTA and also the household factors.

Vicious Circle of Failure: Repetition, Dropout and Poor Performance

There is a strong relationship between repetition, dropout and poor performance and all of them are detrimental to the internal efficiency of the school. It is found that one reason leads to another, and in many cases, the reasons are same for each of these internal efficiency indictors. Therefore, it is important to look at the factors responsible for these problems such as non-detention policy, poor socio-economic condition of students, deficiencies in teaching-learning process, lack of integration of schools, etc. and examine them holistically. An attempt has been made to discuss these issues in detail.

As most of the states follow the non-detention policy at primary stage, a large number of students get promoted to the next stage. Because of this policy, schools have to promote all the students to the next class based on specified attendance, without considering the competency levels. In this process, one can find the collusion of schools, government as well as parents. The school management,

REASON FOR CONSISTANT HIGH PERFORMANCE IN PUBLIC EXAMINATIONS

Internal Factor	Institutional Level	External Factors
System Level ▪ Integration of lower and higher Grades ▪ Low Teacher-Pupil Ratio ▪ Supervision and Monitoring ▪ Support from the Administration	*Academic* ▪ Examination oriented approach with emphasis on completion of syllabus, revision of courses, extended teaching hours, solving model question papers and remedial teaching, supervisory studies, extended hours of teaching-learning etc. ▪ Rigorous implementation of comprehensive and continuation of evaluation of student's performance ▪ Leadership/environment ▪ Good institutional leadership, good interpersonal relationships among headmaster, staff and students and team work ▪ Counseling and Guidance	*Community and PTA* ▪ Cooperation and support from the community and parents *Household Factors* ▪ Household Academic Support and Guidance ▪ Socio-cultural aspects-more awareness about education, higher aspirations of parents, social obsession for education in general and performance in public examinations in particular etc.

Source: Based upon School Case Studies.

REASON FOR IMPROVED PERFORMANCE IN PUBLIC EXAMINATIONS

Internal Factor	Institutional Level	External Factors
System Level ▪ Integration of lower and higher Grades ▪ Fear of disincentives from the government	*Academic* ▪ Academic supervision and monitoring ▪ Examination oriented approach with emphasis on completion of syllabus, revision of courses, extended teaching hours, solving model question papers and remedial course ▪ Comprehensive and continuous evaluation and remedial teaching *Leadership/Environment* ▪ Leadership and Motivation ▪ Setting target	*Community and PTA* ▪ Active role of Parent-Teacher Association *Household Factors* ▪ Dependency on private tuition with exception of few schools

Source: Based upon School Case Studies.

REASON FOR DECLINING TREND IN PERFORMANCE IN PUBLIC EXAMINATION

Internal Factor	Institutional Level	External Factors
System Level ▪ Unqualified and un-trained teachers ▪ Absence of regular headmaster/Principal, lack of subject teacher. ▪ Low integration of schools, high repetition and high dropout rate	*Academic* ▪ Poor academic management, supervision and monitoring ▪ Non-implementation of continuous and comprehensive evaluation *Leadership/Environment* ▪ Lack of interest among teachers ▪ Teacher absenteeism	*Household factors* ▪ Lack of interest among students and parents ▪ Student absenteeism ▪ Good students from better socio-economic background are leaving for better schools

Source: Based upon School Case Studies.

REASONS FOR CONSISTANTLY LOW PERFORMANCE IN PUBLIC EXAMINATIONS

Internal Factor	Institutional Level	External Factors
System Level ▪ Unqualified, un-trained teachers and underpaid teachers ▪ Teacher teaching more subjects is common ▪ Inadequate facilities to some extent ▪ Lack of integration of grades	*Academic* ▪ Low competency level of students when they joint the secondary level ▪ Syllabus not completed in time/not revised ▪ Lack of continuous and comprehensive evaluation ▪ No remedial teaching, crowded classes ▪ Lack motivation among teachers ▪ Teacher absenteeism *Leadership/Environment* ▪ Lack of Regular Head teacher/Principal ▪ Lack of motivation and accountability ▪ Lack of Monitoring and Supervision teachers ▪ External Factors *Community and PTA* ▪ Lack of Community support *Household Factors* ▪ Irregular attendance and indiscipline among students ▪ Poverty and need of students to work/help parents	

Source: Based upon School Case Studies.

Household's Investment on Supplementary Education through Private Tuition

Government Schools and Educational Excellence

Government Higher Secondary School for Girls, Cotton Hill, was established in 1935. This is the largest government school for girls in the state with more than 6000 students and 200 teachers. The school admits students from all strata of the society and is truly representative of the society with different castes and communities. The school has students from business class, high level government officials as well from slums. In fact, 35 per cent of students are from below poverty line. The institutional motto is to provide quality education to future leaders. The school offers both English and Malayalam as medium of instruction. The school emphasizes improving the teaching-learning method *viz.* teachers coming prepared to the class, taking extra classes to finish the syllabus, looking at the problems of individual students and following the practice of comprehensive and continuous evaluation. PTA plays an important role in supporting the school activities, including taking care of children from poor families.

Government Higher Secondary School for Girls,
Thiruvantapuram (2005)

Equity and Excellence

Another example of good performing government schools is the Residential Secondary Schools run by Andhra Pradesh Social Welfare Department. These schools are essentially established to serve the educational needs of the disadvantaged students. The school has higher transition rate and low dropout rate. Despite the school needing improvement in physical infrastructure, its academic responsibilities have never been compromised. The teachers teach only their respective specialized subjects and take remedial teaching for weak students. Teachers are involved in a lot of academic works including monitoring and supervision of students as well as administrative responsibilities. Preparation of institutional plan, teacher management and incentive to successful teacher are the hallmark of the school. Unlike many other schools this school aims at the holistic development of its students and offers career counselling and guidance.

Andhra Pradesh Social Welfare Residential
School (2005)

including the head-teacher and other teachers, are keen to make up the attendance as it serves their interest. Similarly, parents pressurise the school management to promote their wards who would have otherwise been detained. There is the danger that detention may lead to dropout and the fear of dropout discourages detention of students in the same class.

Most of the states, having non-detention policy at the lower levels of schooling especially at primary stage, tend to show high repetition rates at upper primary and secondary stages. This is because all students, including those deficient in learning, are also promoted to the next class/stage during the primary stage. Therefore, one can observe that the repetition rate increases with the increasing levels of schooling.

Consequently, the secondary schools receive students with low levels of learning competency and this in turn makes difficult for these students to cope up with the demands of the system. In some cases, the students entering to secondary level have a competency level of primary schooling and in the context of common curriculum it becomes extremely difficult for such students to meet the new challenges. In the absence of any remedial measures and no help from the school, they remain at the bottom of the class unable to follow the instructions, thereby leaving the schools with no other option but to detain such students. This is more in the case of students from rural schools joining urban secondary schools.

The normal reason for class repetition, according to many teachers, heads of secondary schools, policy makers and administrators, revolves around poor academic levels of students at the entry level. Lack of appropriate facilities and large class sizes are also responsible for low performance and repetition among students. Another important reason for repetition includes vested interests who would like to maintain public image of the school as high performing school in public examinations. This practice is prevalent both in government and private schools, however, more so in the case of the latter. While private schools detain students to record better divisions in public examinations in order to maintain public image and meet market demand, a few government schools also detain weak students to show high pass percentage to restrain administrative targets and pressure. Since the students who fail in public examinations at secondary level have to reappear privately, and chances for clearing examinations without attending classes are much more difficult, therefore, some of the students repeat schooling at Grade X to perform better in public examinations.

There are several factors for dropout, some of them being specific to India, and to local and group contexts. Some of the factors responsible for low transition and repetition also influence dropout rates in the country. The reasons for dropout at secondary level may be much different from those at lower levels of education. The factors effecting dropout can be broadly categorized as academic, socio-economic and cultural. While some of the academic factors push the students out, a few of the socio-economic reasons pull them out from the system.

Because of the poor quality of teaching-learning conditions in schools, students lose interest in continuing, as no worthwhile learning takes place. Some of the interested but academically weak students are also forced to dropout, as their continuance is considered likely to have an adverse effect on results in the terminal examinations. Added to this, some of the academically weak students dropout themselves for fear of failure in the terminal examination. Irregular attendance also adds to dropout, as they find it difficult to cope up with syllabus in the balance term-period. In the Indian context, irregular attendance is very common, particularly among students from poor socio-economic backgrounds. Some of the over-aged students, particularly boys from these communities, indulge in non-academic activities and are vulnerable to lose interest in education. They become irregular in classes and find it difficult to cope with studies, resulting in their lowing interest in studies. For them, it is very difficult or almost impossible to get through the examination. Most of such children are the first generation learners who lack home support. Generally, the schools also lack student counselling and guidance. Lack of proper counselling in schools also adds to dropout of such unguided children at home. At times, the teachers discourage students to continue in the system. All these factors culminate in dropout from the system. Though provision for repetition exists, because of over-age, these dropout students do not want to continue their studies any more. The ultimate result is discontinuation.

Over-age also acts as a negative factor for girls from poor socio-economic background. Social customs and early marriages also act as obstruction for girls to continue in secondary schools. In some states like Rajasthan, social customs demand that girls should be married before they attain puberty. Once married, continuing in school is more or less unlikely. Similarly, lack of separate girls' schools also contributes to dropout of girls before reaching higher classes.

Age also adds, though in a different way, to dropout. With increasing age, students start taking independent decisions, including decision to dropout and earn a livelihood. The opportunity cost of education for students belonging to low socio-economic background increases with age. The family, instead of supporting the child, needs the child's support. Therefore, families prefer to withdraw the child from the school once he/she crosses the age of ten years.

Declining School Performance: Dynamics

This area is highly irrigated and most of the population depends on agriculture. The school was established in 1958 by a philanthropist to provide quality education to students in this area. The school was one of the best performing schools in terms of public examination results till 1990. But its performance has continuously gone down due to lack of quality of education and coming up of new private unaided schools in the vicinity. Only economically poor students come to join this school while affluent students prefer to go to city for secondary and higher secondary education. However, those students who fail in public examinations from other schools get readmission in this school easily. As the study reveals, there are a number of factors responsible for continuous poor performance of the school which include: the absence of a regular principal for a long time, lack of subject teachers, poor infrastructure, irregular attendance and lack of motivation among students, student's preoccupation with earning livelihood, lack of innovative teaching, non-implementation of comprehensive and continuous evaluation etc. However, one of the striking features of this school is that most of the teachers of the school reside in nearby city and travel more than 30 kilometres to reach the school. This obviously has an impact on the teaching, especially in finishing the syllabus in time as teachers reach late and leave early from the school. Similarly, the poor socio-economic status of the students hinders to get support in their studies either at home or outside.

Government Inter College, xxx
Uttar Pradesh (2005)

To sum up it can be said that in this chapter we have examined the internal efficiency of the education system in terms of transition, repetition, dropout rates and performance of students based on the results in public examinations at the end of secondary and higher secondary levels. The completion of the school education cycle depends on the transition, repetition, dropout and achievement rates. The transition rates examined indicate that these have improved over the years, more so in the recent years. The important reasons behind this increase are: (a) access related (proximity to secondary schooling facility; integrating upper primary section with secondary section; no detention and promotion system, etc.); (b) quality related (improvement in quality of education at the lower levels); (c) government interventions in terms of incentives to promote access and expansion (tuition free secondary education; scholarships; free hostels for disadvantaged groups and girls; concession in transport charges; free textbooks and school uniforms for disadvantaged); (d) general economic factors (reduction in poverty levels); (e) social factors (rise in awareness among the people); (f) employment related factors (lack of job opportunities with lower levels of education), etc.

The analysis of results of public examinations is one of the indicators to measure school efficiency. Towards this end, in this chapter, we have analysed the public examination results at the national, state, district and school levels. There have been plenty of variations in the performance of students in public examinations at inter and intra-state levels as well as among the social groups and institutional level. Since the pass percentage in the public examinations does not indicate the extent of school effectiveness an attempt has been made to examine the extent of performance levels in the public examinations in terms of divisions. Similarly, an analysis of performance in different subjects and streams has been done. Despite the increase in the pass percentage rate in some of the states, the numbers of students obtaining first division have not increased, especially in a few of the sample states. The extent of performance in public examinations varies among the schools irrespective of location, and management types. The performance of the schools in the public examinations is determined by common internal factors besides specific interventions at institutional level.

Examination System: Failures and Fallacies

Serious challenges face the credibility and efficiency of public examination systems in India. The results of SSC and HSC examinations in some states are really astonishing. For example, in Bihar, though it is difficult to believe still one can understand high pass percentage of regular candidates, a high pass percentage amounting to 95 per cent for private candidates raises serious questions about the genuineness of these examination results. Mass copying and rigging of examination results are rampant in some of the schools in some states of India. Students manage to appear from particular examination centres so that they may pass in the examination; and this happens more in the case of private students. For example, when Anti-Copying Act was imposed and followed strictly in Uttar Pradesh in 1992, the pass percentage at higher secondary level suddenly plummeted to a new low and after its repeal, needless to mention that the pass percentage has gone up.

One can also cite media reports regarding mass copying and the number of centres whose results have been withdrawn and scrapped as an indicator of the problem. There are examination centres where armed guards and elaborate police arrangements are made to prevent copying, yet examinees do copy. In fact, some schools, notably private management schools, encourage malpractices and dubious methods to achieve a higher pass percentage.

Invigilators and examiners consistently receive threats from hoodlums to deter them from doing their duty honestly. In the absence of adequate protection, some of them fall prey to such threats. It is indeed strange to note that even parents support such blatant cheating, forgery and rigging in the name of career and future of their wards. In fact, this rotten network is so influential that many candidates earn their certificates even without coming to the examination centres. This racket is conspicuous in some states of the country. In the event of such things, the legitimacy of the results of the public examination system itself could be questioned.

REFERENCE

Sujatha, K. (2011): What Makes Schools Effective – Case Study of Secondary Schools, Shipra Publication, New Delhi.

UNESCO (2004): Global Education Digest: Comparing Education Statistics Across the World. UNESCO Institute of Statistics, Montreal.

Annexure Tables

Table A1: Transition Rates by Major States at Selected Points of Time

(in %)

State	*Primary to Upper Primary*			*Upper Primary to Secondary*		
	1995-96	*1996-97*	*1997-1998*	*1995-96*	*1996-97*	*1997-1998*
Andhra Pradesh	78.5	78.7	80.7	91.7	90.9	90.0
Kerala	93.0	93.1	93.8	83.0	83.4	83.3
Maharashtra	86.2	87.8	89.6	86.2	86.7	89.4
Uttar Pradesh	86.6	87.2	87.2	73.5	74.7	81.0
Assam	79.1	77.6	83.6	85.7	82.7	83.2
Bihar	75.9	76.4	73.1	79.9	82.3	81.1
Gujarat	66.8	71.0	73.1	81.1	81.7	81.2
Haryana	80.9	77.6	87.6	49.4	68.0	66.8
HP	86.0	96.0	103.3	62.7	68.6	76.0
J & K	98.0	89.2	94.5	91.7	91.6	109.2
Karnataka	92.9	96.9	97.2	95.5	89.4	87.6
MP	85.3	78.2	79.0	74.6	64.3	63.1
Orissa	92.9	94.9	102.5	85.6	83.1	85.0
Punjab	95.8	95.5	94.9	79.3	85.9	81.5
Rajasthan	101.5	99.5	101.6	79.9	82.5	80.8
Tamil Nadu	80.8	64.7	65.0	59.3	57.2	55.4
West Bengal	80.6	81.2	82.8	83.4	77.0	74.3
All India	84.4	82.9	84.2	78.7	77.8	78.4

Source: Education in India, 1995-96, 1996-97 and 1997-98. Department of Education, MHRD, GOI, New Delhi, 2002 & 2003.

Table A2: Percentage of Repeaters at School Education by Major States

State	*Primary (I-V)*	*Upper Primary (VI-VIII)*	*Secondary (IX-X)*
Andhra Pradesh	0.00	0.00	0.00
Kerala	4.95	8.97	5.98
Maharashtra	5.39	3.13	2.75
Uttar Pradesh	1.06	5.63	22.19
Assam	9.35	9.41	10.47
Bihar	1.98	0.79	0.63
Gujarat	12.30	5.83	2.59
Haryana	7.04	8.73	7.96
Himachal Pradesh	10.07	11.63	7.27
Karnataka	0.50	1.44	2.16
Madhya Pradesh	3.24	7.81	8.48
Punjab	4.36	6.20	5.44
Rajasthan	3.31	5.02	8.58
Tamil Nadu	9.97	11.27	13.59
All India	3.7	4.9	7.4

Source: Education in India, 1997-98. Department of Education, MHRD, GOI, New Delhi, 2003.

Table A3: Percentage of Repeaters at Upper Primary and Secondary Level by Grades Across Major States in India

States	*Grade*				
	VI	*VII*	*VIII*	*IX*	*X*
Andhra Pradesh	0.00	0.00	0.00	0.00	0.00
Kerala	6.36	9.78	10.69	10.79	0.01
Maharashtra	3.61	2.07	3.76	4.88	0.00
Uttar Pradesh	5.88	5.98	4.91	9.16	34.56
Assam	9.35	9.00	10.00	11.24	9.54
Bihar	0.80	0.78	0.72	0.62	0.64
Gujarat	7.49	4.85	4.85	4.75	0.00
Haryana	6.83	6.81	12.69	5.38	10.46
Himachal Pradesh	11.34	9.20	14.42	7.04	7.56
Karnataka	1.25	1.36	1.79	1.93	2.42
Madhya Pradesh	7.60	6.70	9.20	5.00	12.10
Punjab	6.45	5.01	7.16	4.34	6.54
Rajasthan	6.05	4.45	4.18	8.91	8.10
Tamil Nadu	14.50	10.40	9.00	11.00	16.50
All India	5.10	4.37	5.17	5.62	9.38

Source: Education in India, 1997-98. Department of Education, MHRD, GOI, New Delhi, 2003.

Table A4: Dropout Rates at School Education by Social Group in 2001-02

States	*Grade I-V*	*Grade I-VIII*	*Grade I-X*	*Scheduled Caste Grade 1-X*	*Scheduled Tribe Grade 1-X*
Andhra Pradesh	43.03	63.09	70.12	77.59	87.78
Kerala	0.00	0.00	16.64	27.20	57.20
Maharashtra	7.37	37.03	52.28	57.98	73.93
Uttar Pradesh	49.40	60.11	58.98	68.96	43.22
Assam	48.64	69.21	75.61	71.50	77.53
Bihar	61.64	74.79	82.87	90.11	90.22
Gujarat	25.05	52.52	70.22	74.72	82.29
Haryana	30.51	12.35	35.94	64.98	0.00
Himachal Pradesh	16.68	21.90	31.80	48.11	54.64
Jammu & Kashmir	29.27	30.14	48.94	71.37	N.A.
Karnataka	23.87	50.99	61.65	68.91	69.96
Madhya Pradesh	29.55	50.11	69.88	72.76	80.25
Orissa	39.38	60.74	73.05	75.80	83.50
Punjab	20.34	36.99	38.62	60.91	0.00
Rajasthan	63.20	53.56	75.36	81.14	81.58
Tamil Nadu	27.24	40.07	57.66	57.17	75.29
West Bengal	39.86	70.87	78.52	84.93	87.07
All India	39.03	54.65	66.04	72.71	81.17

Source: Selected Educational Statistics 2001-02. Department of Education, MHRD, GOI, New Delhi, 2002-03.

Table A5: Pass Percentage at Secondary and Higher Secondary in Public Examinations in India

Year	*Secondary**					*Higher Secondary***				
	Boys	*Girls*	*Total*	*SC*	*ST+*	*Boys*	*Girls*	*Total*	*SC*	*ST*
1991	51.03	56.21	52.58	43.24	36.32	53.35	60.52	57.85	42.27	43.95
1992	36.24	47.69	44.09	25.94	27.35	38.67	53.51	48.35	43.95	31.83
1993	43.27	54.77	47.21	32.86	35.73	40.14	55.25	47.65	31.83	36.90
1994	44.52	52.89	47.95	32.55	28.12	46.27	56.57	51.92	37.51	32.24
1995	46.40	53.96	49.47	38.37	30.13	47.34	58.36	54.09	36.90	33.86
1996	40.63	48.32	45.13	35.85	28.12	47.06	58.66	50.92	37.88	34.12
1997	43.59	52.31	47.50	35.23	29.98	47.19	59.13	51.23	42.36	37.44
1998	39.12	51.44	44.16	32.11	37.65	50.32	66.06	54.97	41.70	35.46
1999	50.64	60.67	54.31	40.84	40.54	54.00	67.50	58.12	47.28	40.39
2000	49.97	53.77	51.42	33.87	39.93	55.92	65.80	59.64	54.82	52.77
2004*	64.75	60.23	60.00	61.27	52.34	69.00	76.00	71.00	58.00	59.00

Source: (i) Results of Secondary, Higher Secondary and Intermediate/PUC Examinations, 1991-2000, MHRD, GOI, New Delhi.
(ii) Study of Examination Results-2004. Council of Board of School Education in India, Delhi.

*For secondary 24 Boards

**For higher secondary 25 Boards

+Includes 12 Boards for SC and ST

SC : Scheduled Castes; ST : Scheduled Tribes.

Table A6: Pass Percentage in Public Examinations at Grade X and Grade XII in Major States in India

State	Secondary						Higher Secondary					
	1991	1995	2000	2004	Avg.	Rank	1991	1995	2000	2004	Avg.	Rank
AP	48	60	55	80	61	7	21	28	44	55.00*	37	18
Kerala	51	NA	76	59	62	6	60	54	68	59	60	8
Maharashtra	48	51	52	60	53	14	50	49	62	62.78*	54	10
UP	61	61	32	72	56	11	81	73	68	91	78	3
Assam	31	39	47	50	44	17	40	40	45	55	45	14
Bihar	66	NA	59	NA	63	5	98	94	93	86	93	2
Gujarat	61	50	62	53	56	11	56	71	34	61	55	9
Haryana	88	32	57	59	58	10	55	21	75	58	52	11
HP	52	45	63	61	55	12	30	31	53	61	43	16
J&K	79	39	20	50	47	16	61	31	29	39	40	17
Karnataka	59	46	82	58	61	8	35	44	49	58	46	13
MP	39	28	35	29	33	18	57	53	79	65	63	6
Orissa	44	55	46	52	49	15	31	37	42	80	47	12
Punjab	69	68	53	66	64	4	64	56	64	69	63	6
Rajasthan	50	58	68	60	59	9	53	45	69	81	62	7
Tamil Nadu	59	NA	57	77	64	4	64	65	83	NA	70	5
West Bengal	50	62	76	71	65	3	39	46	58	34	44	15
CBSE	66	68	80	77	73	2	68	71	83	80	76	4
ICSE	91	96	95	NA	94	1	92	97	95	NA	95	1
All India	55	53	53	60	54	13	58	54	52	71**	55	9

* State Boards of Secondary and Intermediate/Higher Secondary Education.

** Includes 12 Boards for SC and ST.

Table A7: Performance, Per cent of Boys and Girls in Public Examinations

State	*Secondary (Grade-X)*						*Higher Secondary (Grade-XII)*			
	2000			*2004*			*2000*		*2004*	
	Boys	*Girls*	*Total*	*Boys*	*Girls*	*Total*	*Boys*	*Girls*	*Boys*	*Girls*
Andhra Pradesh	55.31	60.26	55	80.6	80.2	80.4	40.21	49.69	NA	NA
Kerala	55.3	54.73	76	62	55.8	59.2	68.09	67.43	62.01	55.79
Maharashtra	48.94	53.57	52	59.5	60.7	60	56.84	69.06	NA	NA
Uttar Pradesh	48.64	36.44	32	70.1	76.8	69.8	60.37	81.88	89.35	94.08
Assam	43.25	32.92	47	53.8	68.2	60.6	46.06	43.9	55.89	55.02
Bihar	61.08	70.46	59	–	–	–	91.87	94.26	85.15	87.88
Gujarat	58.87	67.04	62	49.1	58.6	52.7	30.72	37.71	53.85	71.66
Haryana	83.39	87.71*	57	54	57.7	55.4	69.86	83.11	NA	NA
Himachal Pradesh	61.05	86.91	63	58	64	60.5	49.02	57.59	57.51	64.04
J & K	23.58	17.01	20	50.2	50.6	50.3	26.69	32.76	35.88	42.86
Karnataka	89.06	69.43	82	52.1	64.1	57.6	41.97	58.93	52.11	64.15
Madhya Pradesh	47.42	24.73	35	27.2	32.9	29.2	75.44	85.38	61.32	72.66
Orissa	44.94	43.84	46	54.1	50	52.3	39.09	45.77	NA	NA
Punjab	61.05	58.23	53	62.4	70	65.9	63.08	64.73	61.56	76.77
Rajasthan	54.24	60.68	68	59	62.8	60.1	66.5	76.79	78.04	88.93
Tamil Nadu	48.58	68.51	57	74.3	80.5	77.4	78.3	87.69	NA	NA
West Bengal	71.96	68.13	76	75.3	66.9	71.6	59.16	55.85	33.86	34.23
CBSE	74.62	75.08	80	75.93	77.6	76.6	79.8	87.43	76.15	85.84
ICSE	94.43	95.73	95	N.A	N.A	N.A	93.8	96.55	NA	NA
All India	49.97	53.77	53	N.A	N.A	N.A	50.12	55.49	NA	NA

Source: Results of High School and Higher Secondary Examinations, 2000. Department of Education

*The figures and percentage for Haryana are for 1999.

Note There are some discrepancies in the source document and hence they cannot be fully reliable.
CBSE: Central Board of Secondary Education, New Delhi; ICSE: Council for Indian School Certificate; NOS: National Open School.

Table A8: Stream-wise Grade XI Results in Sample States, 2002-03

States	*Subject/Stream*	*Pass Percentage*
Andhra Pradesh		
	BPC	30.86
	CEC	34.92
	HEC	17.32
	MEC	42.71
	MPC	55.00
	Others	24.31
Kerala		
	Science	70.15
	Humanities	51.19
	Commerce	53.33
	Vocational/Technical	89.59
Maharashtra		
	Science	74.72
	Arts	55.18
	Commerce	78.83
	Vocational	57.78
Uttar Pradesh		
	Science	67.51
	Arts	50.93
	Commerce	82.43
	Vocational	62.98
	Others	45.59

Source: State Board of Secondary and Higher Secondary Education in the four sample states, 2002.

Notes:
1. BPC-Biology, Physics and Chemistry
2. CEC-Commerce, Economic and Civics
3. HEC-History, Economics and Civics
4. MEC-Mathematic, Economics and Commerce
5. MPC-Mathematics, Physics and Chemistry

Table A9: School-wise Public Examination Results at Grade X in Four Sample States

Schools	*1997-98*	*1998-99*	*1999-00*	*2000-01*	*2001-02*	*2002-03*
			Rural			
Andhra Pradesh						
ZP HS, Begumpet (Govt)	33	60.0	50.0	88.0	100	NA
ZPHS Tirumalagiri (Govt)	21.5	40.3	20	31.0	14.0	NA
ZPHS Huzurnagar (Govt)	46.0	65.0	45	83.0	100	NA
CSI HS, Gundlagudem (PA)	8.8	11.43	44	44.11	31.5	NA
Kanakamatha HS (PUA)	NA	NA	100	100	100	NA
APRES, Sarvail (Govt)	100	98.6	100	100	100	NA
Kodada	96.7	100	98.18	100	98.9	NA
Kerala						
Neduveli (Govt)	NA	47.0	67.0	86.0	80.0	82.0
Tholikodu (Govt)	NA	26.0	26.0	33.0	27.0	32.0
St. Mary Pattom (PA)	NA	99.8	95.3	99.8	98.0	95.0
Arumanoor (PA)	NA	66.0	83.0	83.0	73.0	73.0
Kaniyapuram (PA)	NA	NA	NA	45.0	46.0	50.0
Anad (PA)	NA	47.0	47.0	36.0	54.0	53.0
SN Public School (PU)	NA	NA	NA	100	100	100
Maharashtra						
Someshwar (PA)	38.5	28.1	47.3	26.4	31.9	13.6
Sabnish (PA)	55.0	73.8	54.6	57.3	69.1	NA
Shivaji (PUA)	30.8	36.8	53.7	68.4	54.2	78.7
Bhairownath (PA)	91.5	84.6	67.5	68.9	56.1	NA
Walchand (Govt)	37.1	44.6	31.1	16.1	36.1	NA
Uttar Pradesh						
Jakhni (Govt)	12.0	14.0	9.0	22.7	12.1	
Kasturba (PA)	150	99	85	87	99	
Rohania	NA	88	39	38	84	
Kanier (PA)	16.4	14.5	32.5	47.2	13.2	
Tikri (Govt)	68.9	95.65	86.88	71.57	19.32	
Adampur,	86.07	89.34	58.56	27.05	21.7	
Chiraigaon,				50	32	
			Urban			
Andhra Pradesh						
Miriyalaguda (Govt)	40.00	31.00	35.00	70.00	73.00	NA
Govt Girl High School (Govt)	12.00	20.00	40.00	31.00	33	NA
St Alphonsa HS (PA)	86.52	88.51	98.58	97.33	99.41	NA
Sadana HS, Bhongir (PUA)	NA	NA	NA	NA	57.14	NA
JC Suryapet (Govt)	36.36	83.82	87.87	87.5	91.00	NA
Kerala						
Cotton Hill, HSS (Govt)	NA	79.0	89.0	NA	93.0	86.0
Peroorkada (Govt)	NA	47	36	54	53	47
Kattela (Govt)	NA	100	100	100	100	88.5
SVVM, Vazhuthakad (PU)	NA	100	100.	100	100.	100
Beemapally (PU)	NA	60.0	58.0	75.0	36.0	61.0

(Contd.)

Schools	1997-98	1998-99	1999-00	2000-01	2001-02	2002-03
Maharashtra						
Ashok Vidyalya ()	18.6	35.9	15.8	23.7	46.2	43.8
Balveer (Govt.)	43.8	39.2	66.7	55.5	40.4	30.2
Choski (PA)	90.8	98.5	93.1	99.5	96.6	NA
Muktangan (PUA)	100.0	100.0	99.6	99.2	100.0	100.0
Laxman Rao (PA)	55.8	66.5	62.3	74.6	88.8	NA
NMV (PA)	97.2	97.3	84.6	96.8	99.6	96.9
Poona Night school (PA)	40.9	81.3	22.2	38.5	63.0	45.0
Uttar Pradesh						
Radhakishori (Govt)	48	53	44	37	31	
Queens (Govt)	71	71.3	50.3	78.2	56	
BTS (PA)	72.85	78.52	94.66	66.71	82.55	
Nilkanth (PA)	94.67	81.63	95.74	55.5	64.28	
Aryamahila (PA)	72.3	63.4	45.8	48	40	
Sunbeam (PUA)	92.8	91.4	89.1	89.5	94.4	78.66

Source: Field Survey.

4

Private Tuition at Secondary Level: Trends and Troubles

Internal efficiency in terms of performance of students in public examination at secondary level showed a wide degree of variation among the schools as well as a large number of failures. This obviously demonstrates the inadequacies of formal education system. In India, like most of developing countries, there exists a system of 'private tuition'[1] parallel to formal system of education to supplement the academic support in the household and to overcome school inadequacies. In fact, in terms of its nature, extent and importance is comparable to formal system or, in other words, it is like a shadow (Bray: 1999) of the formal system. Though private tutoring is prevalent at all levels of education it is preponderant in secondary education for various reasons i.e. improving performance in public examinations, preparing for entering into higher, technical and professional education etc.

Despite the prevalence of private tuition and its effect on education there is hardly any study in this area especially at secondary level except anecdotal information. In order to have holistic understanding of the context of secondary education it is imperative to examine the nature, extent, intensity, cost and source of private tuition in sample states. The present study makes an attempt to examine the different aspects of private tuition.

The data with regard to private tuition were collected from a sample of 6,948 students from 49 schools) drawn from four districts of four sample states, represent rural-urban location, different management types, good and poor performing types. The study covered four states i.e. Kerala, Maharashtra, Andhra Pradesh and Uttar Pradesh. The sample districts are Thiruvantapuram (Kerala), Pune (Maharashtra), Nalgonda (Andhra Pradesh) and Varanasi (Uttar Pradesh).

49 schools from four districts of four sample states were chosen. The basis of school selection was their level of performance in public examination at secondary level (X-XII) level in the past five years. The first part of this study provides an overview of the nature and forms of private tuition in India. The second part presents an empirical analysis of the extent, intensity, gender and rural-urban variations, cost, sources and reasons for private tuition. The last part of the study presents case study of private tuition centres in two sample states (Uttar Pradesh and Maharashtra)

PRIVATE TUITION IN INDIA: AN OVERVIEW

The system of private tuition has been in existence in India for a fairly long time but in recent times it has grown manifold affecting the very core of educational system. During the last three decades, the private tuition scenario has undergone a sea change in tune with the changing composition and character of education. Earlier the students in terminal grades/classes only thought of receiving tuition but nowadays children start tuitions right from class one. Instead of being perceived as an indicator of dullness it is now perceived not only as a matter of necessity but also as a symbol of pride and social prestige. The necessity of weak students has now become the universal necessity of all students – weak, average and bright, because every student is keen to further improve one's score in the examination.

The market forces have been responsible in transforming private tuition from the social taboo to a widely practised and accepted reality. The spirit of competition has been exacerbated by the mismatch between the number of aspirants and the limited spaces available at the higher levels of academic ladder. Parents incur extra expenditure on private tuition of their wards in the hope that it will bring them higher returns in future (Tansel and Fatma: 2004; Sahfiq: 2002). In some of the cases tuition is not needed but it is still arranged because students and their parents might feel that they are doing their utmost to meet the challenge of examination.

The phenomenal growth of private tuition in India in recent times can be explained by the 'surrogate system'. Like a surrogate mother, private tuition is expected to take care of students by managing their studies and taking additional care so that they perform well in public examinations. Further, the trend of working parents has created a situation where the parents are willing to invest more in private tuition so that they can get over the guilt of not doing enough for their children. Many parents prefer to send their children for private tuition so that they don't waste time at home either idling or watching television.

TYPES OF PRIVATE TUITION

As the activity of private tutoring finds new means and territories, classes and sites, its nature and type too change in accordance with the demand, groups and locations. Private tuition can be divided into four types namely: home tuition arranged by individuals or by tuition bureaus, group tuition or tutorials, coaching centres and private tuition by school teachers for one or a group of students at one's place or at a place convenient to students.

Home Tuition

Home tuition is generally found in urban and bigger cities among the economically better off classes. It is either on one-to-one basis at the home of the student at individual level or sometimes, more than one student gathers at one student's house for tuition to obtain the benefit of comparatively reduced cost. Normally, the subject-teacher, specializing in a particular subject, offers his services on an hour-to-hour basis. In this case, tutors are appointed either through Tuition Bureaus or on the basis of words of mouth.

In urban areas, a mechanism known as 'Tuition Bureau' links the prospective tutor to the taught and acts as a facilitator in an organized form. Tuition Bureaus operate like Employment Agencies for registered prospective tutors; for example, in one of the tuition bureaus in Pune city, in the state of Maharashtra, about 400 tutors were registered seeking students for home tuition. Tuition Bureaus while mediating between tutors and students decide upon the fee structure, course to be covered, service charge, timings and holidays (see Annexure-I).

Tutorial/Group Tuition

This refers to a system where private tuition is provided to a group of students by one tutor either at his/her residence or at a place convenient to all students. (It is also known as tutorials). The group tuition may be limited to the teaching of one subject or a group of subjects depending upon the tutor's ability and students' requirements. Group tuition has become so lucrative that particularly schoolteachers use unfair means to draw students to tuition.

Same School Teachers

Another category of private tuition is tutoring offered by serving teachers either to their own students or other students. This type of tutoring is available both in rural and urban areas.

Coaching Centres

The more organized and commercialized form of private tuition prevails all over the country in the form of coaching centres/ tutorial institutions. These coaching/tutorial centres provide private tuition to a relatively large group of students in a structured institutional environment. They help the students in their preparation for public examination as well as for entrance examination to technical and professional courses. These coaching centres are highly sought after. The number of such coaching institutions has increased rapidly since late 1980s as a result of introduction of entrance test admission into various courses.

Registration

Though there has not been any policy to regulate the system of private tuition at the central level, there are legal provisions and Acts at the state level at least in some states to legalize and rationalize the private tuition system. While the tuition bureaus and coaching centres are normally registered bodies, other forms of tuition are in the unorganized sector.

In the state of Maharashtra, coaching centres are registered under the 'Shop Act' of the State's Revenue Department, while tuition bureaus providing tutors for home tuition are registered under the Charity Commission Act. The bureaus are registered under the head of educational consultancy and welfare activities. A registration fee of ₹ 500 to 1000 is charged from coaching centres and tuition bureaus, depending upon the number of students. The registration has to be renewed in every three years, which generally does not occur due to the laxity of concerned departments and authorities.

In the largest state of India, Uttar Pradesh, all the coaching centres have to be registered according to Uttar Pradesh Coaching Rules and Regulation, 2002. According to this Act, any one can open a coaching centre by applying to the Education Department after paying a small amount of application fee. Similar process exists in many other states also.

Who Manages Coaching Centres and Tuition Bureaus?

The prevalence of coaching centres is an all-India phenomenon though they display large variations among themselves in terms of size, areas of specialization, subject specialization, infrastructure and clientele, their spread and depth vary from place to place. There are many well-organized corporate type-coaching centres on the one hand as well as dingy little rooms with one or two tutors transacting lessons on the other. Former teachers and businessmen operate some of these centres. In early 1990s, these institutions were set up on the pattern of business houses or in the form of companies. Some of the established centres have introduced the franchise system also to regulate and monitor their quality.

Fee Structure

Generally, the private tuition/coaching centres keep secrecy about financial aspects of the centre and seldom share the information. The fee charged by coaching institutions ranges from ₹ 1,000-8,000 per annum in most of the centres. However, information collected about some institutions, through their brochures, reveals that the per student fee for some subjects and long duration tutoring costs around ₹ 10,000. The private tuition fee package also varies across different grades. It is higher for Classes X and XII. Again, for grade XI and XII, fee package varies depending on the academic stream and combination of subjects. The fee package is generally higher for science and mathematics group. Some coaching centres have fee packages for 2/3 years for secondary students (i.e., for Classes VIII to X), and 2 years for higher secondary students (i.e. Classes XI and XII). The yearly charges for such a package in one of the private tuition centres ranges from a minimum of about ₹ 10,000-12,000 to a maximum of about ₹ 30,000-35,000, depending on the grade and the subjects to be covered. Micro level evidence from sample study shows that a student pays on an average ₹ 3,500 in coaching centres as tuition fees for a combination of mathematics, science and English at lower secondary level. At the higher secondary level, the fees go up to approximately ₹ 8,500. However, the average amount paid for group tuition is lower in rural areas while there is no difference between the charges for group tuition and coaching institute in urban areas.

As a rule, no fees concession is available to socially disadvantaged students in these private tuition centres. Some centres, however, offer discounts to those students who pay the annual tuition fee at the time of admission rather than in instalments. A number of centres offer fee concessions to a few meritorious students so that the centre can use their performance for publicity later. Some of these centres offer 10 per cent discount as brother/sister concession; and if a student scores 80 per cent consecutively in the 8 weekly tests, then 75 per cent of fee is waived off.

Admission Packages and Coaching Centres

The criterion for admission into private coaching centres is very simple. Though many centres conduct written tests and interviews, hardly any student is denied admission as the number of coaching centres with specialist tutors is growing at a faster rate than the demand for tuition; and, in fact, there has been a steep competition among coaching centres to attract students. Ability to pay is the ticket to admission. Most of the private tuition centres have long-term as well as short duration of tutoring. In the first category, the duration of the tutoring is of full academic year either for a subject or for the full course. In the second category, they offer crash tutoring, focusing on one or a few topics in definite schedules. Curiously, two-third of students would join at the beginning of the session while only 5 per cent of them opt for private tuition just before public examinations.

In some cities, students register their names in private tuition centres at the beginning of the academic year, parallel to school registration. Popular centres seem to have a batch size of 30-35 students. Some of them have a separate batch of 20 selected students known as 'Select Students Batch'. Short-term tutoring packages are of varied nature, namely, intensive tutoring, crash tutoring, and capsule tutoring with duration ranging from 40-120 days. The cost of tuition depends on the number of subjects and duration. Of course, it depends on various other factors also like credibility, infrastructure provided, etc. There is stiff competition among private tuition centres over acquiring students, which also determines the package.

Who are the Private Tutors in Coaching/Tuition Centres?

Tutors employed by private tuition centres comprise teachers working in government schools, private schools and colleges, university teachers, unemployed educated, retired teachers, educated housewives etc. Despite ban on teachers working in government and aided schools/colleges on private tuition, the practice continues in many states. Private tutors, in coaching centres, are usually appointed on temporary basis for a stipulated period or are paid on a contractual basis. The contractual tutors are engaged and paid on the basis of number of lectures taken. Some of the centres employ full-time tutors for teaching as well as for preparing the study material. A few large and well-established coaching centres seem to keep a core of full-time teachers so as to ensure regularity in teaching and updating of their study material.

Infrastructure

The infrastructure facilities of private tuition centres vary widely from air-conditioned rooms and modern technology to tin and thatched sheds and congested rooms. Majority of private tuition centres' premises are rented but most of them have minimum requirements pertaining to teaching-learning facility, though some of them may lack adequate space and ventilation.

Teaching-Learning Process

The coaching centres normally run for 10 months (i.e. June to March) covering full academic year. The teaching-learning process involves tutor-student contact ranging from 10 to 29 hours per week in most of the private tuition/coaching centres depending upon the number of subjects and grade. Generally, the duration of teaching a subject varies from 50-60 minutes per lecture. The efforts in private tuition centre obviously focus on preparation of students from the point of view of public examinations by covering the school syllabus with individualised attention. Lot of coaching is given to students as a drill and to practise answering questions correctly as well as managing time during examinations. Model test papers with solutions form part of the teaching material. Frequent tests and feedback are part of private tuition. Some of the Centres regularly revise their study material based on feedback of students, and keep them updated. The noticeable aspect of these coaching centres is the regularity, punctuality and accountability both among tutors and students. Generally the continuity of subject teachers depends upon the students' satisfaction and feedback.

Remuneration of Tutors

The remuneration paid to the tutors in these centres is based on the subjects they teach and their contact hours. Their remuneration ranges from ₹ 100 to 250 per contact hour. Some institutions also pay up to ₹ 400 per contact hour. Teachers employed on regular basis, for full-time, are paid ₹ 12,000-15,000 per month. Consequently, teachers, with good reputation often leave their job to join or open their own private tuition/coaching centres. In well-established registered coaching centres like that of 'Chate' in Pune city, tutors are paid in the range of ₹ 3000-20,000 pm, depending upon the experience, subjects, nature of batch, number of classes and, most importantly, students' feedback and their success rate.

Creating Demand for Tuition

The coaching centres adopt different methods to attract students. To draw more students, better publicity is resorted to through advertisements, leaflets, pamphlets, wall posters in front of schools and residential areas, banners, newspapers, cinema halls etc. They also widely publicize the results of the students, their unique infrastructure and facilities, and experienced faculty. Besides the hiring of the PR firms to ensure a "positive publicity" in the media, the coaching centres have launched a number of "schemes" to lure students.

Extent of Private Tuition

Out of the total number of students (see Annexure-II) covered in the study (6948)[2] 41.32 per cent were seeking private tutoring for one or more subjects at secondary level (Grade-IX-XII). The extent of private tuition varies among four sample states ranging from 44.74 per cent in Kerala to 32.26 per cent in Andhra Pradesh[3]. The extent of going for private tuition is higher at the lower secondary level (44.57%) compared to higher secondary (36.8%) level among all the four states. Out of four sample states, Kerala has the highest percentage (55%) of students going for private tuition at lower secondary level (grade IX-X). It is interesting to note that Kerala is not only an educationally developed state but has also the highest human development index in the county. It is followed by Maharashtra (49.35) , which is both industrially and educationally developed. In Andhra Pradesh the percentage of students taking private tuitions is the lowest (32.26%) while Uttar Pradesh (46.67%) is just behind Maharashtra.

Since the results of public examination in grade X determines admission into higher secondary as well as choice of subjects and streams, higher percentage of students in grade X go for private tutoring compared to grade IX. The average percentage of students seeking private tuition in grade X is 58.8 per cent as against 32.0 per cent in grade IX.

Among the four sample states in Kerala a high majority of students seek private tuition (71.58) in grade-X. Interestingly though Uttar Pradesh shows lower level of propensity towards private tuition compared to Kerala and Maharashtra, in grade-X a high majority of students attends private tutoring.

The reasons behind this phenomenon are the social, economic and educational characteristic of the states. In Kerala universalization of elementary education has ensured a higher base and the state also has higher transition rate at all levels especially at secondary level. This means higher competition for higher secondary education where the seats are limited. The social obsession for higher education in Kerala also makes parents put pressure on children to perform better at all levels of education. All this culminates in private tutoring, considering it as a panacea. Consequently, a high percentage of grade X students rush for private tutoring. The educationally and economically backward state of Uttar Pradesh has witnessed dramatic increase in enrolment at lower secondary level in the last four years; and also since this state has a poor and fluctuating performance at public examination, it is only but natural that students go for private tuition at the final year of terminal examination. Of late, this state also is characterized by increased social obsession towards secondary education (Jeffery: 2004).

Table 4.1: State-wise Percentage of Students receiving Tuition in Different Classes

S. No	*State*	*IX*	*X*	*IX -X*	*XI*	*XII*	*XI-XII*	*IX - XII*
1	Andhra Pradesh	11.3	52.7	32.26	–	–	–	–
2	Kerala	43.0	71.58	55.0	31.5	35.98	33.47	43.68
3	Maharashtra	43.21	56.0	49.35	41.0	38.49	40.0	44.74
4	Uttar Pradesh	31.39	62.0	45.67	31.34	38.59	34.87	40.70
	Total	32.0	58.8	44.57	36.0	53.76	36.8	41.32

N = (IX - X) - 4031 , (XI - XII) - 2917

Contrary to other three states, in Andhra Pradesh the demand for private tuition is relatively low. This interesting trend can be explained in terms of both declines in the demand as well as the supply of private tuition. The declining demand has come through the indirect effect of administrative intervention through accountability of teachers and head teachers for better performance of students in public examination at lower secondary level. In this state a large number of coaching centres have turned into private unaided schools in order to meet the increasing demand for quality private schools. Most of these schools have the provision of extra classes during the morning and evening sessions as part of their schedule. Secondly, increase in the number of private aided schools has made the private tuition redundant, as these schools integrate private tutoring as part of school schedule after school hours. Some schools charge for this facility while others have included this in their fees. This is largely due to increasing competition among private schools. At the supply side the transformation of private tutorials and coaching centres into private unaided schools has taken place to meet demand for private schools on the name of quality of education.

Maharashtra, despite being an educationally and economically advanced state shows a relatively low demand for private tuition in comparison to Kerala and Uttar Pradesh. The state also follows some of the welfare policies like those in Andhra Pradesh which might have affected the percentage of private tuition. However, in all the states, there has been a demand for private tuition at lower secondary level.

Private Tuition at Higher Secondary Level

At higher secondary level both Maharashtra and Kerala have similar percentage of students (40%) attending private tuition. The percentage is relatively low in Uttar Pradesh (34%). Apparently, it looks that fewer students opt for private tuition at higher secondary level, which is not true. Since large majority of students at higher secondary level especially in Science, Mathematics and Commerce groups were attending private tutoring for entrance tests for professional and technical education, the syllabus for coaching for these entrance examinations covers mostly the syllabus of higher secondary level. Therefore, these students do not join separately for private tutoring exclusively for public examinations at higher secondary level. In view of higher demand for technical and professional education entry through entrance examination have meant higher dependency on coaching centres, a shift can be found in the nature of private tuition i.e. from public examination to entrance examination.

Private Tuition: The Rural-Urban Differences

The extent of private tutoring varies among localities. It is usually higher in urban areas than in rural areas (Bray: 1999). The present study shows similar patterns with more students from urban areas going for private tuition than their rural counterparts. However, the gap gets narrowed between the two groups at higher secondary level. In all the four Indian states, the percentage of students going for private tuition in urban areas is much higher than that of rural areas as evidenced in other developing countries. The extent of private tuition in rural areas is much lower (29.03%) especially at lower secondary level compared to urban areas (64.0%).

This clearly indicates inequity in terms of supplementary tuition between these two groups. In other words, it implies that there is lot of difference between the rural and urban students in terms of access to and the amount and quality of private tuition. The increased access and participation rates in rural areas not necessarily provide equal opportunities to rural students to succeed and compete in the sphere of education. In other words though the government policies welcome rural and disadvantaged students welcome in to the system but with compromised quality provisions and lack as resources to supplement the learning through private tuition. While the urban and well off people pursue additional learning opportunities through private tutoring. The private tuition, thus perpetuates the locational disparities.

Table 4.2: Private Tuition in Rural/Urban Areas

States	*Lower Secondary*		*Higher Secondary*	
	Rural	*Urban*	*Rural*	*Urban*
Andhra Pradesh	20.67	38.75	0	0
Kerala	66.53	70.6	41.34	28.0
Maharashtra	29.3	72.72	25.0	51.34
Uttar Pradesh	32.0	52.7	23.65	48.21
Total	29.03	64.0	25.0	45.43

Lower Secondary N = Rural = 1492, Urban = 2539.
Higher Secondary N =Rural = 1152, Urban = 1765.

At the higher secondary level (XI-XII) the pattern in the extent of private tuition between rural and urban areas indicates at the inequities like that at lower secondary level and also varies from state to state.

The highest percentile difference can be found in the industrially and educationally advanced state of Maharashtra. Kerala not only has a very high frequency of private tuition but, unlike other states, the difference between rural and urban areas is marginal, both at lower and higher secondary levels. This also suggests that not only there is little difference in Kerala in terms of rural-urban locations, rather it shows a continuum. This state with higher human development index depicts low-level inequality among different localities even in terms of a negative indicator like private tuition.

There are several reasons behind the more prevalence of private tuition in urban areas than in rural areas in most states. Firstly, parents in urban areas are relatively better off economically and are in a position to afford the cost of private tuition. Secondly, there is more competition in urban areas for admission to different streams such as mathematics and science stream, professional examinations and college education of which the parents are aware. There are also tremendous peer-group pressures and a sense of guilt feeling among parents of neglecting their children besides social obsession and prestige. Also many parents are unable to guide their children academically at secondary level and prefer to send them to private tuition. Parents also feel safe leaving them in private tuition centres as they would not waste their time watching television and idling at home. The phenomenon of nuclear family has given the couples the requisite money to spare, coupled with a guilt-feeling of not taking care of their child, has resulted in sending them to the best tuition centre to overcome that feeling. Further, in urban areas there is more supply of private tuition, which creates a demand.

Management of Schools and Private Tuition

There are different types of managements for schools in India in general and secondary schools, in particular. On the basis of administration, finance and overall control, schools are divided into three types namely, government, private aided and private unaided. There is a perceptible difference between schools regarding quality, efficiency and clientele. This variation is also reflected in the percentage of students seeking private tuition at secondary level.

Surprisingly, the highest percentage of students was attending private tuition from private unaided schools compared to government and private aided management types of schools (Table 4.3).

Table 4.3: Student Receiving Tuition in Different Management Type of Schools Percentage of Private Tuition in Schools by Management

States	*Lower Secondary*			*Higher Secondary*		
	Government	*Private Aided*	*Private Unaided*	*Government*	*Private Aided*	*Private Unaided*
Andhra Pradesh	26.7	51	50	–	–	–
Kerala	67.4	61	93.5	26.19	30.16	86.08
Maharashtra	32.6	63.3	74.1	27.47	36.56	80.14
Uttar Pradesh	42.4	37	57	20.5	36.64	86.20
Total	41.47	55.06	65.72	26.19	35.76	84.14

Similar pattern was found both at lower and higher secondary levels and among all the four sample states. The percentage of students going for private tuition was the lowest among government schools. At lower secondary level while 65.72 per cent of students in private unaided schools go for private tuition as against 55.06 per cent in private aided and 41.47 per cent in government schools. The prevalence of private tuition in government schools assuming their poor quality but existence of the same in private unaided schools, despite presumably better infrastructure, good results and adequate monitoring by management and teacher accountability may be understandable.

Among the four sample states, the percentage of students going for private tutoring from private unaided schools ranges 93.5 per cent to 50 per cent in Kerala and Andhra Pradesh respectively. In Kerala private tuition is not only higher than all other sample states. It is interesting to note that disparities in the extent of private tuition are very low in Kerala compared to other states both at the levels of location and gender. Further, more surprisingly, it is common among the students of government, private aided schools though its quantum is much higher in private unaided schools. This scenario evidently indicate that existence of private tuition is not merely the result of poor quality of government schools, rather it has emerged as a shadow of the formal schooling, irrespective of location, gender and management.

The state Maharashtra, which is an industrially and economically well off state, follows almost the same pattern but to a lesser extent. However, private tuition in government schools is much lower compared to private aided and unaided schools. In Andhra Pradesh, as explained earlier, only a little more than one-fourth of students in government schools go for private tuition while the percentage of students going for private tuition in government and private aided schools is also almost the same. On the contrary less percentage of students in Uttar Pradesh go for private tuition in private aided schools. In Uttar Pradesh, higher percentage of students from private unaided schools go for private tuition followed by government schools. However, unlike other states private aided schools in Andhra Pradesh are largely Christian missionary schools, not necessarily serving the low socio-economic groups, which thus, show the tendency of higher private tuition.

At higher secondary level, the percentage of students going for private tuition in government and private aided schools was very low compared to private unaided schools. A little more than one-fourth in government schools and a little over than one-third of students in private aided schools were receiving private tuition. This was the common trend among all the three sample states.

However, the extent of private tutoring among the students of private unaided schools was very high (84.14%). This can be explained in terms of location and stream. Primarily, most of the government schools are located in rural areas where the percentage of students seeking private tuition is less and secondly, some of these schools do not provide Science and Commerce subjects and most of the students are enrolled in Arts stream who usually do not for go private tutoring. On the other hand most of the private unaided schools are located in urban areas and have more students enrolled in Science and Commerce streams where private tuition is highly prevalent. As discussed elsewhere generally the students from low socio-economic group are largely concentrated in arts stream especially in government and government funded private schools, which are located in rural areas.

Box

The school caters to those who would like to have their children brought up in a modern public school based on values emphasizing all round development of personality and character. There is an atmosphere of friendship, understanding, care and support that pervades in the school – community-parents, pupils and teachers. The school follows continuous and comprehensive evaluation, uses innovative pedagogy and conducts co-curricular activities regularly and systematically. The basic facilities, library and laboratory facilities are excellent. Teachers qualified and selected based on merit. They are efficient and accountable. They feel there is no need for private tuition for their students. Yet, private tuition is widely resorted to by students. According to teachers it has become a fashion among the parents to send students to private tuition even if the school provides necessary teaching learning atmosphere. A high majority of students seek regularly private tuition particularly in Mathematics and Science.

XXX Public School, Chenkottukonam,
Thiruvanthapuram, Kerala, (2005)

The reason behind higher percentage of students seeking private tuition from good performing private unaided schools could be for achieving higher percentage in public examinations and to maintain the cutting edge. On the other hand, in case of government schools, it is for passing the public examinations. Contrary, some of the private unaided schools encourage private tuition to ensure the students get good ranks to maintain better reputation and withstand the competition among the private schools. Parents of students of private schools also encourage their wards for private tuition for obtaining better ranking largely due to their own insecurity.

Gender Differences

Combined in all the four samples states, higher percentage of boys are attending private tutoring than the girls. At the lower secondary level 54.86 per cent of boys attend private tuition in comparison to 39.58 per cent of girls. This means there are 15.28 percentile gender differences. However, at the higher secondary level, this gender difference though exists, the margin gets reduced to a mere 2.64 per cent.

When we examine the gender perspective in private tuition, which involves additional expenditure for household, it showed an interesting scenario. Among all the sample states, except Kerala, the percentage of boys was found to be more than that of girls seeking private tuition at lower secondary levels (Table 4.4) as 54.86 per cent of boys attend private tuition in comparison to 39.58 per cent of girls. This means there is 15.28 percentile gender disparity.

The percentile difference between boys and girls varies from 36.69 in socially and economically backward state Uttar Pradesh to 11.67 in Maharashtra. In educationally and socially progressive Kerala, the difference is in favour of girls while in case of educationally and economically developed state of Maharashtra, the percentile difference is very small in comparison to other two sates. In other words, educationally and economically backward states showed higher gender inequity in accessing private tuition. Firstly girls have disadvantage to reach to secondary level of education, even if they could reach at this level they lack equal opportunity to obtain supplementary tutoring. However, in India girls as discussed earlier perform better than boys in public examinations especially in the sample states.

This shows that despite universalization of elementary education and increased participation of girls in secondary education, the girls still get discriminated in terms of educational inputs and investment viz. private tuition, thus, restricting their choices and opportunities. This is more so, in case of the backward states. Further, when we look the relationship between gender and location, it was found that not only students in rural areas have less private tuition than urban

Table 4.4: Gender and Extent of Private Tutoring

States	*Lower Secondary*			*Higher Secondary*		
	Boys	*Girls*	*Percentile. Diff.*	*Boys*	*Girls*	*Percentile. Diff.*
Andhra Pradesh	39.97	16.55	23.42	–	–	–
Kerala	66.56	72.16	5.6	32.34	34.31	1.97
Maharashtra	62.77	51.10	11.67	37.16	43.86	6.7
Uttar Pradesh	58.25	21.56	36.69	44.53	27.52	17.01
Total	54.86	39.58	15.28	38.16	35.52	2.64

Rural N = (Boys = 754 Girls = 655) Total = 1492.
Urban N = (Boys = 1407 Girls = 1163) Total = 2539.

areas but also it is the girls who have less access to private tuition compared to boys (Table 4.4A) in rural areas. However, at the higher secondary level, the situation is much better.

In fact, in both Kerala and Maharashtra, more girls are attending private tuition than boys. In Kerala even girls are more in number in higher secondary level as far as enrolment in concerned as it has been described elsewhere. Only in Uttar Pradesh, boys are in a more advantageous position than girls in attending private tuition at the higher secondary stage.

Table 4.4 A: Private Tuition Gender and Location (in percentage)

States	*Lower Secondary*				*Higher Secondary*					
	Rural		*Urban*		*Rural*			*Urban*		
	Boys	*Girls*	*Boys*	*Girls*	*Boys*	*Girls*	*Total*	*Boys*	*Girls*	*Total*
AP	27.5	10.01	44.14	22.15	–	–	–	–	–	–
Kerala	64.7	68	66.16	75.26	44.29	38.46	41.34	22.09	32.09	28.31
Maharashtra	35	23.4	78.23	66.74	29.97	17.83	24.86	42.55	62.35	51.14
UP	21.3	7.43	84	31.1	17.27	7.08	10.56	55.12	41.78	48.21
Total	34.01	26.87	64.03	49.26	31.04	18.97	24.91	42.81	46.32	44.59

This dimension of gender and private tuition can be explained in terms economic and socio-cultural background of the states. The inherent gender bias in backward states is reflected at the supplementary tutoring even if the girls could reach to secondary levels of education. This shows the discriminatory tendency of parents in the investment of girls' education though they decide to send their girls to school. In addition, parents may make gender-related decisions. In some settings, boys are considered a better investment than girls because boys are more likely to find wage–earning employment (Stevenson and Baker 1992). According to Buchmann, "lingering gender stereotypes regarding job prospects and gender biases in children's expected contribution to housework may mean that parents are less willing to provide additional educational resources to their daughters, especially in cases where family resources are severely limited (i.e. poor families or those with many children)' (Buchmann quoted in Bray: 2005). As a result of this kind of disparities and inequities, the opportunity for girls diminishes with successive stages of educational development. Needless to add, this has affected the presence of women in higher levels of academic and administrative positions. However, if we discover an entirely different pattern in Kerala, the reasons are embedded in its socio-cultural setting. The matrilineal society, higher levels of education in general and among females in particular, coupled with high mobility particularly the higher work participation of women of Kerala in nursing (medical) and teaching profession have certainly helped in favour of investing in girls. The state of Maharashtra both at secondary and higher secondary level does not follow the expected pattern and shows modernizing trends as a result of industrialization and urbanization, not to mention the cultural development of the sample district.

Social Groups

The access and affordability to education also varies among social groups who are endowed with differential socio-economic status. The supplementary teaching which costs more to the households and further investment in education, an attempt is made to examine the differences in the use of private tutoring among different social groups (Table 4.5A).

The general category of population, who are ranked higher in the social grouping[4], sends higher percentage of children to private tuition but the difference between this community and other backward communities (OBC) is not wide.

Table 4.5A: State-wise students receiving Tuition in different Caste Groups

Caste Group	*Andhra Pradesh*	*Kerala*	*Maharashtra*	*Uttar Pradesh*
General	28.09	62.66	48.56	38.47
Most Backward Class (OBC)	0.00	50.00	43.29	31.65
Backward Class (BC)	8.22	40.29	28.21	34.69
Scheduled Caste (SC)	5.76	28.19	30.10	32.28
Scheduled Tribe (ST)	2.41	9.30	50.91	26.32

The difference between the general category of population and backward castes is substantial. When we look at caste versus gender categories, a general trend emerges, showing that there is not much difference in terms of boys and girls availing private tuition in general category but the difference is quite higher in case of OBCs. The Backward castes too show the higher percentage of boys going for private tuition than girls. The trends are slightly different at the state level viz. in Kerala girls have slightly better percentage for availing tuition among all groups though it is marginally lower among ST groups and same is the case with Maharashtra while U.P. has a different result. Not only private tuition is low among OBC but they are also concentrated in government schools. In Uttar Pradesh, the difference in terms of accessing private tuition is quite high between different caste groups especially between general category and OBCs and STs. This shows the impact of social awareness and modernization among social groups but, more importantly, it explains that in terms of obtaining private tuition, there are only variations in degree among various social groups.

Inter-school Variations

As mentioned earlier, the students covered in the study are drawn from 49 schools spreading over four states. These schools are different from one another in terms of availability of infrastructure, socio-economic profile of students, performance in public examination, management types and !ocations. In view of this diversity among the sample schools, the aggregate level trends discussed represent the average which may conceal variations and interrelated aspects at the school level. Therefore, the school level picture is important in identifying and explaining the specific determinants of private tuition and its dynamics. There is significant variation in the percentage of students going for private tuition - ranging from 93 per cent to

Table 4.5: State-wise Students Receiving Tuition from Different Social Groups (to be replaced) (total–need to be added)

Caste	*A.P.*		*Kerala*		*Maharashtra*		*U.P.*		*Total*		
	Boys	*Girls*	*Boys*	*Girls*	*Boys*	*Girls*	*Boys*	*Girls*	*Boys*	*Girls*	*Total*
General	32.99	2.63	63.92	61.46	44.31	53.34	54.27	28.34	47.48	44.15	45.83
OBC	0.00	0.00	46.15	55.56	41.27	46.04	73.68	7.92	46.94	32.34	39.96
BC	12.82	0.00	38.74	41.74	24.87	33.61	35.98	33.81	28.39	31.01	29.65
SC	7.74	2.27	28.36	28.10	22.81	39.13	33.64	30.49	20.73	23.44	21.99
ST	2.70	0.00	40.00	2.82	50.00	51.61	31.25	0.00	19.38	15.79	17.70
Total	16.10	1.03	46.03	41.74	40.45	49.87	47.12	28.29	38.11	36.52	37.33

OBC: Other Backward Communities; BC: Backward Communities; SC : Scheduled Castes ; ST: Scheduled Tribes

0 per cent at lower secondary level (see Appendix-I). Inter-school variation among the schools is also found in all the four states. In three schools, out of total sample schools, no student was attending private tuition. These schools situated in Andhra Pradesh and Kerala, were fully residential schools run by the government for disadvantaged groups. In all these schools the performance of students in public examinations was also very high. As mentioned earlier there is an inherent mechanism of quality teaching through structured curriculum, evaluation, remedial coaching and individual attention in these schools.

There are large inter-school variations, which can be established from the fact that in six schools out of 49, more than 80 per cent students seek private tuition (see Table 4.6). However, these schools were located in Kerala and Maharashtra in equal number. Kerala and Maharashtra, educationally developed states, are showing higher inclination towards private tuition even among, as only in these states more than 80 per cent of students are seeking private tuition in sample schools at lower secondary level. These six schools cut across locations and management types.

Table 4.6: Inter-School Variations in Accessing Private Tuition

Frequency of Private Tuition	*AP*	*Kerala*	*Maharashtra*	*Uttar Pradesh*
0%	2	1	0	0
< 20%	9	1	3	4
< 40%	0	1	5	3
< 60%	1	3	1	4
<80		4	1	2
80%>		2	2	0

In case of Andhra Pradesh, in 12 schools the percentage of students going for private tuition ranges from 55 per cent to 0 per cent. In Kerala the range of students seeking tutoring varies from the highest of 93.5 per cent to 34 per cent as the lowest. In educationally and economically developed state of Maharashtra too shows a high degree of variation with 93.1 per cent as the highest and 3 per cent as the lowest. In case of Uttar Pradesh, it ranges from 75.7 per cent to 2 per cent. Inter-school variations are not only found in terms of extent of private-tuition but more importantly in the intensity and nature of private tuition ranges widely.

Intensity of Private Tuition

Among students availing of private tuition, most often get tutoring in one or more subjects. The intensity of private tuition varies among four states as there is a variation in the number of students seeking private tuition in number of subjects (Table 4.7)

At lower secondary level while more than one-third of (39.04%) students go for private tuition in three subjects, at the same level more than one-fourth of students get tutoring in all subjects. However, 20.67 per cent of students go for two subjects and only 13.30 per cent of students opt for private tutoring in one subject. The intensity of private tutoring varies among the sample states both lower and higher secondary levels.

The state of Kerala, with highest frequency of private tutoring, also shows a very high intensity. A majority of students who go for private tuition in this state receive private tuition in all subjects. Similarly, in Maharashtra, a high percentage of students (55.30%) go for private tuition in three subjects. However, even in educationally and economically backward state of Uttar Pradesh, majority of students go for private tuition in more than three subjects. In fact, the percentage of students seeking private tuition is higher in Uttar Pradesh than Maharashtra if we combine the percentage of students seeking private tuition in three or more subjects (70.14%).

At higher secondary level, majority of students (49.46%) go for private tuition in two subjects while one-third of students get tutored in one subject. Only a small percentage of students seek private tuition in all the subjects while 12.36 per cent of students receive Private tuition in three subjects. The reason could be attributed to difference in combination of subject and streams.

In all the three states most students go to private tuition in two subjects. However, only in Kerala one-fifth of students at higher secondary level go for private tuition in all subjects. Interestingly in Uttar Pradesh higher percentage of students attend private tuition in three subjects compared to other two states.

Subject-wise Private Tuition

At the lower secondary level, the subjects covered in the school curriculum in India are three languages (Mother Tongue, English, Hindi – choice of languages including foreign languages),

Table 4.7: Intensity of Private Tuition

States	*Lower Secondary*				*Higher Secondary*			
	1 Subject	*2 Subjects*	*3 Subjects*	*All Subjects*	*1 Subject*	*2 Subjects*	*3 Subjects*	*All Subjects*
AP	58.12	36.75	3.42	1.71	–	–	–	–
Kerala	7.02	12.92	12.36	67.60	18.78	47.42	13.15	20.66
Maharashtra	11.98	21.81	55.30	10.90	37.96	55.92	6.12	0
UP	7.85	21.01	46.84	24.30	35.06	40.58	21.75	2.6
Total	13.30	20.67	39.04	26.99	33.04	49.46	12.36	5.14

Mathematics, General Science, and Social Studies etc., which are examined and evaluated. Other subjects include classical language (Sanskrit) and foreign languages, opted by very few students. The largest percentage of students goes for private tutoring in mathematics, closely followed by science and English. This phenomenon is common in different management type schools as well as locations with some variations (see Table 4.8). High prevalence of private tutoring in mathematics is not unique to India but is also found in many other countries (Bray: 1999). Out of the total number of students who are privately tutored, 90.4 per cent of them go for tutoring in mathematics. This varies among three management types of school. Government (90.7%) and government-funded schools have lesser percentage (87.8%) of private tutoring in mathematics compared to private unaided schools (95.3%). This trend is found in all the states, except Andhra Pradesh in case of private aided schools. However, there are differences among sample states as it ranges 98.8 per cent in Kerala to 73 per cent in Uttar Pradesh among different management schools.

In Kerala and Maharashtra out of total students going for private tuition 98.8 and 95.8 per cent of students respectively seek private tuition in mathematics at lower secondary level. In case of Uttar Pradesh and Andhra Pradesh the percentage of students privately tutored in mathematics is 88.4 and 72.9 per cent respectively. In all the four states, more than 90 per cent students attend private tuition in mathematics. However, the percentage of students going to private tuition in mathematics in government and government-funded schools is less in Uttar Pradesh and Andhra Pradesh compared to Maharashtra and Kerala. In other words, while in educationally developed states of Kerala and Maharashtra, we did not find much variation in the extent of seeking private tuition in mathematics by schools belonging to different managements, in case of other two states it is less in government and government aided schools. The low percentage of students going for private tuition in mathematics in Uttar Pradesh can be directly attributed to the availability of mathematics as an optional subject rather than being a compulsory one.

Next to mathematics the demand for private tuition (PT) is more in science subject. Those who go for PT 84.8 per cent of them get private tutoring in science subject. Unlike in mathematics, a large percentage of students (86%) from government and private aided (83.3%) schools go for PT in science compared to students from private unaided schools (79.63%). At the state level, it varies from

Table 4.8: State-wise students going for Tuition in different Subjects according to Management At Lower Secondary Level

States	*Management*	*Math*	*Science*	*English*	*Other sub.*	*M&E*	*M&S*	*M&O*	*S&E*	*S&O*	*M&E&S*	*M&E&S&O*
A.P	Government	83.8	87.0	89.0	44.8	68.8	71.4	31.8	80.5	33.8	69.5	39.0
	Aided	94.3	86.8	86.8	69.8	86.8	88.7	52.8	83.0	58.5	88.7	67.9
	Un-aided	92.9	88.2	83.5	64.7	84.7	85.9	61.2	82.4	57.6	83.5	60.0
	Total	**88.4**	**87.3**	**87.0**	**55.1**	**76.7**	**78.8**	**44.2**	**81.5**	**45.2**	**77.1**	**50.3**
Kerala	Government	99.5	89.2	88.2	76.9	88.2	88.7	76.9	82.3	76.3	82.3	72.6
	Aided	98.1	83.0	94.3	81.1	92.5	82.1	80.2	83.0	78.3	82.1	77.4
	Un-aided	96.6	65.5	55.2	34.5	55.2	65.5	31.0	48.3	27.6	48.3	24.1
	Total	**98.8**	**85.0**	**87.2**	**74.5**	**86.6**	**84.4**	**73.8**	**79.4**	**72.6**	**79.1**	**69.8**
Maharashtra	Government	95.7	74.3	38.6	14.3	38.6	70.0	12.9	37.1	12.9	37.1	9.8
	Aided	94.5	83.2	77.9	12.0	74.2	81.5	10.6	70.3	10.6	69.6	16.4
	Un-aided	100.0	77.4	78.1	22.6	78.1	77.4	22.6	60.3	21.9	60.3	7.1
	Total	**95.8**	**80.9**	**73.7**	**14.6**	**71.5**	**79.3**	**13.5**	**64.5**	**13.4**	**64.0**	**11.0**
U.P	Government	78.3	92.6	82.0	39.2	69.3	73.5	24.9	77.8	37.0	73.5	25.0
	Aided	70.0	87.2	84.4	45.6	61.7	65.6	26.7	80.8	43.3	65.6	28.1
	Un-aided	100.0	81.5	51.9	18.5	51.9	81.5	18.5	51.9	21.1	81.5	21.1
	Total	**72.9**	**89.4**	**81.1**	**40.7**	**64.6**	**70.5**	**25.3**	**77.4**	**39.0**	**70.5**	**26.2**
Total	Government	90.7	86.7	82.5	35.4	66.2	75.9	36.6	69.4	40.0	65.6	36.6
	Aided	87.8	83.3	84.9	49.1	78.8	79.5	42.6	79.3	47.7	76.5	47.5
	Un-aided	95.3	79.6	60.7	37.9	67.5	77.6	33.3	60.7	32.1	68.4	28.1
	Total	**90.4**	**84.8**	**80.4**	**39.7**	**74.9**	**78.3**	**39.2**	**75.7**	**42.6**	**72.7**	**39.3**

89.4 per cent to 81 per cent in Uttar Pradesh and Maharashtra respectively. Except Andhra Pradesh in all the three states less percentage of students from private unaided schools go for PT in science compared to government and government aided schools.

English language is one of the subjects where a large percentage of students' do not secure pass marks after mathematics. Consequently, higher percentage of students secures private tuition in this subject at secondary school students. 80.4 per cent of those, who attend PT, seek tutoring in English language. It varies among the sample states with 87 per cent in Kerala and Andhra Pradesh to 73.7 per cent in Maharashtra. Similarly there is large variation among different management type schools ranging from 94.3 per cent to 51 per cent in private aided and private unaided schools in sample states. In all the states, except in Maharashtra, the percentage of students going for PT in English language is much lesser in private unaided schools compared to government and private aided. This is mainly due to the fact that private unaided schools are largely English medium. However, it may not be true in case of students from rural areas as found in Andhra Pradesh. In rural areas, in most cases, there is no subject teacher especially English is affecting the performance of students. This is more so, in case of rural government and private aided schools.

When we examined the PT in different subjects in rural and urban areas (Table 4.9), it was found that 94.8 per cent of students go for mathematics tutoring in rural areas as against 88.8 per cent in urban areas. In case of Kerala there is not much difference between rural and urban areas in case of mathematics though more percentage of students goes for Science and English than in urban areas.

In Uttar Pradesh and Kerala higher percentage of students seeks private tuition in English in rural areas where the opposite is true for Maharashtra and Andhra Pradesh (see Table 4.7). Higher percentage of students getting private tuition in English in rural India can be explained in terms lack of subject teachers in rural areas to teach English, which has been true in many sample schools. One of the weak areas in teaching at secondary level is poor teaching of the subject and most of the government and government aided schools are located in rural areas do not help it either. Consequently the failure rate in English is higher rendering PT in this subject a necessity for a large number of students. Lack of home support in English for rural students, coupled with poor standard at lower level of school education, creates the need for private tutoring to secure pass marks in public examinations.

Table 4.9: Extent of Private Tuition in different Subjects By Location At Lower Secondary Level

States	Location	Math	Science	English	Other sub.	M&E	M&S	M&O	S&E	S&O	M&E&S	M&E&S&O
Andhra Pradesh	Rural	94.8	85.9	84.8	52.4	82.2	84.8	46.1	80.6	48.2	81.2	50.3
	Urban	76.2	90.1	91.1	60.4	66.3	67.3	40.6	83.2	39.6	69.3	50.5
	Total	**88.4**	**87.3**	**87.0**	**55.1**	**76.7**	**78.8**	**44.2**	**81.5**	**45.2**	**77.1**	**50.3**
Kerala	Rural	98.7	87.2	95.3	84.6	94.0	86.6	83.9	86.6	82.6	85.9	81.9
	Urban	98.8	83.1	80.2	65.7	80.2	82.6	65.1	73.3	64.0	73.3	59.3
	Total	**98.8**	**85.0**	**87.2**	**74.5**	**86.6**	**84.4**	**73.8**	**79.4**	**72.6**	**79.1**	**69.8**
Maharashtra	Rural	92.8	43.2	53.2	2.9	51.1	40.3	0.7	25.2	6.0	25.2	5.0
	Urban	97.0	91.1	79.4	18.0	77.2	90.1	17.3	75.2	17.3	75.0	14.1
	Total	**95.8**	**80.7**	**73.7**	**14.8**	**71.5**	**79.3**	**13.7**	**64.4**	**13.5**	**64.2**	**11.0**
Uttar Pradesh	Rural	87.5	83.3	91.7	6.3	81.3	79.2	4.2	75.0	6.3	72.9	2.1
	Urban	74.4	90.2	79.6	45.4	62.4	69.3	28.2	77.0	41.1	75.9	26.3
	Total	**72.9**	**89.4**	**81.1**	**40.7**	**64.6**	**70.5**	25.3	**77.4**	**39.0**	**70.5**	**26.2**
Total	Rural	94.8	72.7	78.8	46.3	**77.2**	72.7	**33.7**	**66.9**	**35.8**	**66.3**	**34.8**
	Urban	88.8	89.2	81.1	37.3	**71.5**	**77.3**	**37.8**	**77.2**	**40.5**	**73.4**	**37.6**
	Total	**90.4**	**84.8**	**80.4**	**39.7**	**74.9**	**78.3**	**39.2**	**75.7**	**42.6**	**72.7**	**39.3**

The study shows that students going for private tuition usually get tutored in more than one subject at lower secondary level. The combination of the subjects, which students pursue in private tuition, varies (see Table 4.10).

Table 4.10: Frequency of Private Tuition in Different Subject Combinations

States	*First Preferred*	*Second*	*Third*
Andhra Pradesh	Science and English (81.5)	Mathematics and Science (78.8)	Mathematics, Science (77.1)
Kerala	Maths and Eng. (86.6)	Math and Science (84.4)	Math, Science and Eng (79.1)
Maharashtra	Math and Science (79.3)	Maths and Eng. (71.5)	Math, Science and Eng (64.2)
Uttar Pradesh	Science and English (77.4)	Math, Science and Eng (70.5)	Math and Science (70.5)
Total	Maths and Science (78.3%)	Science and English (75.7)	Maths and English (74.9)

Figure in parenthesis indicates percentages.

Note: Subject combination is based on preferences.

In Andhra Pradesh, the highest percentage of students had chosen the combination of Science and English, closely followed by Math, Science and English. In short, it can be said that in all the sample states, most of the students go for private tuition in these subject combination, which slightly varies from state to state. There is difference in other subjects but common among them are Mathematics and Science. In Kerala, Andhra Pradesh and Maharashtra, the preference for tuition is Mathematics, followed by Science, while in case of Uttar Pradesh; it is Science, followed by English. In Uttar Pradesh, Mathematics is not compulsory for girls, thus reducing their dependence on private tuition in this subject.

Higher Secondary

At higher secondary level the highest percentage of students go for private tuition in science stream followed by commerce and arts and this trend is common in all the four sample states (Table 4.11).

Table 4.11: Students of Classes (XI & XII) Receiving Private Tuition in Different Academic Streams

Academic Group	*Kerala*	*Maharashtra*	*U.P.*	*Total*
Science + Maths	45.38	55.71	52.11	52.31
Arts	23.36	19.39	15.03	17.48
Commerce	20.08	17.77	47.37	19.82
Any Other	0.00	1.59	10.00	4.30
Total	33.61	40.03	34.87	36.85

However, among the four states the highest percentage of students goes for private tuition in Maharashtra and the lowest in Kerala. In this context it is important to note that in a students at higher secondary level in the state join for coaching for entrance examinations professional courses rather private tuition per se. A large percentage of students in commerce stream attend for private tuition in Uttar Pradesh unlike in other two sample states. While in arts stream, the lowest percent of students seek private tuition however, in Kerala one fifth of students in arts stream go for private tuition.

Similarly, a higher percentage of students seek private tuition in science in urban areas than their rural counter parts (Table 4.12). However, the extent of PT in particular subject varies from state to state, for example, Maharashtra has the highest percentage of students seeking PT in science, followed by Uttar Pradesh and Kerala in urban areas.

At the same level, management-wise distribution of private tuition shows (see Table 4.13) that higher percentage of students in private unaided schools goes for private tutoring in science and mathematics while in arts and commerce streams higher percentage students from government and private aided school seeks private tuition.

However, the trend is different in case of Uttar Pradesh where higher percentage of students from private aided schools goes for private tuition in science and mathematics. As discussed earlier, generally private unaided schools have science and mathematics while in Uttar Pradesh it is usually the private aided schools that offer Science and Commerce streams. On the other hand, government schools usually have Arts and Commerce streams.

Time Spent on Private Tuition

Duration of private tuition is not only limited to the amount of time

Table 4.12: Stream-wise Students of class (XI & XII) Receiving Tuition

Stream	Kerala		Maharashtra		Uttar Pradesh		Total		
	Rural	Urban	Rural	Urban	Rural	Urban	Rural	Urban	Total
Science& Maths	40.24	49.75	26.77	70.98	12.90	66.00	31.59	64.36	52.35
Arts	1.85	0.00	28.87	5.88	0.00	26.61	9.09	18.29	13.83
Commerce	0.00	3.83	9.47	29.66	0.00	35.14	8.31	47.37	15.60
Others	0.00	0.00	1.59	0.00	10.00	0.00	4.30	0.00	4.30
Total	28.64	41.34	24.86	51.14	5.90	50.77	23.61	45.57	36.88

Table 4.13: State and Stream-wise Students of Classes (XI & XII) receiving tuition in different Management type of Schools

Streams	Kerala			Maharashtra			Uttar Pradesh			Total
	Govt	Aided	Un-aided	Local Body	Aided	Un-aided	Govt.	Aided	Un-aided	
Science	42.78	43.62	70.59	0	50.31	80.14	59.25	90.14	18.84	52.41
Arts	23.36	0	0	20.29	14.81	0	10.74	16.75	21.74	17.48
Commerce	37.5	0	0	50	11.93	0	0	0	47.37	19.82
Others	0	0	0	0	1.59	0	10	0	0	4.3
TOTAL	36.14	36.31	20.87	27.47	36.56	80.14	39.64	36.64	22.17	36.88

Table 4.14: Timings for Private Tuition in Rural Urban Areas

State	Rural				Urban				Total		
	Beginning	Middle	Before Exam	Total	Beginning	Middle	Before Exam	Total	Beginning	Middle	Before Exam
Lower Secondary											
Andhra Pradesh	84.1	12.1	5.4	36.6	81.6	13	5.4	63.4	83	12.7	4.8
Karla	83.9	14.8	2.3	46.4	79.7	18	2.3	53.6	82	16.5	1.9
Maharashtra	77	19.4	2.2	21.6	87.5	10.3	2.2	78.4	85	12.3	2.5
Uttar Pradesh	37.5	43.8	9.2	12.1	64.1	26.7	9.2	87.9	61	28.8	10.4
Total	76.7	18.7	4.7	26.8	79	17	4.7	73.2	78	17	4.7
Higher Secondary											
Kerala	75.2	23.9	0.9	49	85.2	14.8	0	51	80.3	19.2	0.4
Maharashtra	57.4	35.3	7.4	26.3	78.8	19.9	1.3	73.7	73.2	23.9	2.9
Uttar Pradesh	21.1	42.1	36.8	6	62.1	30.2	7.7	94	59.6	30.9	9.5
Total	62.5	30.9	6.6	25.3	73.6	22.9	3.5	74.7	71	25	4.3

spent in tuition centres rather it reflects the extent of investment of households and perceived need and importance attached to intensity of private tuition. Students can either opt for an annual session that teaches them for a full year or take short-term tuitions at particular intervals. The sessions for private tuition have early sessions (during the beginning of academic session), middle and end sessions (before the examinations).

The amount of time spent on private tuition and the duration varies among the four states. About 75 per cent of students join PT from the beginning of the academic session. 21 per cent of students join in the middle of the academic session while a small percentage of students join before the examinations.

Though the states vary in terms of percentage of students joining at different times of session, the degree of difference is quite small. However, both Maharashtra and Kerala show a higher similarity as most students pursue private tuition from the beginning of the academic session. In Uttar Pradesh and Andhra Pradesh, a little less than one-third attends private tuition from the middle of academic year. In Uttar Pradesh nearly 10 per cent of students rush to private tuition just before annual examinations.

A large percentage of students go for private tuition in the beginning in urban areas than in rural areas. There is a glaring rural-urban difference in terms of duration of private tuition in Uttar Pradesh. Though rural students seek private tuition, the intensity is less, which is thus accentuating the inequities. In other words, even if private tuition exists in rural urban and its intensity and quality vary in favour of urban localities.

Source of Private Tuition

Majority of students go to private coaching centres which organises tutoring for public examination as well as coaching for professional entrance examinations. This is more so in case of higher secondary level. Interestingly 19.8 per cent of students get privately tutored by the same teacher who teaches in the school, which, despite being banned in many states, continues to flourish. This source of PT is higher in urban areas (21.31) than in rural areas (see Table 4.15). This clearly indicates the vested interest of teachers in increasing the supply and creating the demand for private tutoring.

Table 4.15: Source of Private Tuition

State	*Group Tuition*	*Coaching Centre*	*Same School Teacher*	*Home Tuition*
		Lower Secondary		
A.P	20.5	16.2	58.1	5.1
Kerala	55.5	27.7	13.1	3.7
MH	16	66.3	14.5	3.3
U.P	21.7	54	22.5	1.8
Total	26.5	50.6	19.8	3.1
		Higher Secondary		
A.P	0	0	0	0
Kerala	52.2	20.9	24.7	2.2
MH	4.2	84	8.7	3.1
U.P	7.1	70	20.8	2
Total	16.3	65.8	15.8	2

Further analysis of tuition pattern shows that in Andhra Pradesh, a high percentage of students (58.12) goes to the same teacher, followed by visiting the coaching centres (24.79), group tuition serve 11.97 per cent of students and the rest 5.13 per cent of students go to any another place for private tuition which includes home tuition. The pattern is different in Kerala with 55.63 per cent of students going for group tutoring by tutorial, followed by in coaching centre (24.54), and 19.83 per cent receive private tuition from the same teacher. In case of Maharashtra, a large percentage of students (74.62) seek private tuition in coaching centres, followed by almost equal per cent of students going for tutorial and the same teacher. As far as U.P. is concerned, 61.32 per cent of students going private tuition prefer coaching centres; Maharashtra, 22.5 per cent go to the same teacher, 16.03 per cent receive tuition in tutorials and less than a per cent (0.84) of students get tuition at home. In total, among all the four states, 57.21 per cent of students go for coaching, followed by 23.40 per cent to tutorials, 18.89 per cent to same teacher and only a meagre half a per cent go to any other places.

Same teacher providing PT is an important issue that needs to be taken rather seriously. In fact, this has significant implication for classroom teaching. Qualitative data from micro level clearly indicates that teachers involved in PT do not take classroom teaching seriously and at times coerce the students to seek private tuition either from them in certain coaching centre. Teachers may stress that the system is not compulsory; but parents know that if they do not pay, their children will be handicapped not only by failing to secure a curricular knowledge but also probably by incurring the disapproval of the teachers. (Bray: 2005). In fact, for many teachers private tuition is an income generating activity (Biswal: 1999).

Amount Spent on Tuition

As discussed earlier, the scale of private tuition has an implication on the household investment. It also depends on intensity, nature of private tuition as well as location. Students receiving tuition from different sources spend different amounts. On an average, a student pays ₹ 260 per month in tutorials, ₹ 350 in coaching centres and ₹ 273 to their own school teachers (see Table 4.16). There is a wide variation in these amount rural-urban areas. A rural student, on an average pays ₹ 153 per month in the tutorial whereas his counterpart in the urban area pays ₹ 330. Similarly, in the rural area per student amount paid in coaching centre is ₹ 135 while it is ₹ 411 in the urban area. Similarly, the same schoolteacher charges ₹ 148 from a rural student, the urban student pays ₹ 340 per month. Thus, the households in the urban areas, on an average, pay more (double the amount) than the rural households. This differential expenditure in rural-urban areas implies the differential quantity and quality of private tutoring too.

Table 4.16: Average Amount Spent on Tuition at Different Types of Centres

Tuition Place	**Average amount spent (in Rupees)*		
	Rural	*Urban*	*Total*
Tutorials	153	330	262
Coaching centres	135	411	350
Same school teacher	149	340	312
Any other place	50	292	273
Total	143	379	321

Reasons for Availing Tuition

The reasons mentioned for getting private tuitions varied and also more than one (see Table 4.17). Based on the perspective of students seeking private tuitions, the reasons could be classified into three categories namely, academic, personal and social. Academic reasons include inability to understand classroom instructions, unavailability of subject teachers, non-completion of course, poor teaching etc. Personal reasons constitute interest to lean more, desire to score higher percentage of marks, not-doing well in the class etc. and social reasons comprise parental expectation, peer group pressure etc.

Table 4.17: Students' Reasons for Availing Tuition

Reason	*A.P.*	*Kerala*	*Maha-rashtra*	*U.P.*	*Total*
Do not understand teaching at school	29.91	10.42	12.39	15.59	13.61
Teachers do not teach well in school	51.28	8.24	8.29	14.33	11.87
Need more understanding	70.09	35.97	47.61	57.02	48.54
Getting poor marks	53.85	23.19	18.03	19.38	21.20
To get more marks in examination	64.10	60.84	54.27	45.93	53.93
To learn more	67.52	29.41	36.58	51.54	40.44
Parent's Decision	42.74	5.55	13.93	9.83	12.18
Because friends also go for tuition	35.90	10.25	5.38	4.35	7.59
Other reasons	24.79	2.02	7.18	3.93	5.90

Academic

The prime objective of tuition being to prepare for examination, emphasis is given on completion of the syllabus in a planned manner, revision of each unit and preparing students for public examinations through critical question-answer exercises. The most important cause of receiving private tuition is, therefore, preparation for public examinations. Crowded classrooms too push children to go for private tuition to seek more individual attention especially in government schools. Other reasons include discontent with the public system i.e. mainstream schooling, competitive educational culture and giving children access to more intensive and advance teaching etc.

Personal

The reason students seek private tuition can also be explained in terms of personal reasons. Desire to learn more, improve one's own classroom performance, personal goals to enter into professional education, interest in particular subjeci, fear for particular subject, and aspiration to perform better in public examinations etc. are some of the personal reasons behind going for private tuition.

Social

From parent's perspective, tuition has become a matter of security and social identity, especially in the high-class society. Because of inadequate parent's support, tuition makes parents feel more secure about their children's academic success. They feel to keep children occupied in academic activities with an apprehension that they would not be diverted towards other non-academic activities. Tuition also enhances parent's self-respect and social identity through the process of social comparison.

> As one parent from Pune overwhelmingly says, "I am very happy that my goal of admitting my son in a good coaching centre is fulfilled. In my colony, he is the only student to get a chance in that good coaching centre. Now I feel very relaxed".

In an environment where parent's identity is determined by their children's achievement, parents sometimes feel under pressure from other parents whose children take tuition from reputed coaching centres. This sometimes leaves parents, having little choice, to send their children to these coaching centres, expecting more benefits.

The responses depict that students receive private tuition to get more marks in the examination (54%), they need more understanding (49%) and wish to learn more (40%). Only 12 per cent stated that teachers do not teach well in the school while 14 per cent do not understand teaching in school. Another 12 per cent go because of their parent's decision. Students think that private tuition in the coaching institutions is very good and very helpful to shape up one's future in a proper way; it is useful because students are prepared and taught according to the new examination pattern; and they know the trends and what could be asked in the examination. These institutions have the right method of preparing the students for particular examinations and, therefore, they suitably put in their efforts needed for a particular subject. They help the students by providing a suitable way of study, to optimize the learning of different subjects.

This shows that most of the reasons for going to tuition are directed towards students' preparation for examinations in which they want to score more marks.

Reasons for Not Availing Tuition

On the other hand, we have seen that from our sample data, around sixty per cent students do not receive private tuition. But this does not depict the true story because there are many students studying in residential schools who do not go for private tuition, for example, in

A.P., Maharashtra and Kerala. If we exclude these students, then there are around 40 per cent who do not go for private tuition. It is also important to know as to why these students do not go for it. The students were asked to give three important reasons as to why they do not go for private tuition, such as: because they understand teaching in school; parent's help at home in studies and because of lack of money. Many students have given more than one reason also.

Table 4.18: Students' Reasons for Not Availing Tuition

Reasons	*A.P.*	*Kerala*	*Maharashtra*	*U.P.*	*Total*
Understand the teaching in school	22	57	46.4	57.8	46.7
Parents help at home in studies	3.2	6.4	5.47	12.8	7.28
Lack of money	18	28	19	18.1	20
Understand teaching in school & parents help at home	57	3.5	19.4	6.34	20.4
Understand teaching in school & lack of money	0	3.5	3.25	2.85	2.53
Parent's help at home and lack of money	0	0.3	0.21	0.48	0.25
Understand Teaching in school, parents help at home & lack of money	0	2	5.67	1.67	2.71
No response	0	0	0.48	0	0.16

Going through the responses of the students, it was found that 47 per cent do not go for tuition because they understand teaching in school and they do not require any type of supplementary tutoring and one can develop one's own potential by different methods. On the other hand, for 20 per cent students, who do not take tuition, the cost of tuition remains a crucial factor. Students are of the opinion that private tuition is of help to the students, but due to lack of money many students are not able to join them. The Government should give help to such students. If tuition is supplementary to classroom learning, logically academically poor students should have a higher representation in the coaching centres. But this is not the case, suggesting the importance of economic factor, as also one of the important determinants of not taking private tuition.

Others have a very different view: as to them, the coaching institutions only aim at making money and the students waste their time and money, learning nothing.

Like in many developing countries, the private tuition in India has evolved from a simple supplementary system of helping students with their studies to a competitive business with gigantic proportions. There are several factors responsible for the transformation, which can be divided into few interrelated segments namely; educational, economic and social.

The defunct school management and organization system have led to poor teaching-learning process in schools in general and government schools in particular. In the absence of adequate monitoring and supervision, schools have lost accountability. This, in turn, has necessitated a desire among parents to supplement school teaching with education through outside support, thus creating a legitimate demand for private tuition. Initially the availability of private tuition led to improvement in performance of students, especially due to individualized attention and pedagogical improvement resulting in the development of the system. With the passage of time, economic forces joined with educational factors to make it a powerful alternative. In the beginning, many teachers used PT as an opportunity foe extra income to supplement their meagre earning. The economic potential of the PT in a later phase led to the professional growth of this practice as a business venture- a transformation from PT to coaching centres. The development of industrial and information technology, communication and management and subsequent professionalization contributed immensely for the growth of professional and technical course and institutions offering those courses started screening the application. The gap between demand and supply ostensibly led to higher competition. This provided further impetus to private tuition as admission to these course on many occasions were based on performances in public examinations and opportunity to choose a particular combination at higher secondary level.

There are also lot of social reasons behind the rise and growth of PT. Peer pressure, culture of comparing and competing with relatives and kin group, the social obsession with education, the great American Dream, as well as the desire to escape from poverty through technical education etc. This has in turn made parents expect and demand more from their children forcing them to spend more hours revising and learning curriculum for better results thus pushing them toward PT.

These things have led to some negative results like creating problems of equity at the levels of gender, class and rural-urban difference. Private tuition, privatization and private school have further accentuated the social divide rendering the society highly competitive and bereft of values. However, more importantly it stunted the progress and revitalization of formal school system making the entire system defunct thus perpetuating a system of inequality and difference.

On the basis of ensuring discussion it can be said that private tuition has emerged as parallel system to that of formal school system almost like a shadow. This is more so in case of educationally and economically developed states viz. Kerala and Maharashtra. Viewed from the perspective of management types of schools, it was found that the tendency of seeking private tuition is more prevalent in private unaided schools. It is interesting to note that these schools were supposed to provide an alternative to government schools. As the study has shown that, despite better infrastructure and better results, students from these schools still resort to private tuition. This means that beyond the academic reasons, there are factors like competitiveness, desire to have a cutting-edge vis-à-vis others also influence the tendency to go for private tuition.

As discussed earlier, private tuition not only perpetuates, the existing inequities but also creates new forms of disparities especially in case of backward areas. The higher access of private tuition in urban areas and among boys reinforces the existing locational and gender disparities. Even in the state of Kerala, with higher human development index, the difference in extent of private tuition is lower.

The dependency on private tuition varies for different student groups. In case of good performing schools in general and private unaided schools in particular, the reason is to improve the percentage of marks. But in general the failure of large number of students in public examination has also necessitated the desire among students to seek private tuition. The study has also indicated that parents with better educational, occupational and economic background tend to send their children for private tuition, thus further extending the gap.

The next part of the chapter describes the salient characteristics and features of coaching centres in Uttar Pradesh and Maharashtra, Varanasi and Pune respectively, where a large percentage of students prefer to go to coaching centres.

Private Tuition in Uttar Pradesh: An Overview of Coaching Centers in Varanasi

In Varanasi district private tuition exists in all forms and is very common though more in urban areas than rural areas. While in urban areas home tuition, group tuition and tuition by coaching centres is a common practice. But in rural areas home tuition is rare and group tuition at the home of tutor is a common practice, and coaching centres are also in vogue in smaller towns. However, the cost of all forms of private tuition is relatively less in rural areas. Most of coaching centers along with preparing students for public examination also provide coaching for entrance examinations of professional courses. The catchment area for the coaching centre ranges 2-3 kilometers and some times beyond. Similarly, and from different socio-economic background students from all management types of schools (Govt., Aided and Unaided) are found attending private tuition.

Registration

In recent past, the number of coaching centres has increased in Varanasi district. Private tuition has become a huge business; it has grown in to a vast enterprise. It employs many thousands of people and provides additional income to teachers, unemployed educated including senior students. Varanasi city has some of the best educational facilities in the northern India like university, a medical college, a post-graduate medical institute, engineering college and a host of others with ever increasing demand for admission in to professional and technical courses. It is estimated to have more than 400 coaching centres in the district. Some are modest in size, number of them is large and few are very big which fall in the category of big commercial enterprise. All of them are running at a profit but only 273 are registered. State Government' Uttar Pradesh Coaching Regulation Ordinance, 2002, No.-8, Article 15 all coaching centres have to be registered according to the Uttar Pradesh Coaching Rules and Regulations, 2002. Any one can opens a coaching centre by applying to office of *Zonal Higher Education Officer* after paying an application fee of ₹100. The application includes information related to personal details, location and address of area where the private tuition centre will be or is operating, whether the building for conducting classes is owned or rented, if rented applicant needs to provide no objection certificate from the owner of the building. The applicant has to justify the significance of location to operate coaching centre by specifying number of students admitted for private tuition for the current year and whether providing private tuition is only profession of the applicant or engaged in any other employment. The registration fees vary based on number of students from INR 250 to INR 25000 for a period of three years.

After submission of application, investigating officer from the Zonal Higher Education Office inspects the location of coaching centre to examine physical facilities. However, it is only a formality and hardly ever an application is turn down by authorities. It is not mandatory for any coaching centre to mention the subjects to be taught, grades or the amount of fees they are going to charge. The government is only concerned with the number of students the coaching center is going to tutor for the specified period of 3 years although the coaching centres need to maintain registers of accounts. According to the registration, the coaching centres should not exceed number of students specified in the MOU. But hardly any coaching centre adheres to this norm. Similarly, not all the coaching centres get registered according government Act.

Association

There is no association of the coaching institutions in Varanasi district since Government hardly ever interferes in their functioning. The role of government almost ceases after registration and initial verification. Only when the state government issued the notification making compulsory for the registration of all existing institutions, they opposed the ordinance and one of the coaching institute called Mishra Coaching institute took the initiative of collecting money to file case against that ordinance. Since then no such crisis has ever risen rather a keen competition exists among the coaching centres to attract more number of students.

Management of the Coaching Institutes

Management of coaching institutions is distinct from the management of formal institutions of education. Coaching centres are not family based. It is basically run by an idea of individual educational entrepreneur (mostly by educated unemployed youth or retired teachers). In Varanasi town about 80 per cent of the coaching institutes were opened by educated unemployed youth who did not have their desired job and retired teachers of Schools/College or university run some of them. Most of the institutions have indicated that having single branch and individual attention is the key to their successful management of coaching centres. There is a general feeling that coaching centres are started by certain section of the society or cast group though this is no necessarily be true always.

Problems Faced by Coaching Institutions

The coaching centres face many difficulties including having basic infrastructure, retaining qualified and good teaching staff and high advertisement charges. In increased competition among the coaching centres good teachers and market oriented good publicity mechanism became important factors to sustain the number of students.

Tutors

Educated unemployed, college/university students retired teachers and teachers of private unaided schools form an important segment of tutors in coaching centres. Due to ban on government teachers to provide private tuition, rarely they indulge tutoring in coaching centres. However, generally they provide private tuition either at their own place or go to the student's home. It is also very common that private tuition by class teachers/subject teachers become a kind of blackmail, because teachers teach important topics in the private tuition only.

The selection of tutors in coaching centres varies from institute to institute. In most of the institutions it is through recommendation or personally the institutional head or management know the teacher; and also through open advertisements followed by personal interview and classroom demonstration. In most institutions demonstration is very important through which there teaching ability is judged. Most important is the students feed back. If the students are satisfied by his/her performance and style he/she is selected and continued.

The nature of appointment of tutors differs from ad-hoc to permanent, teachers are employed on part time and hourly basis, but the tenure of the teacher depends upon his performance and performance of students. As long as the management and students are satisfied the tutors are continued. Otherwise the tutors are easily terminated.

There is no common pattern of amount paid to tutors by the coaching centres. It is different for different subjects. Many institutions do not reveal this information. But it is generally:

- Package based (for specific number of months and number of subjects taught
- Hours/class based, this is according to number of lectures taken. In urban areas it ranges from ₹ 50 to ₹ 150 per lecture, (for class IX to XII) depending upon the nature of coaching institutes. It also depends upon the class size.
- Percentage based (60 per cent of the fees paid to teacher and 40 per cent is taken by coaching centre management).
- Some teachers who are well known and quite experienced and the management thinks that because of him the demand for the coaching centre increases they pay him according to his wish. They compromise on the amount.

Most of the centres pay their tutors at a rate of ₹ 100-150 per hour while a few pay up to five hundred in urban areas. Even on this issue most of the institutions have preferred not to mention explicitly. Despite all efforts coaching centres face more problems pertaining to teachers. They offer good remuneration for retraining capable teachers. This has led to a competition where teachers join a particular centre only for the money it offers and leave it for more money elsewhere.

Students

In Varanasi students from all socio-economic backgrounds join coaching centres though much prevalent among higher and middle-income group. The monthly fees in the coaching centres are not very high in Varanasi district and vary widely. It ranges from ₹ 60 per month onward both in rural areas as well as in the city. The criterion for admission is very simple. If one is able to pay he/ she can get admission. Though many claim that they conduct written test and interview but it is a formality. Some of the reputed coaching centres such as JRS Coaching (for CBSE) and Current coaching (U.P. Board) in Varanasi town conduct entrance test for admitting students in their coaching centres. It indicates that these institutions exercise choice of selection and accept only the hopeful cases. This enhances the chances of success for the students tutored by them.

Demand

The coaching centres adopt different method to create demand. To draw more students, better publicity is required such as: Through Advisements, Leaflets, Pamphlets Posters on the wall in front of schools and residential areas; Banners, News Papers; They publicize the results of the students, profile of tutors highlighting their experience and reputation. class size, infrastructure facilities etc., The coaching centres also advertise their uniqueness of separate special teachers for separate subjects and also guarantee the passing of the students.

Besides hiring of PR firms to ensure a "positive publicity" in the media, the coaching centres have launched a number of "schemes" to lure students. In addition to advertisements in newspapers the most effective means has been through Cable Television offering short, capsule and crash courses, as well as independent modules offering "100 per cent" success. Most coaching centres have taken full-page advertisements in newspapers carrying photographs of students who had been successful with high scoring. A new trend is to organise shows in schools and colleges from where students are "recruited" to these coaching centres. Quiz programmes are organised where winners are offered attractive prizes.

Infrastructure

The infrastructure facilities at coaching centres in terms of classrooms, electricity, water, toilets, libraries and laboratories are much different from what one observes in the formal educational system. There are all types of coaching centres ranging from one room to multi-stored building. They are either owned or rented. Most of them have limited infrastructure facilities, which suits their requirements as they work on a shift system. Effective and optimum utilisation of space and infrastructure is common among the coaching centres. maximum benefit. It has been observed that in the urban areas the space is adequate, rooms are well ventilated, but some of them, which are single room centres, have at least one window.

Coaching centres in urban areas are normally located near the schools, residential areas and market places with better transportation links and where people of higher socio- economic group live. The coaching centres have electricity and all those who run evening classes have power backup (Generators/invertors). Most of the coaching centres have toilet facilities besides blackboards, chair and table or benches for students to sit. Library and laboratory do not really constitute an important part of the coaching system as they are more concentrated on question and answers and preparing the students for a specific task of qualifying the competitive examinations

Teaching-Learning Processes

In all the coaching centres tutoring is exclusively examination oriented. However, coaching centres claim that they adopt innovative teaching methods different from classroom teaching in schools. They have a more flexible time schedule made to suit the students. They generally adopt lecture method followed by discussion, question answers. Students invariably get individual attention and the tutors clarify doubts. Generally in urban areas and in big coaching centres there are separate teachers for each subject. They distribute their own printed, photocopied and cyclostyled reading materials and set question answer material.

One of the most common features in all the coaching centres is regular evaluation of students' performance based on weakly tests. Some of them conduct even daily tests for one or the other subjects. Students' performance in these tests becomes a feedback both for tutors and students. Coaching centres also ensure to emphasis on language proficiency, attention on problem solving, solving sample question papers/previous years question papers, time management in examinations, personal attention to students/extra attention on weak students, and counselling to parents.

Duration of Courses

There are variations in time devoted per week and duration of courses respectively. Generally most of them follow a common pattern. The institutions run:

- Full Term courses from: June to February
- Guarantee Course/Crash Course from: December to February-March
- Duration of Periods: 30 Minutes to 1 hour
- No of Periods: 2-3 periods daily
- No. of days: For class IX, X, XI XII – 7 days a week [6days teaching followed by one day test]. For class VII and VIII – 6 days a week

Size of Batches

While the mainstream schooling is organized in classes comprising 50 to 60 students, these coaching centres are arranged in small batches. The size and number of their batches, varies from institution to institution and there is no general pattern for the entire system. But as observed from various institutions in Varansi district it can be concluded that the number of batch ranges from 1 to 5 for each class and the size of a batch ranges from 10 to 30 students. In order to personalize the attention they try to maintain the teacher pupil ratio of 1:20. Issues like the number of students attended so far or attended during specific year kept as secrete by most of them due to implications such as income tax and other aspects.

Finance

The coaching centres decide the amount of fees and also varies across coaching centres and in different locations. The fees charged for private tuition by coaching centres is not regulated by government. The source of amount of income is very important for coaching institutions as they are financially self-sustained need to make profit. However their source of income also includes charges for study materials. The coaching institutions do not like any inquiry with regard to finances.

Organisation, Management and Infrastructure

The coaching centres have simple management structure there is merely one key person at the hub of administration and management. This key position is designated as 'Director'. The key person-Director looks after the management of the centre. Regular informal meetings are organized once a month where by all old staff (teachers including the manager) meet and discuss various aspects of management. These discussions are focused on status of the completion of courses of different subjects, need and availability of teachers, and any other outstanding issue. In fact this informal meetings do not have any definite agenda but the discussion invariably revolves around improvement of services and management of the centre.

The management reported no major problem as regard the students, barring a scarce few that come up sporadically due to some mismanagement by the tutors. The management deals regarding the capabilities of tutors to cope up with the demand ably. The management normally spends 12 hours daily attending to different aspects of the centre. The support staff works in two shifts, and the academic staff is hand picked on the basis of merit. Full time or part time appointments are made in accordance with the availability of the academic staff. The number of support staff is considerable. For example there are 10 manual workers, which includes peons, security staff, sweepers etc. and other handling administrative activities.

Infrastructure wise this coaching centre operates from the Directors own three-storeyed building with sufficient user space considering number of students. For example there are 20 classrooms with capacity to serve 250-300 students. They have a separate staff room, manager's room, Director's room and a big lobby including a reception. They have all the basic amenities like toilets separate for girls and boys, drinking water, electricity, power backup etc.

Admission Procedure and Academic Practice

The admission process is very simple and straightforward. Any student having a minimum percentage of marks in X standard may seek admission for class XI and XII. In the lower class this is also not required. It is generally on first come first basis. They also have the facilities of educational counseling. Classes are taken in two batches, from 6.30.am to 9.30 am in the morning and 2.30 pm to 8.00 pm in the evening. Batches are formed according to the percentage of marks obtained by the students at the qualifying examination or on the spot test.

Each topic of school syllabus is introduced and explained to a batch of students. After explaining the basics, discussions are allowed. Students are given home assignments. This provides students necessary understanding of the subject, clarity of concepts, good practice to face examinations and to build up confidence. Weekly tests are held and such tests are designed as model of public examination (board examination). The students are, however given opportunity to put up relevant queries to their tutors at any stage and the academic staffs clarifies their doubts and helps solving difficulties in learning. This is what conspicuously absent in schools. In Coaching centres healthy competition is induced by occasionally initiating discussions and debate between brilliant and average students. This inculcates in them the tendency of addressing the problems in the best-suited way.

A unique feature in coaching centres is tutoring subjects well ahead of teaching schedule in school. In other words the students who attend private tuition in this coaching centre have benefit of classroom teaching in the schools as an additional revision as they already had been taught in private tuition. This has certain implications for quality of classroom teaching in schools, as teachers know that the students were already tutored in coaching centre. It is also not so uncommon some of the students who join coaching centres for full year absent from regular classes in school.

Table 4.19: No. of Days and Subjects Taught in Private Tuition in Class IX and X

Sl. No	*No. of Days*	*Subjects*	*Hrs/minutes*	*Amount (Rs)*
1	6	Maths	50	75
2	3	English	50	50
3	1	Social Science	50	45
4	2	Hindi	50	30
5	6	General Science	50	75
Total				275

Table 4.20: No. of Days and Subjects Taught in Private Tuition in Class XI and XII

Sl. No	*No. of Days*	*Subjects*	*Hrs/minutes*	*Amount (Rs)*
1	6	Maths/Biology	50	75
2	3	English	50	65
3	3	Hindi	50	65
4	6	General Science (Physics + Chemistry)	50	130
Total				275

Class VI –VII

₹ 250 for all subjects, 4 Periods of 50 minutes each daily.

- On fees few coaching centers gives 10 per cent as brother concession.
- If a student scores 80 per cent in the 8 weekly tests consecutively, 75 per cent of their fees is waved off.

Private Tuition in Maharashtra: An Overview of Coaching Centers in Pune

In Maharashtra especially in Pune city there is a typical coaching pattern known as "Latur Coaching Pattern", which was started in the Latur district, now is also adopted by some coaching centres in other cities. According to this pattern, 10th class and 12th class syllabus are completed in the second half of 9th and 11th class coaching respectively. All forms of private tuitions being supplementary to mainstream schooling. Private tuition is provided mostly in morning and evening sessions arranged in different batches. The timings are flexible according students choice.

Registration

Coaching centres in Maharashtra unlike in Uttar Pradesh are registered under Shop Act of the State Revenue Department. But tuition bureaus involved in providing tutors for home tuition are registered under the Charity Commission Act. The bureaus register in the name of educational consultancy and welfare activities. A registration fee between ₹ 500/- to ₹ 1000/- is charged from coaching centres depending upon number of students whereas tuition bureaus pay a registration fee of ₹ 1000/-. In every three years, registration is to be renewed following an inspection from the concerned department. This is, however not strictly followed. As a result, many coaching centres expanded without renewal. Registered coaching centres pay 1 per cent tax to Revenue Department as per Shop Act. But tuition bureaus pay 8 per cent service charges to Charity Commission. The service charge is collected from parents/students on the tuition fees. The state government was contemplating with a proposal of enhancing service charges for coaching centres to 8 per cent.

There are about 500 coaching centres in Pune city, which is also the district headquarters. out of which only about 20-25 per cent are registered. Generally coaching centres do not prefer to register unless the number of students increase and also intend to advertise and publicise to attract more students and create demand. Most of the unauthorized/unregistered centres have similar to group tuition. It is found that there is a demand from the association of registered coaching centres to make registration compulsory for all coaching centres.

Who runs Coaching Centres/Tuition Bureaus?

Most of the coaching centres and tuition bureaus in Maharashtra are run by teachers/lecturers (after retirement or with voluntary retirement) and academicians. Only about 15-20 per cent of the coaching centres/ tuition bureaus are run by unemployed youth in semi urban and rural areas, in particular. With few exceptions (i.e. about 5%), almost all coaching centres are individual endeavours. A few coaching centres are family based business. For example, the coaching centres like Subodh and Swadhaya are named after husband and wife who were teachers with good reputation. They run their coaching centre with limited number of students in specific subjects. Some well established coaching centres like Chate, Jog, Lucky etc. have branches in more than one town/city. Most of the registered coaching centres, however run in commercial manner. With tutors' salary, house rent and other maintenance expenditures. Some of the coaching centres have offered franchise.

Students' Registration

In most of the coaching centres, students register their name at the beginning of academic year parallel to school registration. Normally, coaching centres have a limited number of seats. When there is more demand, some coaching centres increase the number of batches and hire part-time tutors depending on the availability of infrastructure. Otherwise, screenings test of candidates is conducted based on academic performance in previous class (marks) and an informal interview. But this does not often happen as number of coaching centres with specialist tutors has grown at a faster rate than the demand for private tuition, and there has been a steep competition among coaching centres to attract students.

Tuition is provided in different batches based on either class or subjects or medium of instruction. Each batch consists of 20-3 students for each subject. The time period for each batch ranges between 2.5-3 hours and duration of class for each subject ranges between 45 to 60 minutes. Normally, students receive tuition for 6 days per week.

Students from different socio-economic strata receive tuition from different coaching centres depending on the fee structure. There are one or two coaching centres in Pune like 'Rohan Classes', which are exclusively for private students.

As a rule, there is no concession for socially disadvantaged students like Scheduled castes and scheduled tribes. The meritorious students from low economic status who are not able to pay fees however are selected with low fees keeping in mind the good results for coaching centre. Discounts are given to the students who pay the annual tuition fee at the time of admission rather in instalments. Children of close associates, relatives and socially well-known/ influential persons are also given some concessions or preferred. Coaching centres normally run for 10 months (i.e. June to March).

Some good coaching centres like Chate and Jog do not admit students in the middle of the academic year or before examination, even if students are ready to pay more. But there are many coaching centres to do so, charging higher fees. It is found that students who are able to afford the cost of tuition register at the beginning of the academic year.

Creating Demand

Coaching centres adopt different strategies to create demand for private tuition. They advertise through papers, posters, leaflets and cable T.V. In the advertisement, in addition to the mention of the working pattern, coaching centres display the names of the merit holders with photos and give assurance for success. Sometimes, top rankers in merit list who had not taken any tuition, are also hired for publicity. Some coaching centres declare, special batches for academically good and poor students. Advertisement is sometimes repeated showing 'limited seats are available' and changing the last date of registration. Mainstream teachers being associated directly or indirectly with coaching centres also create demand. Some coaching centres even employ schoolteachers as counsellors on a commission basis to contact parents and students and motivating them for tuition. This strategy is normally adopted towards the last date of registration or immediately after the last date. Personal contact sometimes becomes more effective than formal advertisement. Tuition bureaus, which supply tutors for home tuition, however are not involved in such large-scale advertisement rather rely on posters and word of mouth.

The demand of coaching centres varies different subjects depending on the name and fame of the subject tutors. In urban areas, coaching centres, which provide tuition in mathematics and science, have higher demand whereas in rural areas, it is English, which creates demand for a particular coaching centre.

Facilities, Teaching-Leaning Materials

Almost all coaching centres run in a pucca building. Adequate infrastructure facilities like sitting arrangements, lights, fans etc. are provided in classroom. Other basic facilities like rest room, drinking water, toilet, phone etc. are also available. Teaching learning materials like charts, magazines, newspapers, textbook reading materials, short notes are also made available.

Tuition Fees Package

Pay package varies widely. Some coaching centres have a separate yearly fee package for a group of subjects as well as and for each subject whereas others have for each subject. In general, fees is higher than other subjects. Students receiving tuition in a group of subjects get discounts in pay package. For example, while for each subject, annual fee is ₹ 10,000, for four subjects it is ₹ 30,000.

The fee package also varies across classes. It is higher for Class X and XII. Again, for Class XI and XII, pay package varies depending on the stream and combination of subjects. Some coaching centres have a fee package for 3 years or two years for secondary students (i.e., for the Class VIII to XI) and 2 years for higher secondary students (i.e. Class XI &XII). Students receiving tuition under these pay packages also get receive discounts. Fee package for Marathi medium tuition is less than English Medium tuition. Pay package in home tuition, which has remarkably less amount than coaching centres, alsc varies across classes, stream and subjects. (see Table 4.21)

Tutors/Teachers

Following an open advertisement, tutors in coaching centres are selected based on an interview and teaching demonstration. In the selection process, preference is given to candidates with higher qualifications (such as post graduation and above) and teaching experiences in schools as well as coaching centres. Teacher training as such is not an important criterion. Despite government restrictions, teachers of mainstream schools engaged in part-time work in coaching

Table 4.21: Home Tuitions–Monthly Fees Chart in ₹

	VIII	*IX*	*X*	*XI*	*XII (Commerce)*	*XII (Science)*
English Math Science	450/- 450/- 450/-	500/- 500/- 500/-	550/- 550/- 550/-	700/- 1500/- Phy.-1500/- Chem. 1500/- Bio.- 1500/-	800/- 2000/-	800/- 2000/- Physics. 2000/- Chem. 2000/- Bio. 2000/-
Hindi	450/- (3 days)	500/- (3 days)	500/- (3 days)			
Marathi	450/- (3 days)	500/- (3 days)	500/- (3 days			
Sanskrit	450/- (3 days)	500/- (3 days)	550/- (3 days			
Social Studies	500/- (3 days)	550/- (4 days)			Eco. 800/- Acc. 800/- Other-800/- (each)	
All Subjects				12,000/-Package for one subject 6 hours a week, for 6 months		15,000/-Package for one subject, 6 hours a week, for 6months

Source: Educational Guidance Bureau, Shri Vidya Vikas Seva Pratisthan, Pune, 2005

Notes: i) For foreign languages like German, French etc ₹ 800/- (3 days in week)

ii) ,Singing/ Music/ Dance etc – ₹ 800/- (3 days in week)

iii) Fees for CBSE and ICSE syllabus 10 per cent and 15 per cent more centres, very often in different names. Different tutors are appointed for different subjects, and sometimes also for different classes. Some tutors work on permanent basis whereas a majority are part-timers. In well-established registered coaching centres, tutors' salary ranges between ₹ 3000/- to ₹ 20,000/- depending upon the experiences, subjects, nature of batches, number of classes and most importantly students' demand. Tutors in small coaching centres are paid an amount ranging between ₹ 1000/- to 3000/- per month.

Tutors' performances are constantly monitored through parents' feedback. Tutors are changed, if parents and students are not satisfied with teaching. Tutors also have to maintain a monthly record of attendance, weekly test and performances of students, known as "attendance card". The tutor is paid through cheque by Bureau, not directly by parents, after a submission of the monthly attendance card by tutor duly signed by parents. As per agreement, tutors get a monthly remuneration of 75 per cent of total tuition fees, and 25 per cent is claimed by Bureau against guidance, supervision and service charges. Parents have to deposit tuition fees at bureau in advance. Fees once paid for one quarter is not refunded under any circumstances. Parents also have to pay 8 per cent service charges as well as ₹ 100/- for counselling fee.

Teaching Methodology

As such, there is no significant difference in teaching methods in coaching centres and schools, as most of the tutors in coaching centres are schoolteachers. It is the precise planning, proper individual guidance, teachers accountability, students involvement in learning, regular home assignment, regular monitoring of progress and remedial measures that help in achieving success. Individual attention is paid in clarifying the doubts of students. A competitive spirit is also created in tuition classes. Weekly tests and annual tests based on examination oriented critical questions are most salient features of each coaching centre.

Association of Coaching Centers and Social Activities

There is an association of registered coaching centres in Pune city. The association is registered under Shop Act. They are now fighting against the ban on schoolteachers' engagement in tuition. It is learned that strong link between members of association and government officials has been instrumental in the secret appointment of schoolteachers in coaching centres. Coaching centre association sometimes conducts educational and cultural programmes. Individual coaching centres being associated with other nongovernmental organizations are also engaged in social activities like sports event, relief work, social service such as eye camp, blood donation camp, animal/bird care and other educational programmes.

To sum, private tuition provided through either coaching centres, home and group tuitions have created a different educational environment in which students are found more involved in learning process. There is hardly any doubt that it helps in preparing for examination paving way for higher education, but it may not be true to suggest that it is the only way to achieve quality education. Students without any home tuition have also been successful in achieving what tutees have achieved. It might not be true that mainstream schools have not been able to meet the needs of students. Much rather depends on how students and teachers interact in school environment. Tuition may have negative impact on mainstream education system. Supplementary nature of private tuition has created a different mind set among students because of which they are not sincerely involved learning process in mainstream schools with the belief that they can master the academic tasks in private tuitions. Moreover, because of more commercialisation of private tuitions, students of low socio-economic status are deprived of such opportunities, as an alternative academic service. As a result, it creates social inequities. Even, teachers despite all restrictions in taking tuitions are more inclined towards private tuition and are involved directly or indirectly in masked manner. All these give rise to growth of parallel schooling systems and increase the cost of education at secondary school level.

Chate Coaching Classes – A Case Study in Pune

'Chate Coaching Classes', named after its managing director Prof. Matchindra Chate, was set up in early 1990s. At present, it has about 100 branches in the state, grouped under 6 regions/ divisions- Aurangabad, Kolhapur, Nagpur, Nasik, Pune and Mumbai. About half of the total branches are found in Mumbai region. Pune region has 13 branches, of which 12 are found in Pune city. With one managing director in the head office in Aurangabad, Chate Coaching

Classes are managed by regional and branch managers. Chate Coaching Classes is mainly concerned with the academic subjects at secondary and higher secondary levels. A limited number of branches however provide tuition for the State Combined Entrance Tests.

'Chate Coaching Classes' adopts different strategies to create demand for private tuition. It presents a market-oriented advertisement in the regional newspapers at the beginning of the academic year covering brief outlines about working pattern and other aspects such as special provisions (i.e., physical facilities, special batches, different medium of instructions etc.), number of branches, selected number of students placed on merit lists of the public examinations in previous years and within different percentage ranges of marks. These factual presentations are supplemented by eye-catching headlines (Box 4.1).

Box 4.1

"May be any subject... but the students of Chate Classes are always toppers in SSC Exam".

"Tremendous increase in percentage... only through Chate Classes"

"Chate Classes... the one and only Classes... which takes care to prepare the students for all subjects"

At the local level, additional effort is made to advertise through posters, Cable T.V. and Theatre Halls. Prospectus of the coaching centre, which is provided to registered students, presents its plan and programme in detail. The presentation of photos of rank holders and their positive opinions about the coaching centres help in mobilizing more students. Some positive statements of rank holders published in the prospectus become more effective (Box 4.2).

Box 4.2

"Teachers in Chate help to develop cutting edge and winning edge"

"Chate is the best in every manner. Only Chate class has capacity to pull the students from lower to upper level"

"When we see blindly, every coaching classes appears same but good teachers in Chate bring the students to the bright success"

"Chate classes help students to reap the harvest of success through motherly love and fatherly discipline".

'Chate Coaching Classes' appoints well-experienced teachers and highly qualified unemployed youth as tutors based on interview and classroom demonstration. Other criteria such as availability of tutors for different batches, subject teachers well known in locality etc. are also considered. Tutors have to complete at least one-year term conditioned by satisfactory performance. Otherwise, salary of one month is forfeited. Appointment is extended after every term (year) based on satisfactory performance. Tutors are well paid as compared to other coaching centres, which ranges between a minimum ₹ 3000 to maximum ₹ 20,000 depending on experiences, number of classes taken and satisfactory performance.

Chate Coaching Classes provides tuition for all subjects together with a belief that it would save the time and energy of students in wandering from one place to another. The yearly fees package ranges from a minimum about ₹ 10,000–12,000 to maximum about ₹ 30,000 – 35,000 depending on the classes and subjects. For example, special batch students of Class X and XII and students in Science subjects pay more normal coaching batches. Similarly, students who register for three-year term at secondary level (Class VIII-X) and two-year term at higher secondary level (Class XI-XII) are given concession in pay package. Tuition fees per year could be paid at the time of admission or in instalments. Payment in instalments however, has to be made through post-dated cheque at the time of admission. Inability to pay instalments within prescribed date is liable to cancellation of admission. Admission once taken is not cancelled, and tuition fees once paid, is not transferred or refunded, under any circumstances.

Teaching Learning Methodology

'Chat Coaching Classes' provides tuition in congenial atmosphere with adequate infrastructure facilities including air-conditioned classrooms and other basic facilities like purified drinking water, toilet, vehicle parking etc. It also has other facilities like fax machine, photocopier, laboratory and comprehensive updated reading materials popularly called as 'Chate Perfect Notes' centre. The coaching also has publication business through which it sales its printed notes in bookshops

Tutoring covers teaching of every unit of syllabus and total revision of entire syllabus, solving difficult problems, regular home assignments, ensuring satisfactory progress from time to time and regular feedback to parents. Emphasis is also given on the improvement in legible handwriting, writing speed, grammatical mistakes and comprehensive writing skill. 'Special batches' are organized for Class X students and Class XII Science students for a thorough preparation for the public examinations. 'Summer Vacation Batches' are also conducted at few branches of Chate Coaching Classes for the students of rural areas who are unable to join regular 'special batches'

All coaching classes are held in three shifts- morning (7-10 a.m.), noon (2-6 p.m.) and evening (3-9 p.m.), according to planned timetable for different batches. Coaching classes for Marathi medium students are normally held in morning shift whereas English medium batches in noon shift and special batch of in Class X and XII students in evening shift. In the tuition timetable, number of periods for different subjects varies.

The notable features of Chate Coaching Classes is creating an atmosphere of examination and helping students to gain confidence. Unit Tests are held on every Sunday and revision tests after completion of the course of a subject. In addition five preliminary examinations are conducted before the school annual examinations. The duration and maximum marks for different subjects in the Unit tests and preliminary examinations at the Chate Coaching centre are on similar pattern as of the public examinations conducted by the board. The question papers in unit tests and preliminary examinations and the valuation of answer papers are done according to the pattern of Board Examination. At the end of the year workshops and coaching camps are also organized for all subjects.

Students are exclusively prepared from the examination point of view with thorough mock exercises. Secondly, tutors don't spare any pains to make students understand the fundamentals of the subject. The tutors are well reputed for their subject command and teaching methods.

NOTES

1. Private tuition refers to supplementation of tutoring, covering subjects which are already covered in the school and the tutoring provided by entrepreneurs and individuals for profit making purpose (Bray: 1999).

2. See Annexure for Sample Students by different categories.
3. Includes only lower secondary.
4. Social groups in India are based on caste lines and divided into general, other backward castes and the deprived castes (SCs and STs). A lot of affirmative action measures have been taken to improve the socio-economic status of these deprived sections. The basis of the grouping is social and economic basis while SCs and STs are Constitutionally recognized groups.

REFERENCES

Bray, Mark(1999): *The Shadow Education System: Private Tutoring and Its Implications for Planners.* Fundamentals of Educational Planning No.61, Paris: UNESCO International Institute for Education (IIEP).

Buchmann, Claudia (2002): 'Getting Ahead in Kenya: Social Capital, Shadow Education, and Achievement', in Fuller, Bruce & Hannum, Emily (eds.), *Schooling and Social Capital in Diverse Cultures*. Amsterdam: JAI Press, pp. 133-159.

Davies, Scott (2004): 'School Choice by Default? Understanding the Demand for Private Tutoring in Canada'. *American Journal of Education*, Vol.110, No.3, pp. 233-255.

Stevenson, David Lee & Baker, David P. (1992): 'Shadow Education and Allocation in Formal Schooling: Transition to University in Japan'. *American Journal of Sociology*, Vol. 97, No. 6, pp. 1639-1657.

Sujatha, K. (2009), Private Tuition in India, ANTRIAP News Letter, NUEPA, New Delhi, India.

Tinsel, Asset & Brian, Fame (2005): 'Demand for Education in Turkey: An Analysis of Private Tutoring Expenditures'. *Economics of Education Review*, Vol. 24, No. 6.

5

Planning and Management of Textbooks and Public Examination

The success of education largely depend on its contents is reflected in the curriculum. In other words, curriculum refers to the process of designing courses and disciplines for an educational system. Rooted in this particular conception curriculum becomes not only a medium of transacting learning but a reflection of socio-cultural context and incorporates issues of importance while catering to the societal needs. In this section an attempt has been made to look at the secondary education in retrospective and national curriculum frame work for secondary and higher secondary education across the country and among a few selected states.

A critical look at the curriculum developed has its history in the observation and recommendations of various educational commissions. The Secondary Education Commission (1952-53) examined the existing school curriculum and observed that it was narrowly conceived, examination-centered, bookish and over-crowded with too many facts and details, that it did not take note of changing sociological needs and that it did not cater to pupil's intellectual needs. The Commission recommended 11 years of schooling and establishment of multipurpose schools providing education in a variety of academic and vocational streams. The Commission felt that education need to be oriented and placed in the broader context of society and blend with national goals while catering to the needs of the community and aspirations of the individual.

The Education Commission (1964-66) recommended for an undifferentiated curriculum and made Science and Mathematics compulsory subjects up to grade X. While a common curriculum including work experience was recommended up to grade X, the +2 stage was to provide for academic and vocational courses. It recommended the establishment of a uniform pattern of education known as 10+2+3. The recommendation of the Commission has become the base of serious restructuring of education in India after the independence.

The curriculum development process can be seen in five stages. The first stage was initiative it received in hand of the Second Education Commission but it did not have much of an effect as it not only recommendatory in nature but also did not affect the states. At the second stage it was the efforts of Education Commission's recommendation that formed the basis of curriculum development. As a 1968 policy was formulated and it laid down a new uniform educational structure in all parts of the country. It was during this time that NCERT given was given the responsibility to develop curriculum. The 1986 policy made systematic effort to establish a uniform school education system and paved the way for curriculum development which came in the form of 1988 National Curriculum Framework. This was followed by NCF 2000 of which we have discussed in detail and the latest one framed in 2005 is yet to be adopted.

The National Education Policy-1986 envisaged the uniform school system across the country, the structure known as 10+2+3 pattern had significant implications for secondary education both in terms of curriculum and diversification of courses. Under this pattern, the first ten years of school education were visualized as the stage of general education with undifferentiated courses with the objective of equipping the children who cease their formal schooling at the end of this stage, to be responsible citizens and providing them with basic knowledge for day-to-day life. Science and mathematics were made an integral part of general education. This meant that for all children, science and mathematics were made compulsory up to the end of secondary stage (Grade X). The extension of undifferentiated general education up to the end of the secondary stage was a major step in the development of secondary education. However, at the higher secondary stage (the +2 stage in the new pattern) diversified courses with accent on vocationalization have been envisaged.

The third stage of development was in the late 70s, when efforts to establish the common educational system, as were envisaged in 1968 policy went through further testing and qualification and actually implementation of it was initiated in the mid-1970s. The delay could be explained in terms of the federal structure of the country in which education was in the state list, regional variations in terms of resources and capacities to restructure the educational system among states, political climate etc. Keeping in view of some of these problems the Constitution was amended 1976 to bring education from state list to concurrent list. This in turn facilitated a uniform educational policy that supported common school system, a centrally sponsored curriculum that provided guidance to states, improvement in the delivery of quality education and

Since till mid-education was under the state list and states were in charge of preparing curriculum it was only natural that educational structure and objectives were determined in accordance with the needs, capacities, ideologies of respective state governments. Coupled with these contingencies were the problems of diversity and plurality of culture, beliefs and attitudes and economic capabilities of states and its population. This in turn led to the creation of divergent, unequal curriculums with little similarity with each other.

As a part of the implementation of the new pattern, a framework of national curriculum for all stages of schools education including the secondary stage was formulated by National Council for Educational Research and Training (NCERT). According to this curriculum framework the objectives of the first stage of secondary education (Grades IX-X) are two fold: preparation for entry into the world of work and preparation for higher-level academic studies or for vocational courses. Since the adoption of the 1968 policy, two Constitutional amendments also had been passed which had implications for national and educational goals and one of them is the amendment of 1976 that brought education into the concurrent list from state list.

The release of 'National Curriculum for Elementary and Secondary Education: A Framework' (1988), a document prepared by NCERT was an effort to create a common schools system and bind them through a common curriculum framework. It had twin objectives: facilitating the process of curriculum change and institutional reforms. The major emphasis of the framework was on child-centered teaching, re-orientation and in-servicing training of teachers, examination reform, and provision on minimum threshold for institutional facilities. It recommended the participation of local community in the management of schools.

In the backdrop of above analysis it can be said that the efforts of educational reform have been towards achieving uniformity and evenness in the system, preparation of a curriculum that will appreciate and appropriate socio-cultural realities and would respond to social change. However, this has been easy considering the mammoth population of the country, their diverse of background and the federal nature of the country that gave enough freedom to states in developing their own educational policies.

GENERAL OBJECTIVES OF CURRICULUM

In curriculum organization, the formulation of objectives has a significant place because of the fundamental role they play in determining the content, strategies and evaluation as components of curriculum cycle. While identifying objectives, it is necessary to proceed towards various degrees of specificity, from very general objectives of curriculum, through somewhat specific objectives for each stage of education, to precisely stated specific objectives of each subject area in the form of expected learning outcomes indicating what exact behaviour a learner would be able to demonstrate after the curriculum transaction.

School curriculum, on the whole, should aim at enabling the learners to acquire knowledge, develop concepts, and inculcate skills, attitudes, values and habits conducive to the all-round development of their personality and commensurate with the social, cultural, economic and environmental realities at national and international levels. Keeping this in mind our curriculum at various levels of education has been revised and restructured.

An important development in the field of education during the past four decades or so has been the professionalization of curriculum development, syllabus design and the preparation of instructional material including textbooks and their evaluation. The NCERT emerged as a nodal agency at the national level in the area of school education. IT was involved directly in the process of curriculum development and preparation of textbooks. This was gradually followed by the establishment of the State Institutes of Education, State Textbook Boards, and the State Councils of Educational Research and Training for providing technical support to research and development activities related to the formulation of curriculum and the preparation of textbooks at the state/union territory level.

The publication of The Curriculum for the Ten Year School-A Framework (1975), and Higher Secondary Education and its

Vocationalization in 1976by the NCERT gave concrete shape to the efforts for restructuring of school education and the adoption of the 10+2 pattern as recommended by the Education Commission (1964-66). The NCERT then developed supporting syllabi and textbooks to be used as models states and union territories. The Curriculum for the Ten Year School: A Framework (1975) provided an impetus to the teaching of environmental studies, science and mathematics as the part of the general education curriculum from the primary level. The reorientation of science teaching first initiated through the introduction of the new curriculum and the development of the activity based instructional materials, gradually developed into a national movement for popularizing science among school children.

The National Curriculum for Elementary and Secondary Education: A Framework brought out by the NCERT in 1988 responded to the major thrusts and recommendations highlighted in the National Policy on Education (1986) and the Programme of Action (August, 1986) by incorporating the socio-cultural, political and economic considerations as well as some important pedagogical concerns.

The pedagogical issues highlighted in the National Policy on Education (1986) were also adequately reflected in the 1988 curriculum framework. Emphasis was also laid on continuous and comprehensive evaluation as well as on utilization of media and educational technology. In its totality, the curriculum framework of 1988 has contributed to the development of a national system of school education by ensuring uniformity of levels and standards. In addition to this, realization of the goals of enshrined in the Indian Constitution was one of the major objectives of the 1988 curriculum for preparing detailed syllabi for different stages of school education. The state governments also took steps for developing their own curricula, syllabi and instructional materials.

The basic features and main thrusts of the 1988 curriculum framework stem from the policy documents on education (NPE 1986, and POA 1986). While briefly reviewing the implementations of the various thrust areas, one finds that improvement was evident in a number of areas like strengthening and restructuring of teacher education, National Literacy Mission, and improvement of Science Education in Schools, it is felt that much still needs to be done. Of the several thrust areas, only a few could be implemented and that too in a limited manner. A centrally sponsored scheme like 'Operation

Blackboard' providing science kits, musical instruments etc. as one time support should have created much better impact. Obviously, efforts for developing a national system of education as envisaged by the policy makers have to be strengthened further.

The National Curriculum Framework (2005) proposed five guiding principles for curriculum development: (i) connecting knowledge to life outside the schools; (ii) ensuring that learning shifts away from rote methods; (iii) enriching the curriculum so that it goes beyond textbooks; (iv) making examinations more flexible and integrating them with classroom life; and (v) nurturing an overriding identity informed by caring concerns within the democratic polity of the country.

Over the last decade, changes in every walk of human endeavour have been much greater in magnitude and impact as compared to those during the earlier five or six decades. The educational and social demands have changed. In fact, education and learning have undergone a transformation. India and many other countries looked critically on their education systems and have come out with a frank and honest assessment thereof. The Challenge of Education (India, 1985), A Nation at Risk (USA, 1983) and Learning to Succeed (UK, 1993) have looked hard at their national systems of education. At the international level the UNESCO document (1996) Learning the Treasure Within has also taken a critical look at the total educational scenario and made long-range meaningful suggestions. Within the ambit of systems and structures, curriculum design has an important role to play. It is generally accepted that in education curriculum renewal and development is an on-going process and no nation can afford to go slow in the matter. The curriculum must need the learner's needs, societal expectations, community aspirations and international comparisons.

CURRICULUM CONCERNS

Curriculum development essentially is a ceaseless process of searching for qualitative improvement in education in response to the changes taking place in the society. As such it is not static but a dynamic phenomenon. A meaningful school curriculum has to be responsive to the society, reflecting the needs and aspirations of its learners. Even in the new millennium, some of the country's important societal concerns would remain unchanged because these could not be addressed adequately in the past. At the same time, many new concerns have emerged in response to the fast changes in the social scenario of the country as well as the world. The curriculum has to lead a kind of education that would fight against inequality and respond to the social, cultural, emotional, and economic needs of the learners. This would not be possible just with the elements of mediocrity and ordinariness in the entire educational endeavour. Nothing short of excellence in every aspect of school education is the first imperative for meeting the multifarious challenges of today and tomorrow. In other words, the curriculum must stand on the three pillars of relevance, equity and excellence.

Education liberates human beings from the shackles of ignorance, privation and misery. It must also lead to a non-violent and non-exploitative social system. School curriculum, therefore, has to aim at enabling learners to acquire knowledge, develop understanding and inculcate skills, positive attitudes, values and habits conducive to the all round development of their personality. In order to empower young students it is necessary to shift educational priorities.

SCHEME OF STUDIES

The general objective of education will be realized through the content and learning experiences related to different subject areas. However, the emphasis would shift from factual knowledge to the process of understanding, thinking and internalizing. Towards all-round development of personality, value education' health and physical education, art education and work education, have to be given appropriate importance in the school curriculum. The interconnection among various subject areas has to be clearly established. A common scheme of studies, therefore, is advocated for classes I to X. The core component areas and values shall form an integral part of the curriculum at all the stages and may suitably be integrated in different subject areas. Flexibility in the selection of content and organizing learning experiences must be inbuilt in the system. At the secondary stage three languages, mathematics, science and technology, social sciences, work education, art education and health and physical education are in the scheme of studies.

At the secondary stage the student is expected to have full mastery over the applied form of language and good acquaintance with literary language in the first language. Learners have to achieve maturity in oral and written expression in response to what they read or listen to. As far as teaching of mathematics at secondary level is concerned it has to serve two complementary purposes. Firstly, the aim should be to further enhance the capacity of the students to employ mathematics in solving problems that they face in their day-to-day life. Secondly, a systematic study of mathematics as a discipline has to be started here and continued further. The curriculum may include the study of relevant arithmetical concepts, number system, algebra, geometry, trigonometry, coordinate geometry, mensuration, graphs, statistics etc. Similarly, scientific attitude and skills developed at this stage would become foundation for further growth. They need to be exposed to the nature and structure of science and the support it provides to the technological developments. At this stage, learning of science would continue to be built around natural and social elements of environment. Focus should continue on understanding of concepts and application in the areas of matter and its properties, energy, relationship of various physical processes and the technological applications of principles of science. The biological sciences will deal with living organism, their organization and life processes. An integrated approach to science and technology leading to their application in areas like health and nutrition, industry, agriculture and animal husbandry and allied areas would establish linkages of science to societal aspiration.

Contemporary India is the focal theme of social studies, it includes the processes and patterns of man-environment interaction and the issues related to environment, its resources, and development. Major development in recent past including India's struggle for independence, and the contributions of various sections/regions/groups especially the role of women and weaker sections in the movement having bearing on the social, economic and political developments and challenges in the post-independent India will also be covered. Issues and challenges of India such as poverty, illiteracy, corruption, and anti-social practices, fundamental rights, fundamental duties and economic development will be covered appropriately. In addition India's role in the world especially world peace, international cooperation and decolonization may be included. Contributions and achievements of Indians in other countries need to be given due place. At the end of the secondary stage, the students may develop the ability to use their knowledge, understanding and skills by undertaking wide range of studies at various scales—local, regional, national.

Work education is viewed as purposive and meaningful manual work, organized as integral part of the learning process and resulting into goods or services useful to the community besides the pleasure of self-fulfillment. It is an essential component at all stages of education and be provided, through well structured and graded programmes. At the secondary stage, the complexities of activities need to be increased keeping the nature of essential activities, by and large, the same. Pre-vocational course will get a prominent place at this stage, which will facilitate choice of the vocational courses at the higher secondary stage and help them acquire the knowledge and skills required for entry into the world of work.

Similarly, the secondary stage is apt for refining aesthetic sensibilities and social values through projects on conservation of natural and cultural heritage by providing opportunities for study of India culture working with artists/artistes in the community, organizing festivals and celebrations of the community at large, display of physical environment and surrounding landscape and the like. Art education at this stage would comprise, study of visual and aural resources and their exploration; projects leading to creative expression and exhibition of works in visual and aural forms; inter-group and interschool activities; study trips and interaction with artists in the community; and exploration of traditional arts forms including theatrical arts available in the community and neighbourhood.

With regard to physical, mental and emotional health of learners, the secondary stage of education is particularly crucial. Rapid acceleration of growth and changes in appearance and functions of the body associated with the onset of puberty indicates the need of provision of appropriate guidance and counseling that would facilitate the adjustment and growth of children. Interests during this period narrow down to fewer games. The learner is likely to be more adventurous comparatively. Physical education should include more vigorous activities of various sports including athletics, major games including indigenous games, gymnastics, yogic exercises, meditation, combatives, judo and swimming. The NCC, scouting and guiding and social service should be encouraged in addition to the compulsory programmes of physical education. In class IX and X, health education should enable the students to learn, in comparatively great detail, about personal health, impact of environmental pollution on health, food and nutrition, control and prevention of diseases, first aid, home nursing, and safety measures.

Scheme of Studies in Sample States

Following the national curriculum framework (2000), scheme of subjects is suggested by NCERT with some flexibility at state level. The states adopt these subjects taking into account their socio-cultural and political contexts. While some states adopt the NCF prescribed subjects, most of the states consider it as a broad framework and work out their own curriculum.

Table 5.1: Scheme of Subjects at Secondary Level

	Core (Compulsory) Subjects	*Optional Subjects*
National	1. 1st Language 2. 2nd Language 3. 3rd Language 4. Mathematics 5. Science 6. Social Science	1. Work Experience 2. Health & Physical Education 3. Arts/Music/Dance etc. 4. Value Education 5. Environmental Education
Andhra Pradesh	1. 1st Language-Telugu 2. 2nd Language-Hindi 3. 3rd Language-English 4. Mathematics 5. Science 6. Social Science	1. Work Experience 2. Health & Physical Education 3. Art Education-drawing, music, Dance, Creative activities, Essay, Quiz etc. 4. Moral Education 5. Games & Sports Education
Kerala	1. 1st Language-Malalyan/Arbic/Urdu/Sanskrit 2. 2nd Language-English 3. 3rd Language-Hindi 4. Mathematics 5. Science 6. Social Science	1. Work Experience 2. Art Education 3. Health & Physical Education
Maharashtra	1. 1st Language-Marathi 2. 2nd Language-Hindi (50 Marks)+ One of the composite Languages (50 marks), Out of 27 *Indian/Foreign/Classical language* 3. 3rd Language-English 4. Mathematics 5. Science 6. Social Science	1. Work Education, Drawing etc. 2. Health & Physical Education 3. One optional Language *(Out of 27 options)*
Uttar Pradesh	1. 1st Language-Hindi 2. 2nd Language-*One out of 23 Indian/Foreign/Classical language* 3. Mathematics or Home Science (for girls) 4. Science (Integrated) 5. Social Science	1. One Extra Optional Subject-Out of 10 Classical (4) & Foreign (6) Language/Music (2)/Commercial Drawing/Agricultural/Home Science/Sewing/Fine Arts 2. Moral Education/Physical Education, SUPW, SSW and Pre-Vocational

The scheme of subjects in four sample states shows some common pattern in case of core curriculum; at the same time differ in degree particularly in case of optional subjects. As per NFC norm, the three sample states have adopted three-language formula. Surprisingly, U.P. deviated from the NFC norm by not making English compulsory where as third language is equated with some optional vocational subjects. However, this deviation is not unique to U.P. rather is common among a host of northern states. In Maharashtra, in case of second language opportunities are provided to have one more language from the list of 27 languages. Similarly in U.P. one has to choose second language out of 23 languages.

Despite a common national framework, U.P. still has an option of home science for girls and mathematics for boys. In case of A.P. and Kerala science subjects are divided into physical and biological streams whereas in Maharashtra and U.P. it is an integrated subject. Although, all NCF prescribed optional subjects are followed by all the sample states, some states add more subjects taking into account social context. It may be mentioned here that, even before NCF prescription of moral education, the state of Maharashtra had introduced the subject much earlier. Some of the optional subjects like value education are introduced because of political intervention on curriculum, as part of ideology of political parties either at the center or at the state. Similarly, the English language is introduced to some extent due to political and social demands.

At the higher secondary level, NCF (2000) declares number of streams. Students have flexibility to choose any subject. However, as the feasibility and infrastructure do not allow for implementation of NCF norms, states have introduced different choices within streams. Though stream-wise subjects vary, there is more flexibility in subject combinations. For example, in Kerala, students can have choices out of 26 subject combinations in Humanities and 7 combinations in Science. But, this is not the case in A.P. The common thing that emerges is that the frontline areas like IT and computer Science as prescribed in NCF are followed by all states as a response to the demands of such subjects in the society. However, it may be mentioned that new and technical subjects have not been accessible to all students as most of the higher secondary schools have only one stream instead of all streams. In case of Maharashtra, IT has been introduced in some schools as a compulsory subject instead of second language. Moreover, because to a large extent the introduction of such subjects require considerable cost and expertise that rural and disadvantage schools have not been able to bear. Thus limiting these facilities to urban and private aided schools. Data from sample schools also shows that the above subjects (IT and Computers) are available only in urban and private unaided schools. In the context of above observations it can be deduced that though in principle schools offer a variety of choices to students in reality these choices are simply not exercised due to variety of constraints inherent in the system hampering equity and equality aspects of education.

At the higher secondary level, all sample states apart from U.P. follow the two-language formula. There is a wide range of choices available to students in terms of choosing the languages in all states (for example, A.P.=11, Kerala=13, Maharashtra=22 and U.P.=3) More option in case of Maharashtra is largely due to the multilingual nature of the state as a result of number cosmopolitan cities in the state as well as large-scale migrant population. The state also shares its border with five major states with different languages. Some foreign languages are also offered. This is equally true in case of Kerala. With wide range of options in choosing vocational subjects (for example, A.P.=17, Kerala=45, Maharashtra=30 and U.P.=35), it is found that in Maharashtra and U.P. general education students can take some vocational courses whereas in A.P. and Kerala and also in Maharashtra and U.P. vocational courses are separately taught. However, it may be noted that the curriculum of vocational courses has devised in such a way that a student continuing vocational education at higher secondary level can enter into general education at higher education level.

MEDIUM OF INSTRUCTION

National policy recommends that mother tongue/regional language should be the medium of instruction at the school level and most of the states have adopted the policy; in addition the states have also adopted other languages as medium of instruction in view of multi-lingual groups and other social demands. For example, in Maharashtra in addition to the regional language of Marathi, the education is imparted in ten other languages. Similarly, in A.P. and Kerala instructions are given in 9 and 6 languages apart from regional language respectively. Normally, the states have a policy to impart education in languages of bordering states. In addition to regional languages, English being a demanding language is also used as medium of instruction especially in private unaided schools in all states. In Kerala it is included in government and aided schools in class-V. In Maharashtra and A.P. the government has also given permission to unaided schools to introduce English from class 1. With the opening of more English Medium private schools, the number of students receiving education through English medium have increased phenomenally. At the higher secondary level, English has however has been only medium of instruction in some states (e.g. Kerala and Maharashtra) though students are permitted to write public examinations in regional languages. In some other states permission is granted to use both regional language and English (e.g. A.P. and U.P.) as medium of instruction.

Table 5.2: Number of Languages used for Medium of Instruction at Secondary Stage

Andhra Pradesh	*Kerala*	*Maharashtra*	*Uttar Pradesh*
Telugu *(Regional)* English	Malayalam *(Regional)* English	Marathi *(Regional)* English	Hindi *(Regional)* English*
Classical Languages-Urdu, Arabic, Sanskrit, Hindi, Tamil, Marathi, Kanada, Oriya	*Classical Languages*- Arabic, Urdu, Sanskrit, Tamil & Kanada	*Classical Languages*-, Gujarati, Hindi, Sindhi, Kanada, Telugu, Tamil, Bengali, Tibetian	*Classical Languages*- Urdu and Sanskrit

* For Science, Mathematics and Computer Course, English is generally used, as only medium of instruction as the study materials in Hindi is not readily available. However, students can write examination in Hindi.

Distribution of Instructional Time

The NCF (2000) has suggested a minimum of 220 working days per year for transaction of curriculum, evaluation, co-curricular activities etc. However, taking into account the number of days that are spend on unit tests and other examinations, school activities and other unforeseen events, it has been felt that the number of instructional days should not be less than 180 days. Almost all the states follow this national norm. The number of working days in a week has been six for all the sample states at the school level. The school hours is five hours at primary level whereas it is six at the upper primary and secondary level of which five hours is devoted for instructional purposes. The school timings are normally uniform across the states i.e. 9.30 a.m. to 4.30 p.m. with marginal variations. However, the school timings are adjusted in double shift schools. Single shift schools have to seek the prior approval of school management committee and the DEO in order to change school timings. Besides, the school timings are also adjusted according to seasonal demands *viz.* schools operate in morning shift during the summers.

The school hours is further divided into certain number of periods. The number and duration of periods varies among states. For example, the number of periods in A.P. and Kerala is 7 while it is 8 in Maharashtra and U.P. The duration of the period in four sample states ranges from 35-45 minutes. Besides the duration of all period too vary in accordance with the specifications of schools. For example, in Kerala at the secondary level, first 3 periods have duration of 45 minutes, next two periods are of 40 minutes and the last period is of 35 minutes.

At the higher secondary level, the scenario however is slightly different. Although the number of working days per year and per week remains same, number of periods per day, duration of period and school timing differ from the secondary level. For example, in A.P., the school timing is from 9 a.m. to 4 p.m. and the duration of a period is 50 minutes.

Table 5.3: Percentage of Teachers Complete Syllabus Taking Extra Class and Other Short-cut Methods

State	*Extra Class*	*Other Methods**
Andhra Pradesh	33	0
Kerala	34	4
Maharashtra	44	18
Uttar Pradesh	49	0
Total	40	8

* Includes methods of discussion, demonstration, selective teaching, self-study etc.

Normally, teachers follow the annual calendars and monthly plan to complete the syllabus. But this has not helped all teachers to complete syllabus according to plan due to involvement in other out-school and non-academic activities and more number of local holidays. This has made teachers to take extra class. The data obtained from sample teachers (Table 5.3) reveals that 40 per cent of the sample teachers take extra classes and 8 per cent adopt other short-cut methods to complete the syllabus.

Instructional Time for Different Subjects

The NCF (1988) had suggested instructional time weightage for different subjects with some flexibility. However, NCF (2000) did not give any clear-cut guidelines. But states adopt their own norms based on expected workload, subject content etc. At secondary level the total number of periods per week varies from 35 in Kerala to 45 in Maharashtra and 48 in A.P. and U.P. Although the subjects are same in view of curriculum, the extent of time allocation varies among the four sample states. Pie Chart shows the distribution of instructional time (in percentage for major subjects at secondary level.

For the teaching of three languages, NCF (1988) suggested 30 per cent of total time. But it varies from 32 per cent to 40 per cent among states. While in case of Kerala and Maharashtra 40 per cent of time is allotted for three-languages in a week, 32 per cent time is allotted in A.P. However, in U.P. two compulsory languages carry 25 per cent of the total time. Among the three languages maximum time is spend for the first and second language in Kerala and minimum in A.P. Among other core subjects, in A.P. mathematics and science have the same percentage of time while in Kerala and Maharashtra science carries more time weightage than mathematics. In social sciences maximum time is given in Kerala followed by A.P. and Maharashtra and minimum in U.P. Although percentage of time given for different optional subjects widely varies, sometimes it so happens that time allocated for optional subject is used for core subjects.

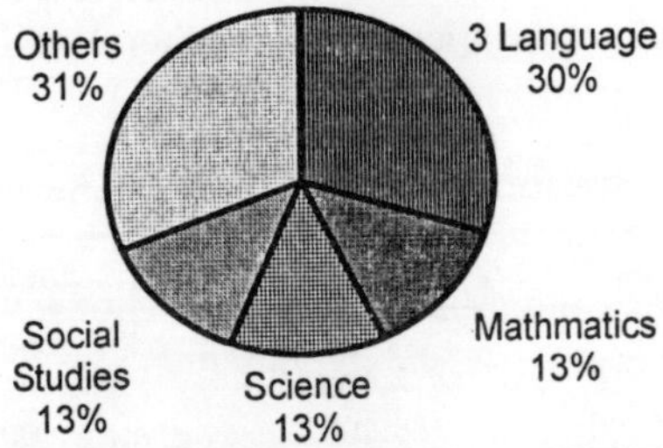

Fig. 5.1: % of Instructional Time as per the NCF 1998

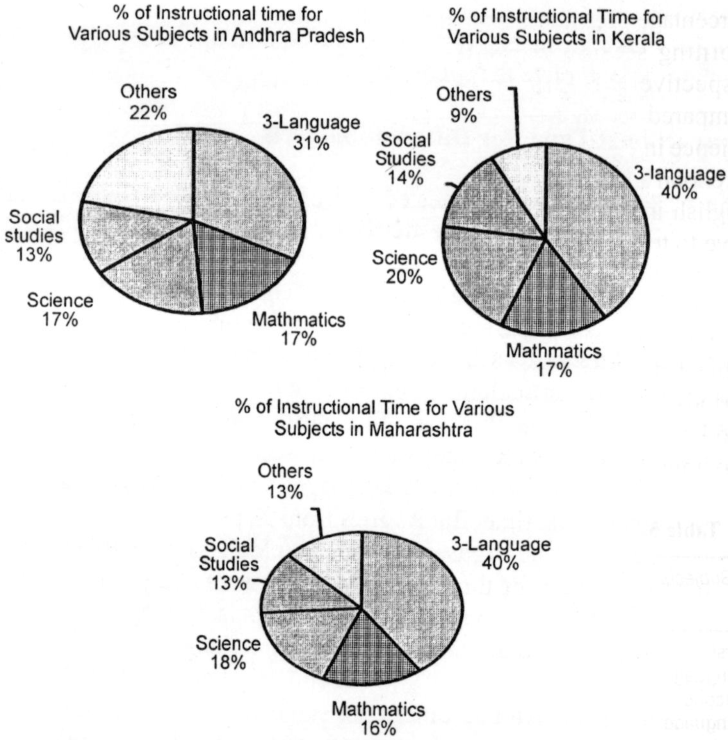

Fig. 5.2: Percentage of Instructional Time

State governments suggests to organize subjects in teaching schedule according to priority. The 'hard subjects' like English, Mathematics and Science should be taught in the first half of the school hour and other subjects like social studies and regional languages in later half. Normally schools teach Mathematics and English during first half. However, some schools adjust the time table according to their convenience and teachers availability.

Table 5.4: Percentage of Sample Schools Teaching Mathematics, English and Science in Morning (Forenoon) Session

State	*Mathematics*	*English*	*Science*
Andhra Pradesh	66	66	55
Kerala	100	83	50
Maharashtra	100	60	80
Uttar Pradesh	81	100	64
Total	84	80	60

Data of sample schools (Table 5.4) shows that at secondary level, percentage of schools teaching Mathematics, English and Science in morning session are 84 per cent, 80 per cent and 60 per cent respectively. Lower percentage of schools teachings science as compared to Mathematics and English is because of two parts of Science in case of A.P. and Kerala in which Science is taught in both forenoon and afternoon sessions. Higher percentage of schools teach English in morning session because in many cases English teacher have to teach social studies.

At higher secondary level subject wise number of periods also vary across the states and streams. This mainly due to the options of optional subjects available in each stream. For the compulsory subject of two languages A.P. and Kerala allots same number of periods (8). Maharashtra allots minimum time periods (6) to these two languages. In U.P. the compulsory subject being one language a maximum of nine periods is allotted.

Table 5.5: Subject-wise Number of Periods at Higher Secondary Level

Subjects	*Andhra Pradesh*	*Kerala*	*Maharashtra*	*Uttar Pradesh*
First Language	7	7	5	9
Second Language	6	6	5	—
Optional Subject 1	7 for Science Group (5 Theory + 2 Practical	8 for Arts, Commerce and Science	6 for Arts & Commerce Groups	9 for Science Group (6 Theory +
Optional Subject 2	12 Mathematics Groups 9 for Humanities	Groups	8 for Science Group (6 Theory + 2	3 Practical) 6 for Arts & Commerce
Optional Subject 3	Group (6 Theory +3 Tutorial)		Practical)	Group
Optional Subject 4				

In case of optional subjects under each stream Kerala allots same number of periods but it varies in other three sample states. Maximum number of periods is allotted for science subjects in U.P. (9) and minimum in A.P. (7). On the other hand time period allotted for arts and commerce subjects is maximum in A.P. (9) and minimum in Maharashtra and U.P. (6).

EVALUATION AND ASSESSMENT

Student evaluation and assessment is a critical area in educational pedagogy, in fact it is crucial to teaching-learning process. With an emphasis on examinations the educational system prevalent in India ostensibly attempted to evaluate students at various stages of learning but more often than not these attempts were haphazard, unsystematic and were certainly not directed towards cumulative assessment of learning skills as a feedback to teachers. It would not be out of context to assert that examinations were held more of a routine and elimination process rather than evaluative of teaching-learning method. However, over the last decade or so attempts have been made to do away with excessive examination of final examination and bring more parity and critical input in assessment and evaluation system. Continuous evaluation and assessment of students performance has evolved as a general norm. The results of these assessments are also being regarded as feedback for measuring teacher's performances so that improvement in those areas can be made. It has been able to de-link students from the fear of examination and has also provided teachers with feedback on their own shortcomings.

Following the national norm, all the state governments have prescribed Continuous and Comprehensive Evaluation (CCE) in terms of unit tests and terminal examinations. All the sample states normally prescribe four unit tests besides half-yearly and annual examinations. However, in A.P. quarterly examination has also been introduced along with other two exams. In case of unit test, syllabus is divided into a few units and tests are being conducted at the end of teaching each unit. Though state prescribes 4 unit tests, at the school level, more or less than four unit tests are also in practice in some schools (Table 5.6). As shown, in the four sample states, about 40 per cent of the schools have more than four unit tests. It may be noted that these schools are normally high performed schools irrespective of management types.

Table 5.6: Percentage of Sample Schools (N = 48) with Number of Unit Tests Conducted

No. of Unit Test	*Andhra Pradesh*	*Kerala*	*Maharashtra*	*Utter Pradesh*	*Total*
2 Unit test	11	0	66	14	26
3 Unit test	22	30	0	0	13
4 Unit test	0	0	33	28	15
5 Unit test	0	30	0	0	7
6Unit test	22	0	0	0	5
More than 6 Unit test	44	40	0	57	31

Source: Case Studies of Sample Schools.

Besides these schools also have weekly and monthly assignments as well as slip tests. Results of all these tests and term examinations taken into account for the promotion to higher classes. The Student Evaluation Profile (SEP) for each student as in the case of Kerala shows the details of the developmental aspects of a student in scholastic and co-scholastic areas in all subjects in an academic year. All these tests help in maintaining continuity in studies and a holistic assessment. In view of bringing significant changes in pedagogy where student's evaluation could be treated as an integral part of teaching-learning process rather than being relegated to a routine work, in recent times the CCE has drawn much attention in the evaluation reform process

National Curriculum Preparation

National Curriculum prepared by NCERT is prescriptive in nature and is not forced either on schools or on states. As result a lot of variation occurs in educational sectors as far as curriculum is concerned. Some states simply follow the national curriculum while other states and agencies adopt the national curriculum with some modifications. However, largely schools affiliated to Central Board of Secondary Education (CBSE), Central Schools, Navodaya Vidyalays follows national curriculum. NCERT takes a lot of care while preparing national curriculum involves functionaries and experts from all states in the process so as to incorporate a pan –Indian perspective. The NCERT expects the states to follow national curriculum with modifications of their own. To this end states normally adopt about 70 per cent of national curriculum. States of course, have more flexibility in determining the optional subjects.

Designing the Curriculum

Curriculum designing is both an interesting and complex issue, which reflects the diversity, and difficulties involved in the process both at the state and national level. Besides, it also provides units for comparison among states in the process of curriculum designing. The NCERT in-house committee discusses the issue of curriculum and is debated upon this later takes the form of a discussion paper. Over the discussion paper a braining storming session is held and experts are consulted and a draft paper is released. The draft paper is widely circulated among the general public, educationists, teachers, subject experts etc. and public attention is drawn towards the issue. National, regional and local level seminars and conferences are organized to highlight the issue.

From time to time the NCERT conducts research and analysis over various points and sub points involved in the draft proposal. While the issue is on the public domain the media plays a significant role in intensifying the debate with strong ideological currents. NCERT consolidates these diverse opinions and prepares its report, which it sends to Central Advisory Board on Secondary Education (CBSE)-an advisory body consisting of education ministers of all states. Once it is passes by the CBSE the document becomes a base document for the country for secondary education. The NCERT then of course, involves itself in the task of preparation of textbooks on the line of curriculum designed by it.

Given the federal nature of the country and inter-regional variation it is only natural that states are given relative freedom in developing their own curriculum. But it is quite interesting to note that despite such freedom rarely the states take any initiative in designing and restructuring the curriculum on their own. As a result states are mostly dependent NCERT for curriculum development and when they restructure, adopt or modify their curriculum on the lines of NCERT the variations can be gauged. Some states follow it in totality, other states adopt it with slight changes and a few other change it substantially to meet their own needs. At the state level it is the Boards of Secondary and Higher Secondary Education are responsible for curriculum designing and where they are either weak or at a nascent stage SCERT takes the task on to it.

Curriculum Designing in Sample States

In Maharashtra and U.P. the Board of Secondary and Higher Education play important role in the process of curriculum designing while in A.P. and Kerala the SCERT has a greater role. In Maharashtra the process of curriculum designing has been a very comprehensive and systematic and the entire exercise is administered under the auspice of Board of Secondary Education (see the diagram). In Maharashtra, the Board of Secondary and Higher Secondary

Education has 38 Board of Studies for different subjects. These Board of Studies are statutory committees and are responsible for designing curriculum for respective subjects for classes of IX-XII. These Boards of Studies comprises of nine members who are drawn from a pool consisting of principals, teachers, educationists, members from the university department of education, representatives from the regional board of education etc.

In Maharashtra the curriculum designing process begins with the dissemination of national curriculum to schools, parents, teachers and teacher's associations, and a vast section of public through media for generating awareness and debate. A cross section of public was involved in the process of opinion making and suggesting alternatives so the needs and demands of various strata of a society could be incorporated. A questionnaire is circulated among head teachers, teachers, parents, educationists, social workers, people representatives, education officers etc. and also is published in the newspaper asking people to respond and suggest for improving secondary curricula. These responses then become the strong base background for preparing a background paper, which later discussed, debated and shared in various forums. Later these views are compiled and given to the subject committees who in turn prepare a curriculum based on the line of national curriculum while including local specifications. The committees are also engaged in making a comparative analysis of curriculum of different states and the draft curriculum is prepared. Once the draft curriculum is passed by the Executive Council and General Body of the State Board of Secondary and Higher Secondary Education, it is send to schools, educationists and parents for comments. Necessary inputs are incorporated and the draft curriculum is submitted to the government for final approval.

Though Uttar Pradesh have a Board of Secondary Education that is entrusted with the task of curriculum designing the realities are far from satisfactory. The state does have subject committees responsible for designing curriculum for respective subjects but its nature is largely ad hoc. Members of these expert committees are drawn from schoolteachers, subject experts, educationists and teachers from the university department of education. There are seven members in the committee and the selection of these members is rather dubious. Many experts do not show much interest to join the committee as there are no honorariums involved and in the absence of serious minded people the State Board has to fall back on same people time and again. There are also political interference and push and pull factors involved in the selection of these members making the process ineffective and routine.

In case of Andhra Pradesh the process of curriculum designing if not as rigorous and systematic like Maharashtra but is more organized than Uttar Pradesh. In A.P. curriculum designing is the responsibility of SCERT in the absence of a strong and vibrant State Board. However, the curriculum development committee formed under the aegis of SCERT consists of teachers, representatives of teacher's associations, students and members from the education department. The department of education constitutes the expert committee on curriculum with sub-committees for different subjects who are responsible for working out syllabus for different subjects and preparing textbooks. This committee prepares the draft curriculum while the entire exercise is coördinated by the SCERT.

In Kerala the task of curriculum designing rests with a body known as State Curriculum Steering Committee (CSC), which acts in collaboration with SCERT. The CSC comprises of 45 members, all the directors of education, representatives of teacher organizations, director of one of the IITs, director of SCERT, education experts from the University and colleges etc. and this committee is chaired by the minister of education. Debates, discussions and inputs of the meetings of CSC are used for further deliberation and the SCERT coordinates the entire exercise. Based on the information the CSC prepares the vision document, publishes, circulates and solicits the responses of public and professionals. For each subject there is a sub-committee of 15 members. The sub-committee for particular subject prepares the objectives of subjects for particular classes. The same committee is also responsible for preparing the lesson-plans and textbooks.

The study of the procedures and practices involved in the exercise of curriculum designing entails us in finding some commonality and units of comparison among various states. First of all, it can be said that curriculum development is entirely a central exercise in the sense that no states come forward to prepare its own curriculum on its own before the national curriculum is published.

Secondly, despite the importance and seriousness of curriculum development and designing, the states have shown a very low level of intensity and activism with exception of few states. Ad-hocism, lethargy and non-seriousness rules the roost as far as curriculum development is concerned. Subjects experts do not come to meetings, are meeting are not held, draft papers are rarely placed before the public, choice of experts are largely arbitrary and suggestions of public rarely incorporated.

Thirdly, the states differ from each other as far as their choice of agency for curriculum designing is concerned. In Maharashtra and Uttar Pradesh is it respective Boards of Education while in case of Kerala and Andhra Pradesh the responsibility is of SCERT.

Fourthly, it is important to involve various agencies, public at large and Non-Governmental Organizations in the consultation process prior to designing the curriculum, as everybody is a stakeholder in the entire exercise. Wider consultation process in framing the curriculum in Maharashtra with its conspicuousness has helped the state in incorporating the contextual reality to a large extent. This is quite uncommon in many a state and is patently conspicuous in its absence in Uttar Pradesh.

It is rather disturbing to note that Uttar Pradesh with its large size and relative lack of diversity and Kerala with its high level of literacy and professionalism have not developed a comprehensive and systematic mechanism for curriculum designing. The reason behind such low level of participation and lackadaisical approach may have been rooted in a general sense of indifference towards curriculum. Curriculum development process in general too suffers from the following lacunas.

Lack of empirical research in the field of curriculum development is solely responsible for low level of awareness and lack of quality in curriculum designing. In fact, over the years according to V Survey of India Education Report research on curriculum has dwindled over the years. There have been only 23 studies conducted on the theme and only four of them are in secondary education.

Lack of rigorousness and professionalism has been the bane of curriculum designing at the state level. The curriculum designing exercise is carried as a matter of routine rather than of rigorousness. For example, in U.P. where the expert committee is ad hoc, experts

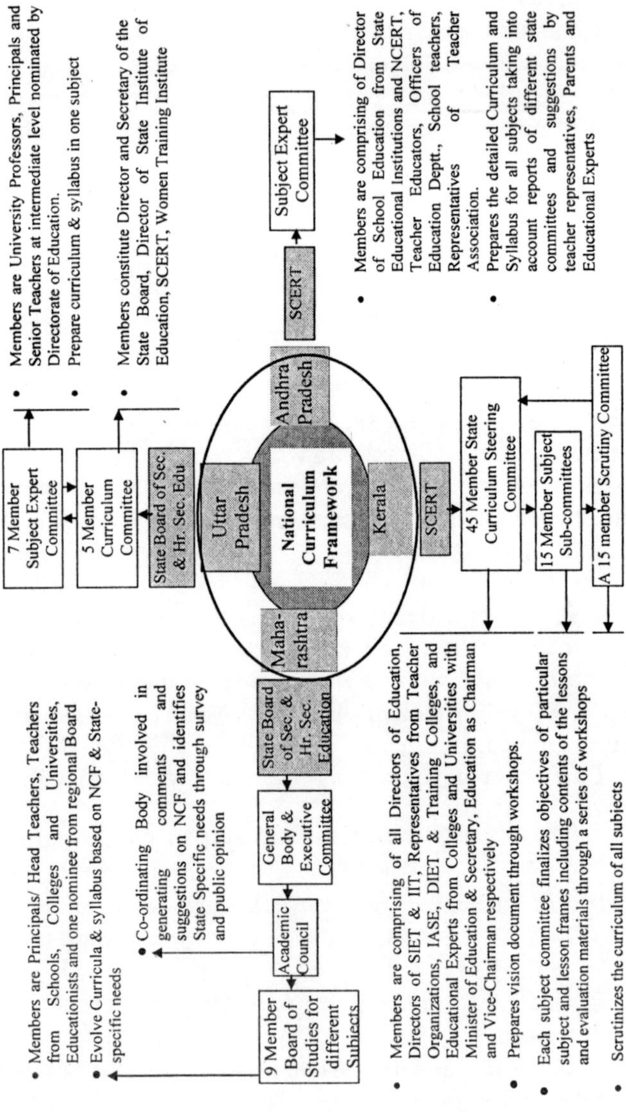

Figure 5.3: Process of Curriculum Development

refuse to become members because they are not given any honorarium, political interference is rampant and work ethic is non-existent. Further, pilot surveys are not conducted on curriculum development making the entire exercise redundant.

Another important dimension of curriculum designing is the political overtones of education. Politicians do not involve themselves or are not party to curriculum preparation which is essentially an academic exercise but of late with publication of the draft document and increasing role of media in dissecting it has brought political attention. Modern politicians also have taken an interest in the curriculum development exercise, as they are required to respond to public debate over the issue. As politics has become a site of communitarian and sectarian debate it is needless to add that education in general and curriculum development in particular has become level playing field for politicians in providing them an opportunity to publicly express their growing tendency of cultural identity.

It would be pertinent to site the case of 'history education' that become a major political issue between the politicians belong to left and right of Indian politics. While the right wing politicians were keen on 're-writing' the history textbooks so that it can glorify the ancient civilization of India and inculcate a sense of nationalist spirit among the children, the left reaction was swift and sharp. Branding the exercise as 'safronization' of education the left opposed the entire exercise tooth and nail though the government of the day saw to it that textbooks are re-written. But with the change of government at the center the 'de-toxification' exercise is on in order to cleanse the system.

This is not only a national phenomenon but has its reflections in the state as well and one can cite the examples of Madhya Pradesh, Uttar Pradesh, Maharashtra, Rajasthan etc. However, it may be added that the politicization of curriculum development exercise is more at work where the power play is on between two mutually exclusive ideologies than in governments of conciliation and compromise.

PREPARATION AND DISTRIBUTION OF TEXTBOOKS

The quality of teaching learning process largely depends on the availability of teaching learning materials. In the Indian context, textbooks are the main source of teaching and learning of the subjects, which are available at both national and state levels. At the national level, National Council of Educational Research and Training (NCERT) publishes textbooks for all classes at the school level. These books are mainly adopted by schools under central government and also private unaided schools affiliated to Central Board of Secondary Education (CBSE). Some of the states also have been implementing NCERT textbooks, particularly at higher secondary level. In the preparation of these textbooks NCERT follows rigorous procedure. It identifies subject experts, practitioners, teachers, educationists and set up different subject committees to prepare the syllabus in different subjects. The finalization of the syllabus takes a considerable time, as it requires a lot of discussion in workshops and inputs from others (especially people associated with education). Like the curriculum and syllabus preparation, NCERT produces the final form of manuscript after a lot of brain storming sessions and reviews. The NCERT prints the textbooks through private publishers and distributes them through registered booksellers all over the country.

The textbooks at secondary level are nationalized in all the states in order to control quality and ensure timely availability and affordability. The preparation of textbooks is a long and cumbersome process. However, the approach and strategies adopted in textbook preparation, the agencies and organizations involved in preparation of textbooks vary among the states. Normally, it is the responsibility of either the State Board of Secondary Education or SCERT in preparing textbooks. States also have textbook bureau (e.g. Maharashtra) or textbook office (e.g. Kerala), which take responsibility of printing and distributions of textbooks. However, in some of the states textbook preparation is also entrusted or offered to private publishers, though the State Board or SCERT provides syllabus and guidelines and also approves textual materials for final printing. This is especially common in case of higher secondary education. Textbook preparation normally takes place when there is curriculum revision. However, every year, before reprinting of textbooks, necessary changes are made based on feedback from teachers and parents.

How Textbook is Prepared?

The preparation of textbook requires professionalism and knowledge of subjects, didactic principles and evaluation methods. In most of the states, textbook is prepared by a team of people (committee) consisting the teachers, subject experts, teacher educators etc. Different strategies are adopted in preparation of textbooks Among four sample states, while in Maharashtra and U.P., State Board of Secondary Education plays crucial role in the preparation of textbooks, in Kerala and A.P., the responsibility is that of SCERT.

In Maharashtra, although State Board takes the responsibility in preparation of textbooks, the textbook bureau is entrusted with the task of printing and distribution. The State Board sets up textbook writing groups, the members of which are normally experienced teachers from secondary and higher secondary schools and universities. One of the members of each of the 38 Board of Studies coordinates the textbook writing. The textbook writers consult Board of Studies, collect relevant materials/literature from various sources, compare the textbooks of other states and then prepare the draft textbooks. The issues related to number of lessons, pages, question paper formats, marking scheme etc. are discussed in workshops and necessary revisions are made. The revised manuscripts later are sent to three reviewers. The comments and suggestions made by the reviewers are incorporated after a discussion with the Board of Studies. The entire work is done under the roof of the State Board. Academic Council in the State Board scrutinizes the revised manuscripts and finally the manuscript is sent to the Executive Committee and General body of the State Board for approval; and once it is approved, the final manuscripts is sent to the State Textbook Bureau for textbooks production and distribution. This rigorous process however is not found in all the sample states, especially in U.P. While in case of Maharashtra, a full cycle of procedure is followed, in U.P. it is very simplified process. The textbook preparation is entrusted to private publishers. A hand full of experts decided by the private publishers writes the textbook. But it is scrutinized by the curriculum committee in the State Board and reviewed by experts under the control of the state Board. In A.P. and Kerala, the process of textbook writing is coordinated by SCERT and it takes ample time in finalizing the manuscript of Textbook, while it goes through several steps. SCERT follows similar steps as the SBSHSE in Maharashtra. In these three states, the important aspect in preparation of the textbook is that the manuscripts are tried out in the schools and necessary modifications are made and final form of manuscript is produced. Finally, the textbook manuscript is send for approval of Board or SCERT and from there to government.

At the higher secondary level (Classes XI and XII), in Maharashtra, the State Board prepares only language textbooks. Private publishers are encouraged to publish other than language textbooks after due approval from the State Board and they submit the manuscripts of the textbooks based on syllabi. The procedure for the production of the textbooks other than languages of classes XI-XII is more or less same as in case of secondary text books in terms of scrutiny, reviewing by experts, approval of several bodies etc. A complete secrecy is maintained regarding the publishers and expert reviewers. More or less similar pattern is followed in case of U.P. In Kerala, except language, the SCERT adopts the textbook of NCERT with slight modification. In A.P., except language, for preparation of other textbooks, the responsibility is given to private publishers. The intermediate Board itself prepares the language textbooks through State Telugu Academy. However, the Boards in A.P., Kerala and Maharashtra have control over the quality and price of the textbooks published by the private publishers.

Printing and Distribution of Textbooks

Normally, textbook bureau and textbook offices at the state level have printing facilities. However, it does not suffice of all the requirements of large quantity. As such, they outsource the textbook printing through private printers but have control over quality and price. While in A.P. and Kerala, the government printing press prints some books; in Maharashtra and U.P. the whole printing business is in the hand of private printers.

Distribution of textbook is a gigantic task in view of length and breadth of the states, transport problem etc., the common problem as such, is of delayed reaching at school level. However, several steps have been taken in recent years, for on time delivery and access of textbooks to all students. Towards this, textbook distribution mechanism is highly decentralized by creating network and involving several agencies at different levels. The states like U.P., A.P. and Maharashtra have been able to establish textbook depots and entrust responsibility on DEOs to ensure textbooks distribution in time. In case of Maharashtra, for the effective and efficient distribution of the textbooks, the Bureau has implemented the schemes of

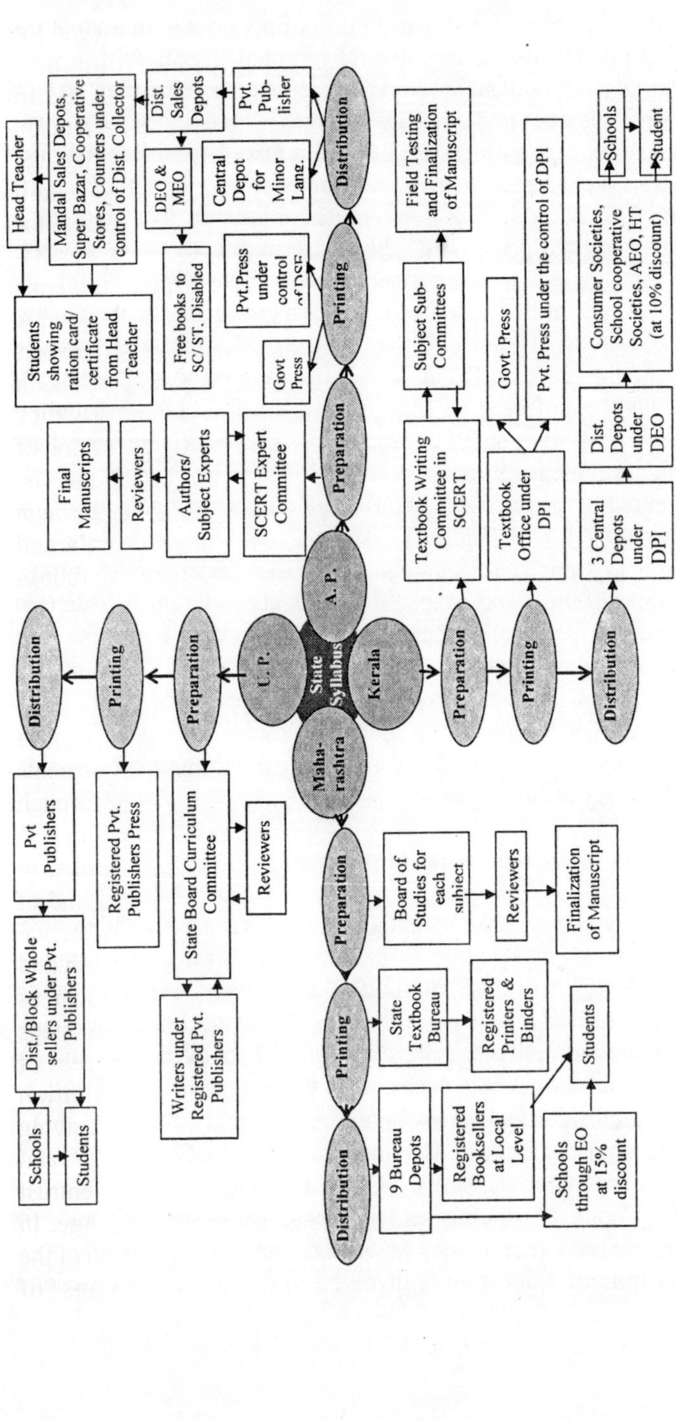

Fig. 5.4: Process of Preparation, Printing and Distribution of Textbooks at Four Sample

decentralization of sale and distribution of textbooks. In addition to Central Book Depots, it has several regional depots with a good networking with booksellers/retailers, consumer societies, school cooperative societies and other agencies registered under the Bureau. The booksellers are entitled to 15 per cent discount on original price of the textbooks, and receive the books from depots with cash payment. The book selling is monitored to ensure that no book is sold above printed price. The schools can buy books directly from depots through education officers in a discount rate, which the booksellers are entitled. It so happens that a group of schools together buy books directly from Depots and this provides monetary benefits to schools. In case of A.P. and Kerala, in addition to state level and regional level monitoring, DEO is given responsibility for distribution. However, in U.P., they solely depend on agencies of private publishers, which is not the case in other states. Under the Book Bank scheme implemented by government, the Bureau makes the books available to the various Local Bodies (District Councils) Zilla Parishads according to their requirements. The Zilla Parishads do further distributions of the books to specified students under the jurisdiction. In general, the price of textbooks in Indian context is not far from affordability of all students. Free textbooks are also distributed to SC/ST students. With all streamlining of preparation, printing and distribution of textbooks, there is still problem of delivery in time, and especially when textbooks are revised. Even though, this problem is tackled it is not fully solved.

Preparation of Instructional Materials

In view of revised syllabi and textbooks, efforts are extended towards effective teaching-learning process by developing instructional materials in the form of handbook for teachers/teachers' guide, workbooks for students, learning kits, model answer books etc. These materials are normally prepared and published by the constituent bodies of state education department those take responsibility in developing curriculum and textbooks. Accordingly, the State Board of Secondary Education in Maharashtra and SCERT in A.P. Kerala prepares these materials. However, in U.P. though the State Board of Secondary Education publishes textbooks, it prepares only modern papers related to examinations for teachers and students whereas the State Institute of Education is involved in developing instructional materials like teachers' training guide, subject teachers' handbook etc. for the secondary school teachers. The instructional materials in all the sample states are normally prepared with the assistance from Association of Head teachers and subject teachers. The process of preparation of these materials is however is not that rigorous and time consuming like the preparation of textbooks.

Curriculum of Teacher Education

Effective teacher education is an essential condition for the quality education. Pre-service teacher education helps in systematic professional induction in all the prospective student teachers to cope with changing needs of classroom situation. Towards this, curriculum of pre-service teacher education particularly at secondary education (i.e. B.Ed.) is revised under the guidelines of National Council of Teacher Education (NCTE) and University Grants Commission (UGC). However, this is not a necessarily sequel to the curriculum revisions for students at secondary level. The B. Ed. course content is largely not revised to suit the changing curriculum and teaching methods at secondary level. Very often the age-old syllabus with slight modifications is used.

However, whenever curriculum at secondary level is revised, in-service teacher training is undertaken at state and regional levels for all teachers. In some states, subject-wise special training programmes are conducted for teachers, especially in 'hard subjects' like Mathematics, English and Science. In fact, all these in-service training programmes at state level are not so rigorous rather a normal practice focusing mainly on content of new subjects. Teachers are only familiarized about the new contents and evaluation procedures. As such, no systematic mechanism has been developed to provide on job support.

The management of quality in B.Ed. course content is affected by many factors. Opening-up of more number of unaided secondary schools has created demand for teacher education. As a result, in many cases teacher education is highly commercialized being under the control of private institutions. Students are admitted based on some sorts of considerations rather merit. Sometimes, course is not conducted as per the need of student-teachers rather for the sake of completion. As in the case of Kerala, some private institutions complete teaching in three to four months (State Education Commission, 1999). The self financed University teacher education centres have less facilities to impart effective teacher training. The changing needs and challenges in the classroom situation are less addressed during training programme. There is no uniformity in the curriculum used for secondary teacher education. The curriculum for B. Ed. differs between conventional University and Open university training courses. There is little scope for the prospective teachers to understand the different dimensions involved in the pedagogy applicable for secondary education.

In recent years, in A.P. and Kerala, reforms in the form of inclusion of new areas, teaching practice, internship, school experiences, assignments etc. are undertaken. Efforts are made to bring uniformity in curriculum. In Kerala, Quality Improvement Programmes (QIP) through teacher training at secondary level is implemented from 2003-04.

The fact that despite all Educational Policies suggesting reforms in teacher education in the context of qualitative improvement in school education, no serious efforts have been made towards teacher education curriculum and in-service training programmes.

MANAGEMENT OF EXAMINATIONS

Examination Frame Work

Evaluation of students' performance include both internal and public examinations. Schools conduct internal examinations for class promotion as well as for screening before selecting them for public examinations. Towards this, the prescribed course content in to various units and unit wise tests are conducted with an objective of continuous evaluation process. In addition to unit tests, quarterly, half yearly and annual examinations are also conducted as prescribed the education department in the sate. The government/local body schools and private aided schools follow the prescribed norms. The number of unit tests may vary among different states.

The results of all unit tests are taken in to account along with half yearly and annual examinations for promotion to higher classes. In some of the states a cumulative record of internal assessment is maintained. Internal evaluation is in vogue for all the classes at secondary level, while at the end of X and XII grades students have to appear for public examinations in all the states.

However, among some of the management schools tests are

conducted more frequently like weekly tests, lesson wise test, slip tests etc. This practice is more often seen among private unaided management schools and also among pace setting schools and residential schools run by central and state governments. One of the common features found in effective schools was adoption of frequent student evaluation called as continuous comprehensive evaluation. This helps to identify areas of difficult for individual students and take remedial measures and addition academic support system. Some of the private unaided schools targeting high performance in public examinations adopt daily tests and also train students in time management during examinations. Even the private tuition or coaching centers too adopt regular testing of students as they prepare students examination point of view.

Process of Conduction of Public Examinations

All the states have state level institutional arrangement for managing public examinations of secondary and higher secondary levels. While in some states the State Board of Secondary /Higher Secondary / Intermediate Education are responsible in conduction of public examinations, where as in others, state level Boards of Examination were established exclusively for conduct of public examinations. In Uttar Pradesh and Maharashtra the State Board of Secondary and Higher Secondary/Intermediate is responsible for managing the public examination through regional/divisional boards, where as in Andhra Pradesh and Kerala Board of Examination is constituted for conduction of public examinations with the assistance District Education Officers. The process and procedure of public examinations at the end of X and XII grade are largely common across the states though are some variations. While in larger states the state board of secondary education has divisional or regional boards as in the case of Uttar Pradesh and Maharashtra, in some states the secondary board of examinations with the assistance of District Educational Officer organize the public examinations. Normally public examinations are conducted twice in a year.

Conduct of Public examination at secondary level is one of the most sensitive facet educational management in India as it involves not only a very cumbersome process but also involves confidentiality. It is also extremely challenging considering the magnitude of examinees, very large number of examination centers and in a culture where passing in the public examination is the ultimate objective of schooling from the viewpoint of education system and society at large. As a result organization of examinations is ridden with risk of encountering several problem like leakage of question papers, malpractices and cheating/ mass copying, mistakes in evaluation and delay in the process of results etc. Above all in recent years any problems in conduction of public examinations has become an opportunity to opposition political parties to pull the ruling party. Equally the media plays a watchdog role to publicise the failures. There has been a common criticism from several quarters on reliability and relevance of public examination system in India as it only test the memory of students and less scope to examine the competencies, comprehension and application of knowledge in addition it lacks reliability.

In recent years many state governments in India have initiated important reforms in public examination system to improve credibility and relevance and to meet emerging challenges in education. However, the nature and extent of policy changes vary among different states. In recent years one of the most important radical change in public examination system was introduction of new pattern of question papers focusing on comprehension and application by objective and short answer type questions in some of the sates like Andhra Pradesh, Kerala, Uttar Pradesh and Maharashtra. The new pattern of question paper reduces scope to students for copying. The change in the question paper pattern also helped to reduce variations in evaluation of answer sheets by different evaluators. In order to restrain the question paper leakages, all the four sample states have adopted a change in strategy of question papers preparation. All the four states get prepared more than one set of question papers by different panel of experts for every subject and select randomly one set in order to arrest the question paper leakage which is a common problem. Flying squads, videography are used to stop copying and cheating in examinations. Some of the states have introduced a new policy of 'SAY'(Save A Year) with a view to save one academic year for those who fail in X and XII grade public examinations, an instant supplementary examinations are conducted with in 20-25 days of publishing results, so those who can pass in this examination can join higher classes without wasting one year. However, this policy is implemented in Andhra Pradesh, Kerala and Uttar Pradesh where as Maharashtra still follows the old method of having supplementary examinations in the month September. The state board of secondary education in Maharashtra, recently adopted the scheme of central evaluation and cross moderation at higher secondary level for subjects like physics, chemistry, biology, mathematics, electronics electrical and mechanical maintenance in order to ensure uniform and reliable assessment.

Copying and cheating in public examinations has been one of the common problems in all the states. Restraining copying is difficult as it involves parents, school staff and community at large. In order to improve the credibility of public examinations and to control copying and cheating in examinations, some of the states have adopted innovative strategies to restrict the chances of copying and cheating. One of the changes was that students are allotted examination center other than their own school, and invigilators are drawn from other than the examination center school. In Andhra Pradesh, jumbling system has been adopted to allot examination centre. In this method students of same school are allotted to different examination centers by drawing random numbers. Same procedure is adopted while allotting invigilators to different examination centers. In order to facilitate speedy evaluation and to arrest malpractices in evaluation of answer sheets most of the states have introduced the system of spot evaluation method through different subject centers.

Considering growing size of examinees, one of the important initiatives has been espousal of information technology in managing the examination system. To improve the pace and accuracy of processing the examination results and to eliminate malpractices in organization of examinations computerization has been adopted. While all the four sample sates have been using computers in managing public examinations, there are variations among sates in the extent of use and for different functions. The processing of applications, issuing of examination hall tickets, preparation of results have been fully computerized in Maharashtra, Andhra Pradesh, Kerala and Uttar Pradesh. Similarly Maharashtra has introduced 'Bar' code system on answer sheets to conceal the seat number and identification of students in order check malpractices and manipulation at the stage of evaluation. The states like Maharashtra and Andhra Pradesh provides on line information about examination results and other details. In fact the state secondary board in Maharashtra going a step ahead by developing on line 'Question Bank' and its data bank collects and disseminates information regarding examinations.

Organisation of Public Examinations in Sample States

The State Board of Secondary and Higher Secondary/Intermediate/ Board of Examination is (are) responsible for the entire process of conduct of public examinations with the assistance of Regional/ Divisional Boards and District Education Officer. The process and procedure adopted for conducting public examinations by different states have similarities as well as some variations. In all the states the policy regarding pattern of public examinations, norms and rules are framed at state level by the secondary and higher secondary education boards or examination boards and get the approval of state government. The state level boards decide the general conditions governing admission of regular and private candidates. It undertakes tasks related to selection of question paper setters, moderators, translators, examiners for evaluation of answer scripts, printing of question papers, process and declaration of results and award of certificates etc. in addition to facilitating smooth conduct of examinations by the regional/division boards and District Education Officers.

Conducting of public examinations is long, complex and arduous, therefore, execution of examination is largely decentralized. In states like Uttar Pradesh and Maharashtra the regional/divisional boards of secondary education are responsible for looking after all the logistics and smooth conduct of public examinations including registration of students, organizing examinations and evaluation of answer scripts in their jurisdiction with the assistance of district education officers etc. In Andhra Pradesh and Kerala the District Education Officers are responsible for conduct of public examinations at the directions of state board of examinations. Preparation for the public examinations starts as early as in the month of July. Applications are invited from schools through the regional/divisional boards and DEO for sanction of examination center. According to norms and rules the examination centers are sanctioned to schools based on number of students, existing centers in vicinity etc. Registration of students to appear in public examinations for regular and private students is made through DEO and regional/divisional boards. The Examination Committee of State Board of Secondary Education or the Members of Examination Board select the question paper setters, examiners of answer scripts from the applications forwarded by the regional/division boards or DEO. The selection is based on educational qualification and seniority. In all the states, it is mandatory for all the teachers of government/local body and private aided schools to accept the duty for invigilation of examinations. During the first quarter of academic year the schools send the names of students for registration to appear for examinations. The private candidates have choice either through the examination centres or DEO who in turn send to regional or division/state level board. The nominal rolls of students are prepared and hall tickets sent to respective schools. The hall ticket shows student identification and in some states the it has the photo of the students for avoiding any impersonation.

At state level the selected experts prepare the question papers for different subjects. While the entire process of question paper preparation is a confidential, still the states adopt several strategies to prevent the leakage of question papers. In recent years in some of the states including Uttar Pradesh, Andhra Pradesh and Kerala, 4-5 sets of question papers are got prepared and after moderation one or two sets are randomly picked up for final printing preferably outside the state. However, in case of Maharashtra only one set of question paper is prepared. The paper setter submits the question paper in a sealed cover and the same is sent for printing without opening out side the state. This methods some times results with errors in question paper which are detected only during examination. In Uttar Pradesh and Andhra Pradesh two sets of question papers are printed, if the question paper leaks before examination, the second set is used. In case if the information about question paper leakage is known later and no time to for using the second set, re-examination is held on another date. To arrest the question paper leak the state Andhra Pradesh has adopted different strategy, two sets of question papers are sent to all examination centers and only one hour before examination commences state level administration announces the number of set to be used for the day. This method has been effective in preventing the question papers becoming public before the examinations. In most states, the sealed packets of question papers are dispatched to the storage points with safe custody under the police escort. The storage points vary among different states. The police stations, banks, treasuries are identified as storage points in different states. While in Andhra Pradesh the Question papers are kept in sealed trunks day wise in nearest police station to the examination centers and arrangements are made for delivery of question papers at the examination centre just one hour before the commencement of examination. The chief superintendent of the examination centre and the custodian/officer of educational department jointly unseal the packet. The whole process of day today conduct of examinations is closely monitored from the state head quarters by conducting teleconferences every day evening. For the last six years the state has been successful in conducting examinations without having any complaints of question paper leakage. In Uttar Pradesh and Maharashtra, the sealed packets are deposited in banks, treasure, or under the direct custody of District Magistrate. In some states the sealed question papers are under the custody of one of the examination centers in the area. Accountability is fixed up at every level. With all precautions, there are cases of question paper leak in some states and the leak out can be from different sources including from printers. There are cases of question papers are sold and people purchase paying good amount. One of the main problem is the large size and involvement several people at different levels. The keen competition among the private sector schools to evince high performance, in such cases the managements adopt unscrupulous ways and means to acquire question papers in advance. Cases of such fraud were made big news in recent years in some states.

One of the important aspect in managing public examinations is manning the examination centres and making sure that no undesirable means are adopted by the students. There is variation among the sates with regard to allocation of examination centre for students to write examinations. Earlier students of a school where the examination centre is located are allowed to write examinations in the same school along with other candidates from other nearby schools. The invigilators are deployed from other schools to overlook the examination halls. This practice is still in vogue in Kerala, Maharashtra and in some other sates. The practice of allocating examination centers of same school has provided scope for restoring to unfair means like indulging in malpractices, helping the students of their schools, forming syndicate to help one another etc. Similarly, drawing invigilators from out side examination centre school though to some extent help to restrain malpractices but it is equally difficult for invigilators coming from out side to control the interferences during examination as parents, relatives, community at large also involved to help the students to copy in examinations. Instances of assaulting is not very uncommon in certain areas. Cases of invigilators being killed was also reported in some parts of the country. In view of above problems, some of the states including Uttar Pradesh and Andhra Pradesh have discontinued the earlier practice of allowing students to appear for examinations in the same school where they studied. The students of the school where examination centre is located have to write their examinations in another examination centre located in other than their own school. However, in Uttar Pradesh while girls are allowed to write examinations in their own school if it has examination centre where as boys have to go other examination centre near by.

This strategy though to some extent check the malpractices, but due to vast expansion of secondary schools especially under private sector a competitive trend to achieve good results emerged. At the same time pressure on government/local body/private aided schools has also been exerted, targets are fixed. Head teachers and teachers are made accountable for achieving better results to encounter the public criticism and keep pace with private sector schools. In order to club all such evil practices during recent years (1999) the state Andhra Pradesh has further adopted innovative strategies in managing examination centers. Firstly while sanctioning examination center to the school, strict norms are followed. While in rural areas, the secondary school in Mandal (sub-district) head quarters is the examination centre, in urban areas a maximum of 10 examination centers are permitted. However, a minimum of 250 students in urban areas and 100 students in rural areas is essential to sanction an examination centre for the school. Secondly a system called 'Jumbling' was introduced. In this system, institutions functioning with in a radius of 5-8 kilometers were formed in to a educational zone. In each district educational zones were formed. Students from a school are allotted to different examination centers in the zone by adopting jumbling method-that is to say students of school are not allotted to a single examination centre. Hall tickets (identification number for admission) numbers are given by the state level examination board, before allotting these numbers to a particular examination center, their numbers are jumbled in such away candidates of on school are posted to several examination centers not in serial order but in a jumbled and scattered fashion. All this process is carried in computer. Andhra Pradesh has adopted another major change that teachers who do not teach secondary classes are drafted for invigilation of public examinations. Jumbling procedure is adopted also for allocation of examination centers to invigilators. However, some times the invigilators are shifted from one centre to another locally depending on need. Though this procedure has created a little inconvenience to students, helped to curb malpractices to some extent.

In addition to invigilators flying squads make surprise visits to examination centers. If a student is caught cheating in examination hall, he/she is debarred from appearing public examination for three consequent years. The flying squad comprises education officers, head masters and senior teachers from government schools and colleges.

Evaluation of Answer Scripts

Most of the states in India follow spot evaluation system where in the examiners correct the answer sheets under close supervision and scrutiny at designated subject camps of evaluation centers at district or regional/divisional level following evaluation scheme provided by the state examination boards. This method has been adopted to eliminate malpractices, reduce delay and to minimize subjectivity among examiners. Among all the four sample states similar method is followed in organizing the evaluation. The process of evaluation is generally completed in 8-10 days. While in Kerala and Andhra Pradesh the District Education Officers over look the entire process of evaluation in the centers and send the marks sheets along with answer scripts to State Board of Examinations. The marks sheets are sorted on the basis of registration number and entered in to computers. The entries are verified at least twice However, in Maharashtra and Uttar Pradesh the marks sheets and answer scripts are sent to Divisional and Regional Boards of Examination respectively. The State Examination Boards in Andhra Pradesh and Kerala and Regional/ Divisional Boards in Maharashtra and Uttar Pradesh declare the examination results. The entire process of evaluation and declaring results is completed in 30-40 days in different states. The examination results are published in news papers, posted on web site. The certificate and marks sheets are supplied through the respective schools. The examination Boards have grievances cells for representing any injustice happened to students.

Normally there is provision for re-evaluation of answer scripts in many of the states except in Uttar Pradesh among the four sample states. The students can request for re-evaluation or recounting of marks by applying through the heads of schools. Re-evaluation manuscripts and recounting of marks for different subjects can be requested through the heads of schools within 2 weeks of examination results are declared. If mistakes are found, necessary correction is made and accordingly the marks are revised. In Kerala the photocopy of answer scripts are provided to students if they request the same. In Maharashtra, when cases of malpractice and improper conduct of examinations affect the results of examinations, the Divisional Boards of Secondary Education on the recommendations of Standing Committee amend the results of examinations or take necessary action as it deem fit. Similarly in case if question papers contains questions on out of syllabus and as a result pass rate is affected, the boards can give grace marks for the particular subject. In Maharashtra, if a student falls short of 3 marks in aggregate to get the first division, 3 grace marks are given for the purpose of awarding first division. In Uttar Pradesh up to 4 grace marks are awarded and can be distributed among two subjects if a student is short marks to pass the examination, however in case of higher secondary the 4 grace marks are given for one subject only. In Kerala also the practice of giving grace marks is in vogue where as there is no grace marks system in Andhra Pradesh. Kerala, Andhra Pradesh and Uttar Pradesh have adopted a policy of save a year by conducting re-examination with in one month for those who fail in the examination. But in Kerala instant examination is only for those who failed in one subject.

Discussions with State Boards of Secondary Education in Sample States.

REFERENCES

NCERT (National Council for Educational Research and Training). *National Curriculum for Elementary and Secondary Education. A Framework* (revised version). New Delhi: NCERT, 1988.

NCERT, *National Curriculum Framework for School Education: A Discussion Document.* New Delhi: NCERT, 2000.

6

Administration and Management of the Secondary Education

In the process of educational reconstruction in order to meet the diverse needs of a changing society, the administration and management system has significance for the orderly development of education. The administrative machinery sustains the quality of education through effective utilization of available resources. The educational administration in India has evolved from colonial legacy. There have been significant reforms in administrative structure of education to meet the emerging challenges and priorities.

After independence, there was a analogous pattern of administrative set-up in most states, with a Minister who is assisted and advised by a secretary at secretariat level in policy planning. Directorate of Education (DOE), the executive body under the direct control of secretariat responsible for planning and carrying out the educational policies and programmes. Besides the department of education, at the centre as well as at state levels, different departments and Ministers had responsibilities for various spheres of education such as technical, agricultural, vocational etc., especially for the age group of 10 to 17. The Secondary Education Commission (1952-53) popularly known as Mudaliar Commission has suggested a hierarchical structure of educational administration, establishment of Boards of Secondary Education to deal with all details of secondary education in addition to national system of education in India. In view of the report of the Secondary Education Commission for a national system of education in India, the Kothari Commission (1964-66) recommended for a unified structure for education at school level to allow an integrated view of education development, with the assumption that the creation of separate directorates/department for elementary and secondary education and sometimes for higher secondary education would create problem of overlap and coordination. It thus recommended 10+2 pattern of school education, with +2 stage as higher secondary. The National Policy on Education (NPE), 1986 further also suggested that all states should adopt a uniform structure of education, which is of course, yet to be realised. Similarly, the NPE and POA envisaged establishment of District Boards of Education and State Advisory Boards of Education and effective educational administration machinery at different levels, particularly in major states, with a mechanism of coordination for programme implementation. While most of the states accepted the 10+2 pattern, its implementation however had not been uniform across states.

Educational administration in general and secondary education in particular, has evolved in last few decades ensuing upon the recommendations of several Education Commissions, Committees, and National Policies on Education in order to manage the large education system. Considerable changes in organizational structure and educational administrative machinery have taken place both at the centre and state levels. In recent time one of the major trends observed is that of bifurcation of school and higher education at Ministry and Secretariat levels, further divergence of school education at directorate level and holding of responsibilities of secondary education by local government and non-governmental agencies at the district and field level. However, the non-realization of uniform structure of education and variations in the development of the education system across states has resulted in varied pattern of administrative structure.

EDUCATIONAL ADMINISTRATION AT THE NATIONAL LEVEL

At the national level, ministry of education has undergone structural changes because of shifting of focus on specialization. Till 1999, the Department of Education (DoE) had been one of the constituent units of the Ministry of Human Resources Development (MHRD) along with other departments such as Culture, Youth Affairs and Sports. The DOE is responsible for all matters on education, including overall policy making and planning of programmes. The MHRD is headed by a minister of cabinet rank and assisted by ministers of state. In policy making and planning, the minister is assisted by education secretaries who in turn is assisted by joint secretaries, deputy secretaries for different aspects and sectors of education. However, in recent years not only two separate secretaries for school and higher education have been appointed but also secondary education has been bifurcated from school education and clubbed with higher education. The DOE as the apex body at the center is more concerned with policy making, planning and running special schemes and monitors the educational programmes. However, in view of large and diverse education system and in federal political system, the central government has limited role in administering education in general and secondary education in particular. However, DOE of MHRD runs two categories of secondary schools which include a chain of Kedriya Vidylayas (Central Schools) for the children of transferable central government employees and the Navodaya Vidyalaya (Pace Setting Schools for the rural talented children). To administer and manage these schools separate administrative bodies at national and regional level were setup by the DOE. Though there are few other centrally sponsored schemes and programmes like improving quality of science education, computer literacy, girl's hostels etc. at secondary level, they are implemented through the state level administration.

Reorganization of DOE and separating secondary education from school education though helps to provide undivided focus on universalisation of elementary education, but merging with higher education repeat same disadvantages for secondary education like earlier with low priority compared to higher education and lack of importance for either expansion of secondary schools to meet the demand or to improve quality.

However, in a large country with a federal system where school education is responsibility of states, the administrative and management responsibility of education vests largely on state governments.

EDUCATIONAL ADMINISTRATION AT THE STATE LEVEL

Educational administration in general and that of secondary education in particular varies among different states. The administrative structure for secondary education has evolved in the states according to geographical, political and educational context. Generally secondary education is covered under school education and the states have minister/s for school education who is assisted by education secretaries in policy making. In some cases there are separate minister for secondary and higher secondary stage. But in few states higher secondary is clubbed with higher education ministry. All the states have administrative system with horizontal and vertical structures from state, to school level for execution of educational policies and programmes.

The administrative system of secondary education is broadly of four categories *viz.* i) entire school education system from primary to higher secondary under one administrative structure; ii) primary to lower secondary being under one administrative body and higher secondary falling under higher education; iii) while secondary education (both lower and higher) under one administrative structure and iv) primary to lower secondary under one administrative body and higher secondary having separate administered structure. Each state follows one or the other pattern.

Some of the states in recent years restructured secondary education by separate administrative structure arrangement for secondary including higher secondary. While few states have integrated administrative structure from primary to higher secondary level. However, few states have school education covering from primary to lower secondary, separate administration for higher secondary or clubbing with higher education. In some states in recent years higher secondary level has been de-linked from higher education department to make it part of school education. Majority of educationally backward states have bifurcated the DOE both at Ministerial and secretariat levels in view of the focus on elementary education and realization of importance of secondary education for the human resource development. Moreover, in all states educational administration is characterized by decentralization with multi-tier structures from the state to regional, district, block and school levels.

In the context federal system and education being listed in concurrent list, the educational administration at state level plays important role in fashioning education system and to monitor implementation educational programmes.

ADMINISTRATION IN SAMPLE STATES

The educational administration at ministry and secretariat level varies across states depending on size and political contexts. Among the 4 sample states, in a large state like Uttar Pradesh school education is headed by a cabinet rank minister who is assisted by minister of state and minister of independent charge who are overall in charge of secondary and basic education respectively. While in case of Andhra Pradesh there are two ministers-minister of school education, who covers up to lower secondary education, and minister of higher education who looks after higher secondary (intermediate) education besides higher education. In case of Kerala minister of general education is in charge of both secondary and higher secondary education. Similar is the case in Maharashtra, where the minister of school education looks after both secondary and higher secondary education. But there are two ministers of state who assist the minister of school education in the areas of primary, and secondary and higher secondary education respectively.

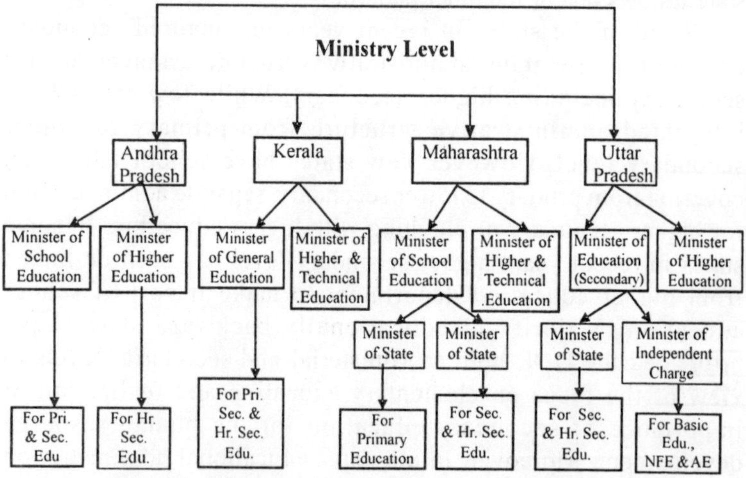

Fig. 6.1: Educational Administration in Sample States

In larger states like Maharashtra and Uttar Pradesh large number schools, primary schools are operated by local bodies and secondary schools are run under private aided sector necessitates to have separate ministers.

In all the states, the ministers are assisted by secretaries in policy making and planning. However, there is variation among states in terms of structure of secretariats and areas of coverage. In case of U.P., the minister of school education is assisted by principal secretaries who discharges responsibilities with the help of two secretaries-i.e. for basic education and secondary and higher secondary education. There are special secretaries below the rank of secretary, who is assisted by joint secretaries, deputy secretaries and under secretaries. In case of U.P., there is also standing committee for advising the ministers of education in education matter. In A.P., there is a principal secretary for primary and secondary education who is assisted by joint, deputy and assistant secretaries. Like the ministry level, the principal secretary for higher education takes care of higher secondary (intermediate) education, besides higher education.

However, the secretary of the general education in case of Kerala as well as the secretary school education in Maharashtra, takes the responsibility of primary, secondary and higher secondary education. In Kerala, the secretary is assisted by the additional, joint, deputy and assistant secretaries while in Maharashtra, he/she is assisted by one joint secretary and two deputy secretaries in charge of primary

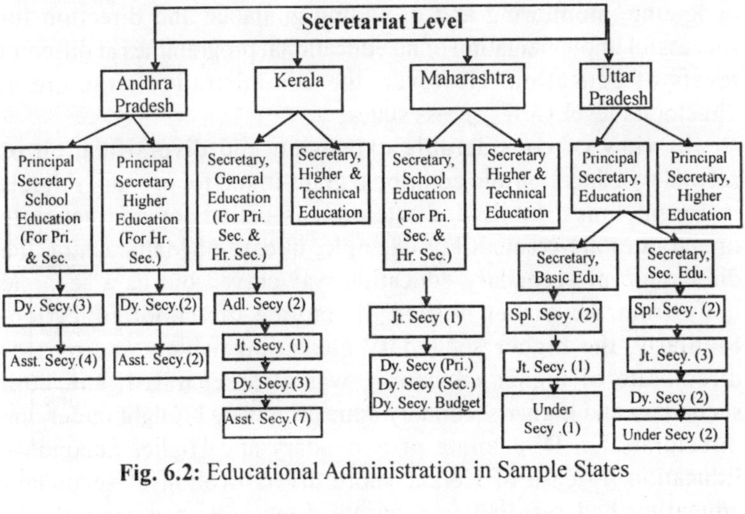

Fig. 6.2: Educational Administration in Sample States

and secondary education. Among 4 sample states, in U.P. the administrative structure for secondary education is bifurcated from primary education. The secretary of secondary education is assisted by special, joint, deputy and under secretaries.

The secretariat functions as nodal agency at the state level. It provides assistance to ministers in formulating policies and takes major decisions on all administrative and academic matters. Other major functions of the secretariat include coordinating with national bodies; supervising, monitoring and providing directions to lower level offices for execution and implementation of various policies and programmes.

Directorate Level

Directorate of Education at state level is responsible for implementation government policies and programmes. All the states have different directorates for school and higher education. However, there are differences among states with regard to levels education covered by Directorates. While in some states there is single Directorate for school education covering primary secondary and higher secondary levels where as in a few states the separate Directorate of for secondary and higher secondary several directorates are made responsible for planning and innovations, programming, budgeting, monitoring and providing guidance and direction for successful implementation of all educational programmes at different levels of education. However, the administrative structure at directorate level varies across states.

In view of considerable expansion and diversification of secondary education and additional grant-in-aid for primary schools in recent times, undivided attention is called for and separate directorates are created. For example, in case of Maharashtra, the directorate of secondary education was craved out as a separate body from the earlier unified directorate of school education. Similarly, the higher secondary education, which was part of directorate of higher education, was also separated; and both secondary and higher secondary education were brought under one directorate i.e. Directorate of Secondary and Higher Secondary Education. In case of Kerala, more diversification of secondary education had resulted in separate directorate for general and vocational higher secondary education. In case of A.P., though there was one directorate for higher secondary (intermediate), the responsibility for vocational and general education was divided between two joint directors.

Among the 4 sample states, the present administrative structures at directorate level show that in A.P. and Kerala, one directorate manages secondary and primary education. Similar is the case for secondary and higher secondary education in Maharashtra and U.P. In other words, while higher secondary education is looked after by one directorate in A.P. and Kerala, it is primary education in case of Maharashtra and U.P. For the management of vocational education, there is a separate directorate in Kerala, whereas it is under the jurisdiction of directorate of higher secondary (intermediate) in A.P., and under the directorate of secondary and higher secondary education in Maharashtra and U.P. In case of Kerala it is interesting to note that in view of different directorates and under their jurisdiction schools having both secondary and higher secondary grades, some schools are under a dual administration of concerned directorate, i.e. Directorate of Public Instruction (DPI) and Directorate of Higher Secondary Education (DHSE). Moreover, if a school has vocational courses at higher secondary level, then the school is under the jurisdiction of DPI, DHSE and Directorate of vocational Higher Secondary Education (DVHSE).

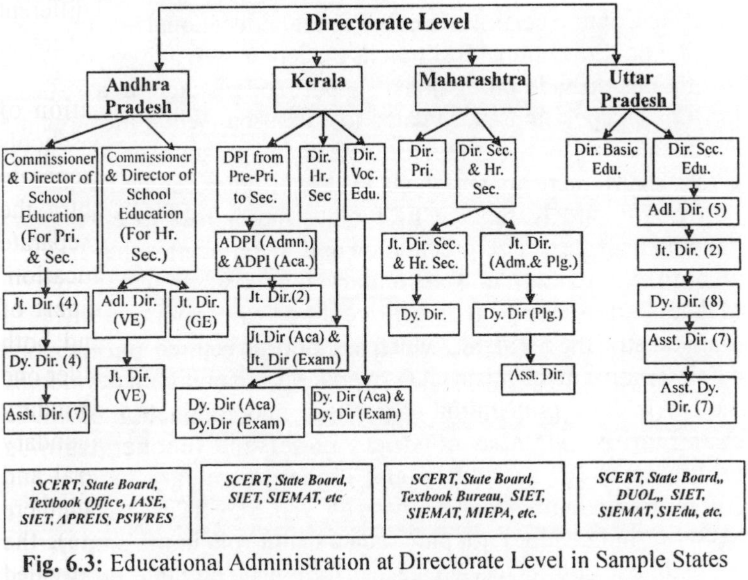

Fig. 6.3: Educational Administration at Directorate Level in Sample States

The directors, as the executive heads at the directorate level, are not only responsible for planning and execution of policies but also advise the government on all issues related to educational matters; supervise and control the educational institutions, provide technical advice for regional and district levels authorities for proper implementation of educational schemes. The directors for different sectors of education are assisted by additional, joint, deputy and assistant directors on various educational matters.

There are also state level autonomous bodies, which render academic and professional support to Directorate of Education (DOI); and often decentralize the administration responsibilities. These are State Council of Educational Research and Training (SCERT), State Board of Secondary and Higher Secondary Education (SBSHSE), State Institute of Educational Technology (SIET), State Institute of Educational Management and Training (SIEMAT), State Institute of Education (SIE) etc. Some of the state constituent bodies like SCERT, SBSHSE and SIET are in line with the central level educational institutions like NCERT, CBSE and CIET respectively. In addition to the above constituent bodies commonly found in every state, there are other state-specific institutions/societies like Bureau of Textbooks in Maharashtra, Bureau of Psychology in U.P.; State Institute of Language, State Social Welfare Residential Educational Society, State Residential Educational Institutions Society in A.P. and so on. These institutions provide professional support and managerial assistance to DOE on specific issues related to education. While the structure and function of some of the constituent bodies are more or less similar across states, there are variations in case of other bodies.

In A.P. and Kerala, SCERT plays major role in curriculum development, textbook preparation and in-service teacher training at both elementary and secondary levels whereas its role in Maharashtra and U.P. is largely confined to elementary level. In Maharashtra, the SBSHSE, which has more structured and elaborate administrative mechanism takes overall responsibility in developing the curriculum, preparation of textbook and conduction of public examinations. It also conducts in-service teacher training programmes for secondary and higher secondary teachers in collaboration with Open University and SCERT. However, the SBSHSE in U.P. does not play such a major role in the preparation of textbooks and in-service teacher training. The State Institute of Education (SIE) and other subject-specific state level institutions like Institute of Science Education, Institute of Languages and Institute of Advanced Studies in Education (IASE) take major responsibility for teacher training; and private publishes play important role in the preparation of textbooks. In A.P., IASEs also play important role in in-service teacher training programmes for the secondary school teachers. The SBSHSEs in A.P. and Kerala act as the coordinating agencies for secondary education at state levels and play major role in the conduction of public examinations.

Regional, District and Block/Mandal Levels

In view of the 73rd and 74th constitutional amendment, state governments have decentralized educational administration and management at regional, district and block levels. The educational administrative structures at these levels, however, vary among states depending on their geographical area, population size and development of education. Among 4 sample states, in case of A.P., Maharashtra and U.P., districts are grouped under different regions whereas in Kerala educational districts are grouped under several revenue districts. In case of A.P. and U.P., a joint director heads the educational administration in each region whereas in Kerala and Maharashtra, it is a deputy director. The regional head is assisted by regional deputy directors in U.P., by assistant directors and deputy education inspections in Maharashtra. But this type of hierarchy is not found in Kerala and A.P. However, in A.P. there are separate regional joint directors for secondary education and higher secondary (intermediate). The variation perhaps due to increase in private management school institutions at secondary level in case of Maharashtra and U.P. and de-linking of higher secondary education from school education in A.P.

The regional directorate holds several administrate responsibilities. It co-ordinates the educational activities and is responsible for implementation, monitoring and supervising almost all education programmes in the region. The administrative power of regional directorate however varies across states. In case of Maharashtra, the regional deputy director is delegated with power of granting and withdrawing recognition of secondary schools, giving permission for upgradation of schools, recommending for grant-in-aid to private unaided schools and appointment and transfer of secondary school teachers. In Kerala, the deputy directors of each revenue district play crucial role in establishing schools, teacher management, conducting of public examinations etc. In A.P. and U.P., the regional directorates mainly carry out coordination and implementation activities and establish link between DOE and DEOs.

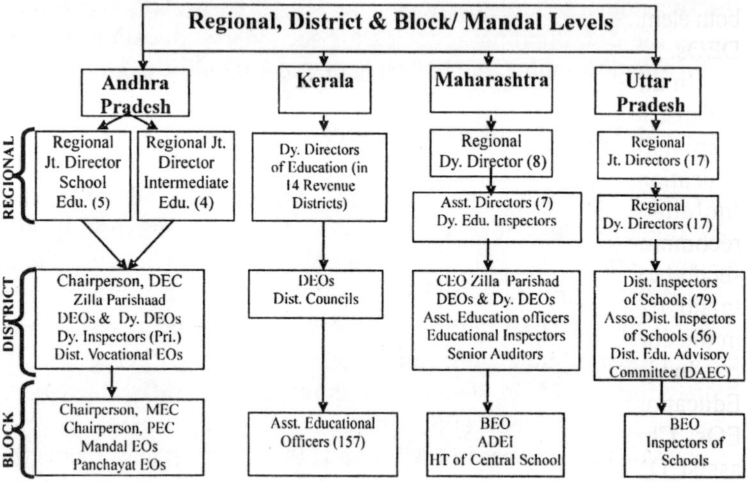

Fig. 6.4: Regional, District and Block/Mandal Levels in Sample States

The educational administration at the district level also varies across states. In some states, district educational officers (DEOs) are in overall in-charge of elementary as well as secondary education whereas in some others, there are separate DEOs for primary and secondary education. DEOs are assisted by a number of officers in the implementation of educational programmes and supervision of schools. However, in some states, other officer or committee heads the educational administration at the district level. Among 4 sample states, in case of Kerala, DEO is the head of district educational administration, who is assisted by District Councils whereas in U.P., it is the district inspector of schools (DIS), assisted by associate DIS and District Education Advisory Committee (DEAC). In case of Maharashtra, the Chief Executive Officer (CEO) of Zilla Parishad is responsible for educational administration at district level assisted by DEOs of primary and secondary education, deputy DEOs, assistant education officers and educational inspectors. Similarly, in A.P. District Education Committee (DEC) comprising of chairman and CEO of Zilla Parishad (District Council), DEO, some members of school committees, headmaster, representative of local bodies, educationists etc., is responsible for the overall development of secondary education. There is a district education board headed by district collector, which acts as advisory body to DEC in implementation of programmes. Unlike Maharashtra, one DEO working under Zilla Parishad looks after both elementary and secondary education with the assistance from deputy DEOs.

In all the states, although different committees or officers head the district educational administration, DEOs assume very crucial responsibility in planning, implementation and monitoring of educational programmes in the district. The main functions of DEOs include inspection and supervision of secondary schools, recommending for opening and recognition of secondary schools secondary, recommending for withdrawal of recognition and grant-in-aid, fixing of staff, releasing salaries of teachers, rendering support in the conduction of public examinations etc.

In view of large number of schools, education officers like Block Educational Officers (BEOs), Education Officers (EOs), Assistant EOs., Chairpersons of Education Committee at Block/Mandal levels assist DEOs in academic and administrative aspects of school management. Although the officers at Block level assist DEOs and deputy DEOs in the supervision of secondary schools, they assume more responsibilities for primary schools.

School Level

For effective functioning of schools, the management at school levels has a lot of significance in terms of regular institutional planning and formulation of academic activities. The state governments have evolved policies in managing schools. Various administrative mechanisms are constituted at the school level in order to bring the values of decentralization, delegation and accountability in the management of schools. However, in view of different management type of schools, there is no uniformity in the administrative and management structures among all schools in a state. The school level management in different management type schools even varies across states. However, since all recognized schools have to confirm to standards and directives of state government, there are common administrative and management units like School Management Committee (SMC) and Parent-Teacher-Associations (PTAs) in case of all schools. The SMC looks after all internal administrative and monitoring activities in a school and is responsible to government for the functioning of schools and PTAs play supportive roles in school activities.

In addition to SMC and PTAs, the number of other committees at school level and their structure and functions vary across states. In case of Maharashtra, there is an academic council comprising of teachers, which assists head teacher on all academic matters and facilitates various academic activities in the schools. Supervisors appointed especially in schools with larger student population also assist the head teacher.

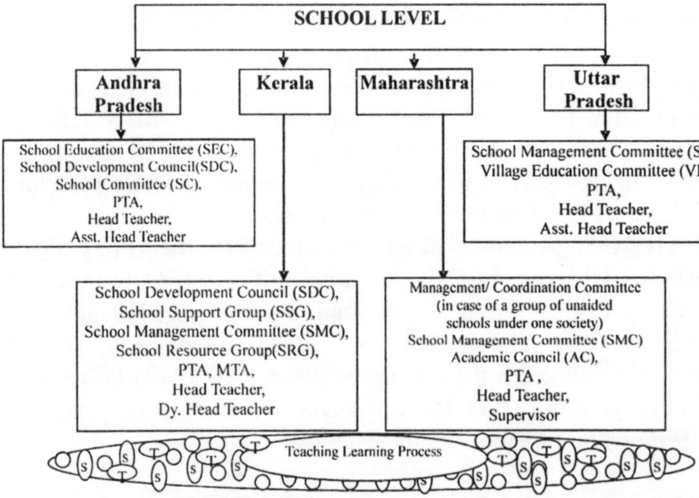

Fig. 6.5: Administration at School Level in Sample States

In Kerala, for all government recognized schools, besides SMC and PTAs, there are School Development Council (SDC), School Support Group (SSG), School Resource Group (SRG) and MTAs. The SDC which is a broader body comprising of head of local elected body (i.e. *Panchayati Raj*), people other than parents, members of local NGOs, head teacher, teacher representative etc. plays an important role in school development. It advises school management committee on both academic and administrative activities. The SSG comprising of members of PTAs, elected members from local body, local experts etc., plays an advisory role in administrative and academic matters. Like the Academic Council in Maharashtra, SRG in Kerala assists head teacher on academic matters. As observed, in Kerala, many committees/bodies associated with school management have duplication of roles and functions, resulted in role shifting and very often insignificant contribution towards effective functioning of school. Of all the committees/ bodies, PTAs however play important roles in planning, academic, co-curricular and developmental activities of the school. In A.P. the functions of the School Education Committee (SEC) is similar to SMC in other states. But, the unique feature is that it has a student representative, generally of Class X securing highest marks in Class IX. Like Kerala, in A.P., the SDC is responsible for overall development of schools. The School Committee, an elected body of parent members with head teacher as convenor advises School Education Committee on both administrative and academic matters. In U.P. SMC and PTAs assume responsibility similar to that of other states. Besides PTAs, the Village Education Committee (VEC) also plays important role in monitoring the school activities.

Despite different committees at school level, the head teacher's role remains crucial as day-to-day functioning of the school depends on his/her style of management with the assistance from deputy/ assistant head teachers, teachers and other non-teaching staff. For that, different committees while rendering managerial inputs and professional supports to head teachers have to take the confidence of head teacher into account. Moreover, teachers in the schools are immediate human resources to provide support to heat teachers in the management of academic and administrative activities. The quality, commitment and accountability of teachers have a lot of significance in the school management process, hence, there is need for an effective management of teachers.

INSPECTION AND SUPERVISION

School inspection system in India was inherited from colonial legacy. Colonial rulers introduced school inspection as a part of grant-in-aid to control proper utilization of finances to supervise quality of education. Even after independence, the inspection system has continued though schools are largely funded and managed by the government. Inspection of schools has been made compulsory. Guidelines and instructions regarding frequency and covering different aspects during school inspection are provided by department of education of state governments. Inspection assumes special importance and mandatory in case of private aided schools for continuing grant-in–aid and to regulate proper functioning of schools and appropriate use of funds. Most states have two kinds of inspection and supervision. One is by the educational administrators in the form of school visits, surprise visits and annual inspection focusing mostly on administrative, financial academic issues. The other category is called panel inspection by a team of different subject experts concentrate exclusively teaching –learning and other academic aspects. District level administration inspect and supervise functioning of secondary schools. Generally District Education Officer with the assistance of Deputy Education Officer and Block (Sub-district) Education Officer conduct the school inspection and supervision. The team for panel inspections is constitute by District Education Officer by nominating the subject teachers, heads of schools and other experts in the district. However, there is wide variation among different states with regard to norms of inspection and persons in charge of inspection at district and Block levels. The differences are evident among the four sample states as the norms of inspection and persons responsible vary. While most of states follow a routine approach for inspection system, the state Maharashtra has introduced an innovative inspection system and supervision both to meet targets of inspecting large number of schools and also to make inspection as a diagnostic tool to help schools consequently to improve functioning and quality of education. The norms, process and procedure, inspecting authorities, frequency of visits, nature and duration of inspection, format used for evaluation of schools vary among the states although there are certain common practices. In most states District Education Officer plays an important role in monitoring regular inspection and supervision of secondary schools in addition to inspecting few schools. Normally the District Education Officer is assisted by Deputy Education Officers, Block (sub district) Education Officers in inspection and supervision of secondary schools. In some of the states like Maharashtra and Kerala the Education Extension Officers who have to inspect only primary schools are also entrusted with inspection of secondary schools in view of large number of secondary schools and shortage of administrative personnel at district level.

The number of Deputy Education Officers at district level who are responsible for school visits and inspection vary among different states. Among the four sample states the number of Deputy Education Officers in a district vary as 4-7 depending on number of secondary schools. DEO and Division/regional Directors inspect the higher secondary schools or Junior/Intermediate colleges.

The number of school visits and inspection schedule etc. are prescribed at state level. A common practice in majority of states found was that the inspecting officers prepare month wise annual plan for school visits and inspection and the same is approved by the DEO. Monthly report of visits and inspection are submitted to the DEO who in turn reports the same to regional or divisional level educational administrators. As per school code in Maharashtra, there should be three inspection visits to each school in a year. While the first visit is meant for general observation or pre-inspection whereas the second visit contains inspection and third visit as a follow up. In Maharashtra according to the state norm the DEO and Deputy Education Officers are expected to visit minimum 20 and 40 secondary schools per year respectively. Besides, Block Education Officer is required to visit 20 secondary schools. Although Education Extension officers are required to visit only primary schools, because of shortage of manpower for inspection, they are also assigned the task of inspection of secondary schools. In Andhra Pradesh the inspecting officers are expected to visit at least twice all the secondary schools in the district. According to state guide lines DEO is expected to inspect monthly two secondary schools, the Deputy Education officer should undertake inspection of 5 secondary schools and visit 10 secondary schools for a month. In Kerala the DEO is the sole authority of inspection and supervision. The DEO needs to visit all the secondary schools twice, one as surprise visit and another one planned inspection. The number of days need to spend in a school during inspection is also prescribed as 2-3 days in different sates. However, only in Kerala the duration of inspection is prescribed based on number students in a school. According to state norms a DEO has to visit a school and spend full day if a school has less than 500 students and two days in a school with 500-1000 students and if they have more than 1000 then the visit should be of three days. Clear guidelines and format exists for covering various aspects during school visits and inspection. However, the guidelines and aspects that need to be observed vary among states especially in case of private aided schools. Inspection of a school is done according to an evaluation format. During the inspection according to Education Rules of Uttar Pradesh, Maharashtra, Kerala and Andhra Pradesh the inspecting officer has to observe the suitability of physical facilities, the normal functioning of the school at work, order and discipline, examination results examine the financial accounts and records maintenance, teaching (periods, time table, assignments etc.) and learning process and quality of instruction etc. Although there are specific evaluation criteria or observation schedule for inspection, inspectors may go beyond the issues mentioned in the format. In Maharashtra detailed information about the finances however, separately collected by the audit official from private aided schools.

The inspection procedure suggests holding feed back sessions after inspection with school staff. While in Maharashtra, generally after the inspection, the inspecting officer holds a feed back session with the head master, teaching and non-teaching staff. However, it would be difficult to believe that the block Education Officers who are junior in cadre to heads of schools really make them effective. It is also not uncommon among private aided schools that inspecting officers are more obliged to the school management as the secretary or president of private managements are influential and powerful persons. In case of Andhra Pradesh, Kerala and Uttar Pradesh though such norm exists, it depends on inspection officer, availability of time for having feed back session. The data from school case studies evince that headmasters and teachers of sample schools find the inspection very superficial and mere formality rather useful and effective in improving functioning of the school. Similarly, the feedback sessions are a formality rather meaningful to advise and motivate the head master and teachers. However, later the DEO formally sends over all feedback normally after 2-3 months.

The frequency, duration and aspects to cover suggested are desirable albeit it is practically impossible for following in view of large number of schools and limited number of inspecting officers and the work load and responsibilities of DEO and other education officers at district and Block levels. Not only the administrative work load of DEO has increased enormously due to phenomenal growth and expansion of schools but also responsibilities have increased due to several other programmes and schemes. The DEOs are mostly busy with teacher recruitment, transfers, attending several meetings, conferences, conduct of public and other types of examinations, distribution of text books, mid-day meals, organization of sports and games, exhibitions, in –service training programmes etc. in addition to many other foreseen responsibilities from time to time. In case of Kerala, Maharashtra and Uttar Pradesh the district level administrators are fully busy with responsibilities related with granting recognition, releasing salaries for private aided schools, administering the teacher provident fund and pensions, regulating service matters etc. In Maharashtra, Uttar Pradesh and Kerala the DEOs are also caught up with legal court cases appealed by teachers of private aided schools, as teachers make government also one of the parties in their legal cases the DEO and even other higher level administrators are often summoned by the courts. Therefore, contrary to the norms and prescribed procedures of inspection and supervision, administrators at district and block level spend more time on planning and routine administrative aspects rather than on inspection and supervision. From the case studies of sample schools in four states it was evidently found that there were 40 per cent schools not visited in last one year and around 35 per cent schools which were not inspected since last three years. There were also schools, which were not visited since 1997. It is generally known fact that inspection and supervision are the weakest aspects in educational administration. A common problem across the states is that number of secondary schools has increased many folds in all the states; but the number of inspecting officers did not correspondingly increased to fulfill the norms of frequency and duration of inspection. DEO and other administrators can neither frequently visit schools nor conduct effective inspection especially related to academic aspects. Another important issue is with the expansion of schools, large number schools were established in rural and remote areas, and inspection of these schools is effected for want of transport facility. As the inspecting officers lack vehicles take more time to visit schools in rural areas. As a result the inspection has become a rare phenomena in many states especially in case of government and local body schools where as in case of private aided schools minimum one visit is absolutely essential for continuing grant-in-aid. The managements of private aided schools are expected to act upon the inspection reports and deficiencies found out are to comply with. In case of serious lapses are found during inspection, the private aided schools are asked to provide explanation on different issues in a given time. If the explanation is not convincing, then as a form of punishment, the administration makes 5-10 per cent cut in the non-salary grant in some of the states like Maharashtra in order to make inspection more effective and to make private aided schools more amenable to established procedures. In follow up inspection if no improvement is noticed, then a special order is issued to the management to take specific action on headmaster or teachers. If the management fails to take necessary action and problems continue, the district administration in Maharashtra make the Deputy Education/Block Education Officer in charge of the school for one or two years. However, this kind of cases are very few and rare as the private managements normally manipulate with the administrators and avoid any action. In Kerala not only the private managements are influential and have political clout and PTA support even the teachers lobby is very strong, taking any action based on inspection is not only difficult but also at times proves fatal for administrators with transfers. Similar situation prevails mostly in other states too where private aided schools are predominant. In case of government and local body schools, if the schools do not comply with inspection reports, the district level administration can take appropriate action but follow up action by the schools largely depends also on administration who responsible to provide facilities and adequate staff etc. Thus both in case private aided or government schools the impact of inspection is very limited.

Panel Inspection

For a long time there has been a criticism that the conventional inspection system is devoid of academic input as they mostly concentrate on administrative and financial aspects and also lack expertise to cover to supervise or inspect all the school subjects. Coupled with this the scanty inspection system has very little scope for covering academic aspects. Recognising the fact that the conventional inspection system can not provide academic guidance to schools, panel inspection has been introduced by many states including four sample states in order to improve quality of teaching learning. A team of subject experts apart from education officer conducts panel inspection. Generally the panel comprises of different subject experts drawn from among the senior teachers, school heads and retired teachers etc. Panel inspection is planned and monitored by District Education Officer. The department provides a format for panelist for close observation and scrutiny of several aspects concerned to academic management. During inspection the subject experts observe both subject knowledge and pedagogical skills of teachers and competencies of students, evaluation methods, examination results etc. The experts during panel inspection conduct staff meeting and ascertain teachers' academic problems and also assess training/capacity building requirements of teachers. The panel inspection report comprises the observations of different subject experts along with suitable recommendations addressed both to subject teachers and school in addition to administration for necessary action. From the case studies of sample schools it is evident that the teachers find panel inspection as a useful exercise and a peer group review though many times lack follow up action if the teachers have subject or pedagogical constraints. However, the sample states like Maharashtra and Kerala take in to account the panel inspection review reports and their recommendation to prepare teacher hand books and guides in addition to in-service training programmes.

Innovations in Inspection

Realising the importance of inspection and supervision on the one hand and on the other the existing constraints for the regular and frequent visits to schools, the state Maharashtra has evolved an innovative strategy called institutional self-evaluation as complement to the routine inspection system for improving accountability and performance of schools. The institutional self evaluation tool is based on 5 point scale i.e. A to E, covering different aspects *viz.* academic efficiency, infrastructure facilities, utilization of resources, co-curricular activities etc. In the gradation process the schools are given opportunity for self evaluation using the standard evaluation tool prepared by the department. School grading is done after the Headmaster of school fills in the grading format/booklet and the information given is verified by an inspection. A committee of experts at Block (sub-district) level consisting of awardees teachers, educationists and education extension officers examine the performance of the school based on self evaluation presented by the headmaster. At school level the headmaster does rating in consultation with teachers. Schools in remote areas however, are given some relaxation in evaluation parameters. The schools with grade E, D, and C which are low according to the continuum, receive preference in the inspection schedule. Despite having better physical facilities the schools with low pass percentage of less than 20 per cent pass rate in public examinations of X grade are also given priority in inspection. In case of schools with continuous zero per cent results in public examinations for two to-three years the recognition may be withdrawn.

Constraints

Some of the weaknesses of inspection system prevalent in most states are inadequate staff for inspection and supervision, lack of follow up action both in terms of provision of necessary facilities and capacity building of teachers, diminutive institutional arrangement for professional development of teachers. Though numbers of secondary schools have grown considerably, the inspection supervision staff at district level remained same. And also the functions and responsibilities of inspection officers have been widened resulting with reduced time for academic and supervision of schools.

Discussions with state level educational administrators in Sample States

7

Management of Teachers

Teacher is one of the most important factors that effect quality of education. The quality of teachers depends on several issues related to teacher management. Broadly speaking teacher management involves aspects pertaining to recruitment and deployment, transfer, promotion and career prospects training and capacity building of teachers, incentives, scrutiny and evaluation or performance appraisal of teachers etc. Considering the enormous size of the educational system and magnitude of teaching personnel, teacher management is not only a big challenge but also crucial for effective functioning of schools in India. Teacher management in India characterizes variation among different states though there are some common aspects. The basic prescribed educational qualification i.e. graduation being the same across the states, pre-service teacher training qualification is relaxed in few states due to lack of adequate trained personnel. The norms for class size, provision of number of teachers, teaching load, process and procedures of teacher recruitment and deployment, method of teacher appraisal, incentives etc. differ among the states and there is variation even among the four sample states. State governments prescribe the norms and procedures related to teacher management encompassing both government and private management schools. However, some of the aspects of teacher management especially process of recruitment, transfer, promotion, punishment, incentives are slightly different for private schools compared to government schools. Not only teacher management procedures of private schools vary among different states but also there are differences between private unaided and government aided private schools. In some of the states, varied teacher management practices are adopted even among government schools of different types like residential schools, schools for disadvantaged groups, special schools for physically and mentally challenged.

In recent years some of the states have adopted reforms in teacher management especially in recruitment, deployment and transfers. These reforms aimed to eliminate biases and undesirable practices like political interferences, corruption in teacher recruitment, placement and transfers of teachers in addition to improve quality, commitment and efficiency of teachers. In view of 73rd Constitutional amendment, few states have adopted decentralised approach and local bodies were entrusted with teacher management especially recruitment, placement and transfers. The extent and nature of decentralization differ among states particularly at secondary level. In some of the states decentralization of teacher management has ensued up to community and school levels to the extent of hiring and firing of contract/Para teachers and payment of their salaries, monitoring etc. The teacher management practices in four sample states obviously illustrate the changes and reforms introduced having commonalities and differences in teacher management strategies. As the four sample states vary in terms of, number of schools and teachers, management type besides political, spatial and demographic profile, accordingly evolving the teacher management practices among them.

Qualifications

Generally the prescribed qualification for teachers in secondary schools in India is Bachelor's degree or first University degree along with the professional pre-service teacher training i.e. B. Ed. However, in few states the pre-service teacher training had to be non-compulsory due to lack of trained personnel. At higher secondary level the prescribed educational qualifications include Masters degree in concerned subject and B.Ed. But there is variation among states with regards to requirement of teacher training qualification for teachers at higher secondary level. In Uttar Pradesh, Maharashtra and Kerala teachers in higher secondary must have a Master degree or a post-graduation in concerned subject and pre service teacher training. But Andhra Pradesh, teachers at higher secondary level ought to have only Masters Degree in concerned subject. In recent years most of the states have been appointing contract and Para teachers at secondary level with a policy of appointing locals as temporary teachers if necessary by relaxing training qualification if trained persons for certain subjects are not available. On the other hand despite prescribed minimum qualifications in some states considerable per cent of teachers possess higher educational qualification than prescribed.

The composition of teachers with differential qualification varies based on structure of schools i.e. number of classes. This varied structure of secondary education becomes important in the context of recruitment of teachers and allotment of classes to teachers. For example, in case of integrated schools, the prescribed number of periods for a secondary teacher could take into account the upper primary and higher secondary classes one teach. This some times prompt to appoint teachers having more than minimum qualification. However, at the school level, number of teachers per subject is normally prescribed according to the level of education and number of sections, even in case of integrated schools.

TEACHER MANAGEMENT IN SAMPLE STATES

Norms for Fixing Teaching Staff

The number of teachers at secondary level is provided according to state norms, particularly on the basis of workload. The number of sections and class size determines the workload for a teacher. Fixing of staff in a school depends on the number of classes and sections, recognized subjects offered and students enrolment. There are prescribed state level educational norms and guidelines clearly indicating number of teaching hours or periods per teacher based on students' enrolment. Extent of workload in terms of number periods or hours per week and prescribed maximum number of students per section vary among different states. The prescribed size of class among four sample states ranges between 40 to 60 students in Uttar Pradesh and Andhra Pradesh respectively.

In Andhra Pradesh, the optimum size of class is 40 students. However, second section would be sanctioned if the class size exceeds 60 students and third section is formed if the number of students exceeds 110 and so on. If any school has more than one section and secondary classes have more than 5 sections, additional teachers are sanctioned in order of priority of subjects, i.e. Mathematics, English, Science and social science. The number of teaching periods ranges 24 as minimum and 30 as maximum per week. For regional language an additional teacher is sanctioned, if workload exceeds 30 periods per week. In reality even if the class size is more than 60 students rarely second section is sanctioned as most of the schools in the sate are under local body and state government.

In Kerala, one section constitutes maximum 50 students and teaching load per teacher is 25 periods per week. Promptly second section is sanctioned if the class size increases to 51 and a third section is made if when number of students ranges between 96 to 131. Kerala has a distinction following strictly the norm for class size both for private aided and government schools. Similar to in Kerala, the prescribed norm in Maharashtra envisages the class size as maximum 50 students and provision of second section if it exceeds, however the teaching load varies based on number of students. If the strength of a particular class is above 50, the workload is reckoned at the rate of 17 hours per teacher. If student strength is between 30-50, the workload is calculated at the rate of 18 hours and if less than 30, the rate is 19 hours per teacher. In Uttar Pradesh the norm for class size at secondary level being 40 students and at higher secondary 50 students as second section is permitted if the number of students exceeds. Normally the number of teachers for a schools is calculated as 1.5 teacher per class or 45 periods per week for Class VIII to X. in The prescribed norms regarding class size and provision of additional teachers is more of a norm rather than practice in most states except in Kerala where the norms are generally strictly adhered and additional sections and teachers are sanctioned. In case of Maharashtra, Uttar Pradesh and Andhra Pradesh, though permission for additional sections and sanction and appointment of additional teachers is seldom done. This problem is more in case of private aided and local body schools due to financial constraints. Therefore, the schools are normally run with crowded class-rooms. However, state governments in recent years allowed to appoint Contract or Para teachers at school level and provide matching grant to local resources mobilised by School Development/Management committee. In some cases Contract teacher's salaries are also supported by the PTA.

In Kerala the private managements of aided schools adopt dubious methods to get approval for new sections and sanction for additional teacher posts. As the private managements appoint the teachers in private aided schools, lot of corruption and money is involved in recruiting teachers due to high demand for teacher posts. The administrators admit that the private managements some times espouse dubious methods and show fake and inflated enrolment and also woo the parents to admit students by offering concessions in order to get additional teacher posts. In recent years Kerala has witnessed decline of number of students due demographic changes resulting with a problem of surplus teachers in private aided schools. The surplus teachers were absorbed by government and are called as protected teachers. O is the major provider of Their services are deputed to government schools where ever necessary. In other words, many times the private managements recruit excess teachers as money changes hands, and the surplus teachers become liability for government. The situation in Uttar Pradesh and Maharashtra is different from Kerala although as the state governments hardly ever sanction additional teacher posts according to norms even if enrolment increases and class size goes up.

Recruitment

Recruitment and appointment of teachers is one of the important functions of the educational administration in the states. Generally at secondary level teachers are appointed both by direct recruitment and through promotion from lower levels of education. The proportion of direct appointment and through promotion varies among the states, for different subjects and also among different management type schools. The process and procedure of recruitment and appointment of teachers differ among different states. Although promoting teachers from lower levels to secondary schools is based on seniority and fulfillment of required qualifications the actual procedures and norms can be different among states and different management type schools. Teacher selection and appointment is done either at district or regional level although the norms and procedure is common across the state. Generally secondary school teachers are appointed at district level, region becomes the unit for higher secondary level teacher selection and appointment. Among four sample sates while in Uttar Pradesh and Andhra Pradesh region and district are the unit of selection for higher secondary and secondary levels respectively, in case of Maharashtra and Kerala district is unit for both secondary and higher secondary teacher management.

The procedure and criteria for direct recruitment varies among different states. Normally the department of secondary and higher secondary education is responsible for selection and appointment of teachers for government and local body schools while the private managements are free to select teachers for private aided schools although they have to follow norms and rules set by government. However, in case of Uttar Pradesh the state secondary education service board recruits and selects teachers for both government/local body and private aided schools.

All most all the states in India have a policy of recruiting secondary school teachers both by direct selection and on promotion from among the teachers working at lower levels. However, the proportions of teachers selected by direct recruitment and on promotion vary among different states. While the state Andhra Pradesh follows 30:70 ratio for direct recruitment and on promotion respectively. In case of Kerala, the proportion of direct recruitment varies for different subjects with 50 per cent, 40 per cent and 30 per cent for science, social science and language respectively. And also out of total vacancies in secondary schools in Kerala, 10 per cent in science, 20 per cent in social studies and 30 per cent in language are reserved for primary school teachers and 10 per cent of the vacancies are filled up by clerks/stenos having required qualification and training. Of the total vacancies, 30 per cent are filled up with inter district transfers based on seniority. In Uttar Pradesh half of the teacher vacancies in secondary and higher secondary level have to be filled by promotion and rest by direct recruitment. The state Maharashtra also follows filling up of secondary school teacher posts both through direct selection and promotion.

All most all the states have to follow the policy of reservation of certain proportion of teachers' posts of both direct and promotion for Scheduled Castes, Scheduled Tribes and backward communities. Similarly, some of the states have policy of reservation of one third of teacher posts for women. A small percentage of posts are also reserved for physically handicapped persons.

Process of selection of teachers by direct recruitment and by promotion vary while direct recruitment depends on performance in entrance examination, interview, merit in qualifying examination etc, where as seniority with required qualification is the sole criteria for selection of teachers on promotion from among the teachers working in lower levels. However, in some of the sates, confidential reports are also taken in to account while selecting teachers from lower levels. However, the process of selection and appointment on promotion vary across the states and among government/local body schools and other management type schools.

Recruitment by Promotion

In Uttar Pradesh teacher vacancies in secondary and higher secondary are filled as 50:50 through direct recruitment and on promotion from among the teachers working in lower levels. Appointment of teachers through promotion is mainly based on seniority, fulfillment educational qualification and confidential reports. If teachers posses required qualification and complete five years of continuous service, they are automatically considered for filling up of vacant positions of secondary teachers or lecturers of higher secondary by a district selection committee in Uttar Pradesh. Similarly, private aided schools have to send seniority list of eligible teachers to District Education Officer and after the approval of district level selection board, the private management is asked to issue appointment orders at school level. In case of non-availability of vacancies for appointing on promotion the teachers are given higher grade of salary in their current position. In case of Kerala and Maharashtra too the district level selection committee selects the teachers on promotion. In addition to seniority and prescribed educational qualification, confidential reports are also taken in to account while appointing teachers in secondary schools form among the lower levels.

In Andhra Pradesh while 70 per cent of teacher vacancies in secondary schools under government and local bodies are filled-up on promotion from among the primary and upper primary school teachers based on seniority and required qualification, the state adopts more rigorous and detailed exercise while appointing secondary teachers on promotion from lower levels. In order to avoid malpractices and political pressures, the existing vacancies on promotion basis are notified and applications are sought. Qualified teachers working in Upper primary and Primary schools have to send their application to District Education Officer. District Level selection Committee chaired by District collector and having Chef Executive Officer of district local body, DEO and teach union representatives as members select teachers based on seniority. Although seniority and necessary educational qualification are the criteria for selection of teachers from the lower levels, posting to the school is based both on seniority and on entitlement points accrued out of nine point scale.

The entitlement points are based on a nine point scale for aspects like number of years working in current place, category of the place working in terms of rural and urban locality, occupation of the spouse, single women, widows and divorcees teachers, health condition etc. Available vacant places and the list of teachers according to seniority and entitlement points scored is also displayed in advance at district level both through internet and also in District Education Officers' Office. After notifying the vacant posts, no additional or new vacancies can be filled up. Teachers are given opportunity to exercise their option in choosing the place according to their seniority and the entitlement points they accrued. The list of teachers with the rank order with seniority and entitlement points is displayed and teachers are provided counseling for choosing the place accordingly. This strategy had helped to a large extent to eliminate manipulation, corruption, political pressures in teacher appointments and placement. This method has facilitated to provide opportunity to move teachers to better places if they were working in interior and rural areas.

Although the policy of pointing secondary teachers on promotion form lower levels is considered as an appropriate way to motivate teachers by providing an avenue for upward mobility. No doubt this policy benefits teachers with promotion and also helps secondary schools to have teachers with prior experience of teaching. But there are several issues related with quality and efficiency of these teachers since seniority and fulfilling prescribed qualification are the sole criterion. Performance appraisal obviously not present at upper primary and primary levels and coupled to it the selection process on seniority lack any systematic academic criteria and evaluation to judge the quality and efficiency of teachers. Mere seniority need not ensure efficiency among teachers. In case of Kerala even steno or a clerk who has no teaching experience can become a secondary school teacher by virtue of seniority. An important issue is that it takes many years for one to fulfill the seniority criteria, as number of teachers working at primary and upper primary levels is so enormous. In other words the senior teachers working in primary and upper primary schools might have passed out of colleges or university many years back, and their experience is limited to teaching for lower classes where pedagogy and content of subject are of at different levels, it is obvious that efficiency and quality of teachers can not be high order. In this context there may be a wide gap between the subject knowledge that is required and the teachers capacities. It is not uncommon many of these teachers find difficult to teach at secondary level especially the subjects like mathematics, science, English as the secondary level curriculum has undergone significant changes and what they have studied more than decade or fifteen years ago in graduation was much different. Given the measly in-service training and professional development programmes for secondary teachers in India, the promotee teachers find it difficult to cope with teaching at secondary classes. This can be one of the factors for poor quality of secondary education.

Direct Recruitment

The agencies/bodies responsible for direct recruitment of teachers different among states. The process and procedures too vary among the states. In view of several problems in teacher recruitment, since last few years some of the states have brought in reforms in recruitment process and selection criteria and appointment The present criteria in few of the states largely focus on merit by lessening if not totally eliminating the biases, corruption, nepotism and political pressures in teachers' selection and appointments which other wise is rampant. Some of the states are using art of technology especially computers in recruitment and selection process to restrain manipulations and malpractices in addition to reduce the delay. Except Maharashtra in all the three sample states teachers are recruited through sate level common written examination/test and interview. Normally district/region is the unit for selection and appointment of secondary teachers, while the state level bodies are responsible in conducting examinations/tests. While, in Uttar Pradesh and Andhra Pradesh teachers' selection and appointments are made at regional and district level for higher secondary/ intermediate and secondary level respectively. In Kerala and Maharashtra the district is the unit for teacher selection and appointment for secondary and higher secondary levels.

The agencies and process of teacher selection differ among states. Only the state Uttar Pradesh has an exclusive body called State Secondary Education Service Selection Board that is over all in charge of recruitment and selection of teachers in the state. Uttar Pradesh has unique system that the state level secondary education service selection board select teachers for government and private aided schools. In view of large number of schools, it has become essential for having an exclusive secondary education service selection board in Uttar Pradesh. In other sample states not only such exclusive secondary education service selection boards are absent but state governments recruit teachers only for government/local bodies schools where as private managements of aided schools are free to select teachers for respective schools under them following the prescribed norms and procedure set by the respective state governments. While in Kerala the State Public Service Commission is responsible for recruitment of teachers for government secondary schools, in Andhra Pradesh and Maharashtra state and regional level educational administration are the recruiting bodies respectively. Department School Education/Directorate of Intermediate Education in Andhra Pradesh and Directorate of Secondary Education through Regional Selection Boards in Maharashtra recruit teachers at secondary level.

In Uttar Pradesh the Secondary Education Service Selection Board that conducts examinations and interviews by constituting specific subject selection committees at regional level recruits teachers of government and private aided schools. The selection committee comprises subject experts from colleges and university departments, nominees and representatives' of private school managements and administrators from education department at regional level. The Secondary Service Selection Board recruits teachers for government, local body and private aided schools. The teachers are selected based on scoring marks in examination conducted by the secondary education service board, performance in the interview and for special qualifications. The total weightage points are distributed as 85 per cent for merit in the written examination, 10 per cent marks for performance in the interview and 5 per cent for possessing special qualifications and higher degrees. In case of government schools Regional Joint Director of Education appoints teachers according to the merit list provided by the selection board through directorate of secondary education. Though teachers are selected by the State Selection Board, appointing authority in case of private aided schools remains with the private management from selected merit list. The selected list is supplied to private managements of aided schools who in turn issue the appointment orders to teachers. In Uttar Pradesh the state government plays an important role in teacher selection and recruitment for private aided schools unlike in Andhra Pradesh, Kerala and Maharashtra where, the state governments plays very limited role of prescribing norms and educational qualification. The private aided schools select the teachers through their own selection committee comprising chairman /secretary of private management, subject expert and representative education department.

In Andhra Pradesh 30 per cent of teacher posts are filled through direct recruitment. The state Directorate of School Education and Directorate of Intermediate Education are responsible for recruitment of teachers for government and local body schools and intermediate colleges. The few private aided schools select and appoint their teachers by the respective managements following government norms and rules. The state has adopted several reforms in policy and procedures of teacher recruitment in the state to improve quality of teachers and to reduce undesirable practices. A common state level written examination is conducted for recruiting teachers after notifying the vacancies and inviting applications from qualified persons. On behalf of Directorate of School Education, State Council For Educational Research and Training conducts the examination. Though state level examination is conducted, final selection and appointments are made at district level according to merit. The entire process of conduction of examination, evaluation, preparation of merit list is computerized and confidential. District being the unit for selection and appointments, the district selection committee selects teachers from among the successful candidates of common examination on the basis of order of merit and marks obtained in Bachelor of Education (B.Ed.) and appointment is made through interview and counseling. The district selection committee is chaired by District Collector and comprises Chief Executive Officer of District Council, District Education Officer and representative of Teacher Union etc. While selecting teachers 85 per cent marks are given for the rank obtained in entrance examination and 15 per cent marks are accorded for merit obtained in Bachelor of Education (B.Ed.). The 15 per cent weightage, which was earlier given for the performance in the interview, has been done away as a result of recent changes in recruitment procedure. The teachers have to be on probation for two years with a consolidated salary. In case of directly recruited teachers, merit and nativity become major points while appointing to different schools. However, most of them are posted to rural and interior schools as a part of first appointment The recent reforms in teacher appointment has especially helped to have fair distribution and providing different subject teachers to rural area by rationalization.

In Kerala State Public Service Commission is responsible for recruiting teachers for government secondary schools. The private managements are free to select and appoint teachers at school level following the norms and procedures set by the state government. After assessing state level vacancies in government schools for direct recruitment, the Director Public Instruction informs the State Public Service Commissions. District level Deputy Directors of Education in turn forward actual requisition of number of teachers to the district level officer of state Public Service Commission after carefully assessing the vacancies. As per state rules once vacancies are notified to the public service commission, it cannot be changed. The mode and process of selection is decided by the state public service commission and publishes the merit list. Both written examination/ tests and interview remain the basis of recruitment of teachers' by public service commission. However, the managements of private aided schools select teachers through interview following prescribed norms related to age, education etc. The private managements run one or more schools. They select teachers for individual schools although later send them to different schools. In case of private aided schools, the selection committee comprises the manager, representative of education department and local experts. But as a formality permission has to be taken from DPI through the DEO for final appointment of teachers in private aided schools. The private managements exercise full freedom in selecting teachers of their choice. Normally in Kerala religious groups or specific caste/ community groups run the private aided schools. It is a common practice that, private aided managements prefer to appoint teachers either form their own community/religious group. In fact, in Kerala it is a open secret that people pay heavy amount of money to private managements for getting selected as teachers though the salaries of teachers are met by the education department. A general estimate of the amount paid for secondary school teachers would be any where between 6-8 lakhs and for lecturer posts in higher secondary the amount is much more than at secondary level. Recruiting more teachers means more profit for the private managements. This is one of the reasons that private aided schools some times inflate the enrolment figures in order to get additional teacher posts. Though the private managements follow norms regarding qualification, apparently teachers are selected based on other consideration rather than merit. Ever since higher secondary stage has been de-linked from collegiate education and integrated with secondary level, the state has adopted alternative strategies in appointing teachers.

Teachers in government higher secondary schools are appointed form among the secondary school teachers based on seniority and educational qualification (having Masters Degree in respective subject with B.Ed.). The same condition applies in case of private aided schools too. In case of non-availability of teachers for particular subjects, a state level selection committee-comprising member, state public service commission, subject experts and Director, Higher Secondary Education make fresh appointment.

In Maharashtra the process and procedure of direct selection of teachers for government schools is of different from other three sample states. Teachers are selected based on merit in prescribed educational qualifications like graduation and Bachelor of Education without having an written examination or tests like in other states. The vacant positions are widely advertised, are selected by Regional Selection Board through an interview. The regional selection board is headed by Regional Deputy Director of Education and consists of experts and representative of district level local body. Though interview is compulsory but no weightage is given for performance in the interview. Private managements of aided schools are free to recruit their teachers by the Management Committee following prescribed norms related to qualification and selection criteria. The selection criteria in case of private aided schools is of the same as in case of government schools i.e. merit in the qualifying examinations. The selected list of teachers in private aided schools needs to be sent for information to District Education Officer. In all the cases the essential qualification fixed by the government has to be followed giving wide publicity to the advertisement. Only qualified persons have to be appointed for the permanent vacancies. In case of genuine unavailability of qualified teachers, the private management is allowed to appoint untrained person as teacher only on temporary basis with prior approval of the Regional Deputy Director.

In Uttar Pradesh and Maharashtra the recruitment and appointment of government higher secondary teachers called lecturers are appointed by the same procedure and agencies as in the case of secondary school teachers. However, in case of Andhra Pradesh a separate administrative structure called Directorate of Intermediate selects and appoints teachers for Junior/Intermediate colleges. The selection is based on state level entrance examination and interview. In Kerala the higher secondary teachers are drawn from the qualified teachers of secondary schools and in case of non-availability of qualified teachers, state level selection committee chooses higher secondary teachers through interview.

Teachers' Transfer

Generally states governments have guidelines and norms for transfer of teachers working in government/local body management schools. Teachers are transferred among the schools of same management. However, the transfer policies and procedure vary among the states based on extent of secondary schools under the direct management of government/local bodies. The rules regarding teacher transfer among private aided schools is more or less the same across the states. In case of private aided schools, teachers normally work in the same school for which they have been recruited or some times they can be transferred to other schools under the same private management/society if it has more than one school. Normally every year teacher transfers of teachers working in government/local bodies are carried out at the end or beginning of academic session. Secondary and higher secondary teachers are generally transferred with in the district and region respectively. Inter district and inter regional transfers are done on request but subject to availability of vacant posts. Mutual transfer is allowed at inter district level in special cases like women, widows etc. However, teacher transfers is the most politicised process with lot of corruption. Those of teachers who have political influence could get transferred to towns, urban areas and better places while those who lack such influences have to work in rural areas and have remote chances to get transferred to urban areas. As a result, teachers develop vested interest or lack motivation. At times transfer is also used as weapon to punish teachers both by the administration and political leaders. As most of the teachers prefer to stay in urban areas and towns, a common problem is that while urban schools have surplus teachers rural schools suffer for want of teachers for different subjects. Many states still continue with the age-old transfer procedures, while few states in recent years as apart of quality improvement initiatives, have adopted innovative teacher transfer policy to reduce the political pressures and corruption on the one hand and on the other to have equitable distribution of teachers in different localities besides providing equal opportunity to teachers to work in better places and towns.

While Uttar Pradesh and Maharashtra with smaller proportion of government schools have similar norms for teachers' transfer. In Uttar Pradesh teacher transfers is not a regular activity unless there are requests or complaints on teachers. In Maharashtra also there is no prescribed number of years or tenure to work in a school. As secondary schools under government/local body management are very few, in Maharashtra teacher transfer is neither a major issue nor a regular phenomena. In case of Uttar Pradesh, no teacher can be transferred before a minimum period of five years in a school. Even after 5years, teachers are not transferred unless there is a request from the teachers or there are any sound administrative grounds for doing so. Interestingly, in Uttar Pradesh this policy effects the rural schools. While large number of teachers manage to get posted in urban schools and never request for transfer, there is hardly any chance to provide adequate number of teachers in rural schools. Though Kerala has considerable percentage of schools under government management, yet there is no prescribed length of service or tenure for general transfers of teachers. A minimum five year service is required for acceding to the request of inter educational district transfer with in the revenue district. In Kerala normally teachers applying for transfer can suggest three places of their choice in order of priority in addition to any other school. The names of such teachers are registered separately. In case of unavailability of preferred schools, transfer to any other school depends on seniority of applicants.

Teacher transfer is a crucial aspect of educational administration in the state of Andhra Pradesh where majority of secondary schools are under government and local body management. Teacher transfers was one of the most politicised aspect in the state as largest number of schools are under district level local bodies. Realising the problems of political influences and administrative manipulations in teacher management, the state government has evolved a more transparent policy with clear guidelines and procedure using state of art technology for teacher transfers similar to teacher recruitment and appointment. This policy essentially aims to eliminate political pressures and corruption in teacher management and to have equitable distribution of teachers among urban and rural schools, rationalisation of teacher positions and redistribution of surplus teachers to needy schools. In other words the policy provides equal opportunity for teachers to work in good places and teachers have choice of place according to their entitlement, while it necessary for all the teachers work in rural and remote schools also. In view of clear guidelines and systematic procedure involved, the teachers and teacher unions have accepted the policy. Directorate of School Education has developed teachers' data base having systematic and detailed information about each and every teacher in all the schools in the entire state. Teachers are transferred mainly due to promotion and more than 10 years working in a school. According to entitlement points based on 9-point scale evolved by the education department, teachers can choose a school.

The transfers are effected through counselling to the place of teachers' request based on entitlement points they earn. Entitlement points are accorded for different aspects. Habitations/towns in the state are classified in to four categories based on admissibility of house rent allowance (as house rent allowance is based on type town/rural area). Teachers earn points according to service rendered category wise. Service recorded in remote areas having no road network with less house rent allowance earn more points. Similarly retiring teachers, husband and wife as teachers, performance of students in the subjects taught in previous academic years etc. President and secretary of recognised teacher unions are considered as special categories and 10 entitlement points are given for each category.

List of vacancies and applicants are displayed on the notice board of District Education Officer and also on the web site of education department seven days before the date of counselling. No vacancy can be added after the list is once displayed. A District level Committee being constituted for executing the transfers. The Committee comprises Chairman of Zilla Parishad (District Council) as the chairman, Chef Executive officer of the District Council as member and District Education Officer as the member secretary. The transfers are done through counselling. The selection committee call the applicant teachers according to higher entitlement points following an a order of priority of widows, legally separated single women, teachers/spouse/dependent children suffering with serious diseases, physically handicapped, unmarried women and other teachers. The teachers have choice to select the school according to the entitlement points accrued. Normally transfer orders are issued on the spot through computer generation letters. The administrators and teachers believe that the present teacher transfer policy has been successful in eliminating external pressures and corruption. Since the entitlement criteria being very transparent and no scope for manipulation at any level, teachers are happy and willing to accept the place they get according to their eligibility. Though it may be some kind of loss for politicians to evince their influence on transfers and there by political support of teachers, still in the state the policy has been in operation for the last five years without any hindrances. Similarly, the transparent approach has cut the corruption and administrative manipulations. The state has established a model of teacher transfer policy which is replicated by some other states like Karnataka.

There is a crucial difference between teachers working in government/local body and private management schools. While teacher in government schools are recruited for the system and posted and transferred to different schools, where as in case private schools, commonly teachers are recruited for a particular school and seldom transferred to schools even with in same management. This has both positive negative implications for school effectiveness. If the teachers are efficient and continued in the same school it would be highly useful to the school. On the contrary, if a teacher is inefficient, lack motivation, and commitment, the problem would be of serious in nature as the school has to endure him. Since, most of the private aided schools are located in rural areas, there would hardly be any chance for teachers to get opportunity to move in to better places. One of the reasons for low performance private aided schools can be attributed to this factor.

If the management resort to any action, teachers go to Tribunals or courts leading to legal cases making government as also as a party. In some of the states like Maharashtra and Uttar Pradesh educational administrators at district and state levels spend considerable time to attend the court cases find no time for regular administrative work.

TEACHERS' SERVICE CONDITIONS

There is no uniform policy regarding teachers service conditions like salary structure, pay scale, promotional avenues among different states. Although there are promotional avenues for secondary teachers working in government and Local Body schools to get administrative positions like heads of schools, field level educational officers etc., Being seniority as the criteria the opportunities are far and few in view of large number of teachers. In case of teachers working in private schools, promotions to higher levels is limited and confined only in same management. Normally private managements apply efficiency as criteria in addition to seniority while selecting heads of schools and rarely they have any other higher administrative positions. Therefore, the most possible carrier promotions are derived from higher grades pay scales, which are normally time bound.

The teachers working both in Government/local body and private aided schools in a state have same salary structure and different grades although the service conditions are vary in different stats. The service conditions of government/local bodies apply to teachers working under their respective managements. While the service conditions of teachers in private management are governed by the Private School Employees Service Conditions in case of Maharashtra, Kerala Education Act and Rules in Kerala and Secondary Education Service in Uttar Pradesh.

The pay scale, salary structure, criteria and conditions for higher grade of pay scale vary among states. The higher scale of pay are called differently as higher grade, senior grade,, senior selection grade etc. in different states. During their service, secondary teachers in Kerala and Andhra Pradesh can get three higher levels of pay scale while in case of Maharashtra and Uttar Pradesh two higher grades of pay scales are provided. However, in Uttar Pradesh the final grade is given only for 20 per cent of teachers eligible on seniority at any point of time. Number of years of experience required for getting first higher grade of pay scale varies between 8 to 12 years among the four states. Similarly to reach to the highest grade of pay scale the number of years experience ranges between 12 to 24 years among different states.

In Andhra Pradesh teachers get senior grade scale after 8 years of service, a service selection grade after 16 years and selection grade after 22 years. In Kerala and Uttar Pradesh the secondary teacher gets higher grade after 10 years of experience where as in Maharashtra the senior grade accorded after completion of 12 years of experience. However, to qualify for the senior grade scale in Maharashtra it is essential to fulfil certain conditions *viz.* twelve years of teaching experience as trained teacher, in-service training and a certificate of recommendation from the school committee. In Maharashtra teachers having completed 24 years of experience with in-service training are eligible for selection grade pay scale, but in case of private aided schools, management wise sanction is made by education department covering 20 per cent of posts in the school on the basis of seniority. However, in case of government schools the all the eligible teachers get the selection grade by seniority. In Kerala the teachers get senior grade and selection senior grade after 18 and 23 years of experience respectively. While in case of Uttar Pradesh promotion scale is given after 12 years based on seniority but at any given point of time this cadre will not be more than 20 per cent of total teachers. In case of Maharashtra the teachers have to wait for 24 years to get selection grade which is the final pay scale. The higher pay scale though linked with experience, confidential reports and in-service training (Maharashtra), but in many states increase in salary scale is not automatic as there is limit of only one fifth of teachers can only get it. Secondly, seniority policy does not encourage merit among teachers as they have to wait so many years despite efficiency. In other words, efficiency is not the criteria for higher pay scale. In a system every thing is based on seniority and number of years of experience, there is more chances of teacher burnout and lack motivation.

Promotion

Normally, teachers are promoted to higher levels based on qualification and seniority. The secondary teachers working in government and Local Body schools have promotional opportunities. The secondary teachers are promoted as lecturers in higher secondary level, head masters of secondary schools, field level administrators, officers of Nonformula and Adult Education. However, the promotions depend upon the availability of vacancies. In some states like Uttar Pradesh in the absence of required vacancy, the teachers receive a promotional grade of pay scale. In some states, as in the case of Maharashtra, in addition to the qualification and seniority, the confidential report (CR) of teachers is also taken into consideration for promotions. If a teacher has a poor CR consecutively for three to five years prior to the promotion, the chances of promotion could be blocked or delayed despite having seniority. On the other hand, having an excellent CR does not facilitate the early promotion. Seniority of teachers is counted only within the management.

Teacher Incentives

In all the states, teacher incentives are in operation to motivate, reward for their performance and as a welfare measure. However, type and nature of incentives may vary across the states and also among different levels education. At secondary level most common incentive is teacher awards for academic and social development are in vogue in all the states, where in teachers are selected based on set criteria at district, state and national levels for the best teacher awards every year. Teacher awards include a recognition certificate and additional increments in the salary. In some of the states special awards are instituted on the name of renowned social reformers and activists to recognise the contribution of teachers especially in the field of girls education, education of children with special needs etc. In order to systematically manage and monitor teacher incentives in the states, a National Foundation for Teachers' Welfare (NFTW) was set up in 1962. Financial assistance from the National Foundation is granted to teachers for construction for Teacher Homes (guest houses for teachers), paid holiday to eminent teachers who rendered meritorious service, support for professional education of children of school teachers, medical reimbursement to teachers suffering from serious ailments, gratuitous relief to teachers in cases of serious accidents, subsidy for academic activity of teachers and assistance to teachers and their departments in indigent circumstances. According to the provisions of NFTW, each state has constituted a state level executive committee under the chairmanship of minister of education. Director of school education is the secretary of the committee. This committee allocates assistance to teachers from the grants received from NFTW.

Since the year 1958, under the aegis of NFTW Teachers' Day is celebrated on 5th of September every year by launching a scheme of state and national level awards for teachers with the objective of raising the prestige of teachers and giving public recognition to the meritorious teachers working in schools. Each award carries with it a merit certificate cash award and a silver medal. Teachers are selected based on criteria at sub district, district and state level by a committee. Although there is set criteria and a selection committee, still cases of favouritism, influence of political and teacher unions is not totally ruled out in teachers selection for at district and state level and to recommend for national level award. Certain number of national level awards is earmarked to each state based on size of population.

In Maharashtra some of the private managements have instituted awards to recognise teachers for good performance of students in public examinations The government provides fee concession for children of teachers in higher education. Teachers are encouraged to improve professional qualification by giving permission without hindering the normal duties. The state has established special awards for teachers working in schools for physically handicapped. Special awards are given to women teachers to recognise their meritorious work in women's' education. In Kerala, there are several welfare measure for teachers which include assistance for education of children and marriage of daughters. The welfare corporation of teaching and non-teaching staff provides housing loans. Kerala Teachers Santoria Society has constructed hospitals and planned to construct health resorts and holiday homes for teachers.

Selection of Heads of Schools

While headmasters head secondary schools the higher secondary schools have principals. The secondary school headmasters are selected from among the teachers of secondary and higher secondary schools based on seniority and educational qualification in different states. However, it varies among different management schools and in different states. In Kerala the post of headmaster of government secondary school is gazetted post and the prescribed qualification is master degree and degree in education selected from among the teachers of secondary schools. The head masters are selected based on seniority and confidential reports by departmental promotion committee. In case of private schools, all the schools have to appoint a manger with the approval of district education officer. Normally the managers are the representative or secretary of private management/society. However, government does not provide any salary for the manger. At school level the management designate one of the senior teacher as headmaster with or without honorarium. In Uttar Pradesh the head master and principal of government secondary and higher secondary schools are selected like teachers by secondary service board. In case of private schools the management selects the headmaster/principal from among the teachers working at secondary/ higher secondary following prescribed qualification and minimum 12 years of teaching experience. In Case of Andhra Pradesh, the headmasters of secondary schools are selected from senior teachers of secondary level having prescribed qualification. The principals of higher secondary are drawn from senior teachers same level. In Maharashtra the essential qualification for the headmaster of the secondary school is Bachelors Degree with B. Ed and five years of teaching experience. The headmasters for government schools are selected by the State Public Service Commission, in case of private management schools they are selected by the respective managements based on seniority and experience.

Discussions with State level educational administrators in Sample States.

REFERENCES

Majumdar, Srilekha, Kalpande, V.A. and Tyagi, R.S. (2002). Educational Administration in Maharashtra: Structures, Processes and Future Prospects. New Delhi: Vikas, p. 291

Matthew, A. 1990. Ministry of Education: An Organizational History, New Delhi: NIEPA.

Tyagi, R.S. and Shardindu. (1999). Educational Administration in Uttar Pradesh: Structures, Processes and Future Prospects. New Delhi: Vikas, p. 230.

Tyagi, R.S., *et al.* (2002). Educational Administration in Kerala: Structures, Processes and Future Prospects, NIEPA, New Delhi.

Tyagi, R.S., *et al.* (2008). Educational Administration in Andhra Pradesh: Structures, Processes and Future Prospects, NIEPA, New Delhi.

Index